A PENTECOSTAL BIBLICAL THEOLOGY
TURNING POINTS IN THE STORY OF REDEMPTION

A Pentecostal
Biblical Theology

Turning Points in the Story of Redemption

Roger Stronstad

Roger Stronstad

CPT Press
Cleveland, Tennessee

A Pentecostal Biblical Theology
Turning Points in the Story of Redemption

Published by CPT Press
900 Walker ST NE
Cleveland, TN 37311
USA
email: cptpress@pentecostaltheology.org
website: www.cptpress.com

Library of Congress Control Number: 2016950547
ISBN-13: 978-1-935931-58-4

CONTENTS

Introduction... 1

Part One: Old Testament Theology
Cycles One through Five

Chapter 1
Cycle One:
From Creation to the Flood (Genesis 1.1–8.22)................................. 7

Chapter 2
Cycle Two:
From Noah to the Tower of Babel (Genesis 9.1–11.9)..................... 19

Chapter 3
Cycle Three:
From Abraham to Israel's Wilderness Wanderings
(Genesis 12–Deuteronomy 34).. 27

Chapter 4
Cycle Four:
From Joshua to Exile (Joshua 1–2 Chronicles 36) 55

Chapter 5
Cycle Five:
From Joshua and Zerubbabel to the Jewish Revolt 87

Part Two: New Testament Theology
Cycles Six and Seven

Transition and Introduction 105

Chapter 6
Cycle 6:
The New Covenant... 109

Chapter 7
Cycle 6, Continued:
The New Start According to John the Evangelist 133

Chapter 8
Cycle 6, Continued:
The Growth and Spread of Christianity 153

Chapter 9
Cycle 6, Continued:
Paul – Apostle and Prophet-Teacher to God's New People 187

Chapter 10
Cycle 6, Continued:
Judgment – The Climax of History 207

Chapter 11
Cycle 7:
From the Second Coming of Jesus to Everlasting Blessedness 223

Bibliography 229
Index of Biblical (and other Ancient) References 233
Index of Authors 248

INTRODUCTION

This introduction will discuss general introductory issues to the book's approach to biblical theology. It will prepare the reader for the first of the seven cycles of 'turning points' in biblical history and theology. The first cycle takes the reader from the biblical creation narrative to the judgment by flood waters in the time of Noah.

A wise man in ancient times once observed: there is no end to the making of books. Such has come to be the case in biblical studies, generally, and in biblical theology, in particular. So, one might ask, why another book in the field of biblical theology. As an instructor of biblical theology courses at the undergraduate level, I have often struggled to find good, user friendly textbooks. Two primary factors underlie my dissatisfaction with many contemporary biblical theologies: 1) They are too lengthy. No undergraduate needs a 600-800 page Old or New Testament theology. 2) They (properly) engage the critical issues; but, at the undergraduate level, students need the opportunity to grapple with the text.

This study of turning points in the biblical story of redemption addresses the above issues. It discusses the entire scope of the Bible – from Genesis 1 to Revelation 22 – but I have kept it to a modest length. Also, of the two approaches to doing theology – search or statement – I have minimized the discussion of critical academic issues, the theology of search, in favor of emphasizing faith issues, the theology of statement.

From the beginning, Bible readers have sought to discover the unifying theme(s) of the Bible. This attempt has defeated the best minds because the Bible was written book by book in different historical settings over a period of, perhaps, 1500 years. Proposals for the unifying theme include: 1) the presence of God, himself, 2) the history of salvation, 3) the formation of the people of God (Israel; the Church), 4) the covenants (Noahic, Abrahamic, Mosaic, Davidic, Jesuanic), and 5) the Continuation Narrative (Old Testament promise; New Testament fulfillment). Each of these, and other approaches for finding a unifying theme has its own combination of strengths and weaknesses. This theology finds its unifying theme in recurring cycles of turning points in biblical history and theology, an approach that also has its own combination of strengths and weaknesses.

This study will develop the unifying theme of 'turning points'. These turning points are the seven cycles of the complex pattern: 1) start/new start, 2) the spread of sin, 3) divine judgment, and 4) a subsequent new start. This pattern is most easily seen in the early chapters of Genesis, but it continues to appear, historically and prophetically, throughout biblical history. The following chart illustrates the structure or pattern of the cycle.

Pattern	First Cycle	Second Cycle	Third Cycle
Start	Adam and Eve	Noah and sons	Abraham and Sarah
Command	Be fruitful and multiply (1.28)	Be fruitful and multiply (9.1)	I will multiply you (17.2)
Spread of sin	Earth was filled with violence	City building and false worship	Israel grumbles against the LORD
Judgment	Flood	Confusion of languages	First generation of exodus dies

The pattern or structure of these first three cycles continues to appear throughout the biblical narrative, not ending until history itself ends. This is illustrated by the following graphic:

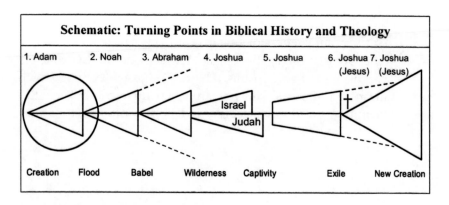

Key to Schematic:
Timeline: The history of humankind and/or God's people from creation (Genesis 1–2) to New Creation (Revelation 21, 22).
  Left facing arrowhead:
  • Point identifies the start/new start
  • Names (top) identify the agents for the start/new start
  • The prone 'V' lines illustrate the numerical growth and spread of the population
  • The closing vertical line identifies the divine judgment upon a sinful population
Circle: identifies each complete cycle in the sequence of turning points
Cross: Identifies the penultimate turning point in the sequence.

As illustrated (above) the first five turning points are reported as the Old Testament narrative advances; the sixth cycle is the subject of the New Testament (Matthew 1 to Revelation 20), and the seventh cycle is transformed into eternal bliss (Revelation 21, 22).

This unifying theme of seven 'turning points', despite its obvious limitations, commends itself for several reasons:

1. It focuses on key turning points in human/biblical history.
2. It focuses on key biblical characters, such as Adam, Noah, Abraham, Moses, Joshua … John the Baptist, Jesus, the Twelve, Paul, *et al.*
3. It discusses every covenant which God makes with humankind, such as the Noahic, Abrahamic, Mosaic, Davidic and Jesuanic.

4. The fact that there are seven cycles of start/new start speaks of the completeness or fullness of God's grace.
5. The fact that the agents of the new start of the last four cycles have the name Joshua (Hebrew) = Jesus (Greek), which means 'God saves', illustrates the repetitive triumph of Redemption over human cosmic and global sinfulness.

PART 1

OLD TESTAMENT THEOLOGY

1

CYCLE ONE: FROM CREATION TO THE FLOOD (GENESIS 1.1–8.22)

Some of the most sublime words ever to be penned are found in Genesis 1: 'In the beginning God created the heavens and the earth' (1.1). These words of creation might be rivaled by the visionary words of re-creation, namely, 'For I saw', John writes, 'a new heaven and a new earth; for the first heaven and the first earth passed away' (Rev. 21.1). But these words of re-creation fall short of the word about creation in the same way that every 'announcement' falls short of the established reality. Perhaps the most sublime words of all are the agonized last words of Jesus from the cross: 'It is finished' (Jn 19.30). In the big picture, creation is finished in 'redemption' (compare the complementary visions of God as Creator and Redeemer in Revelation 4.1–5.14). Therefore, by any eternal standard, God's complementary words about creation/re-creation and redemption stand supreme. Therefore, in a manner of speaking, whereas creation is God's 'good, good' work, redemption through his Son is his most sublime work.

The first cycle of turning points in biblical history and theology is, obviously, about first things. Moses' narrative is not a complete record about what happened; it is selective. The first cycle of turning points focuses upon the following four points. One, God creates the heavens and the earth ... and all their hosts (Gen. 2.1). Two, God creates and commissions human agents to function as his sub-creators (1.26-30). Third, Moses reports about the growth and spread of the descendants of the first human, their fall into disobedience, and the spread of sin (3.1–6.7). Four, God judges human-kind by destructive flood waters (6.8–8.22). These aspects of the 'start' cycle become the pattern of the entirety of the biblical report of human history. The following schematic illustrates the place of the first cycle of turning points in relationship to the six cycles which make up human history.

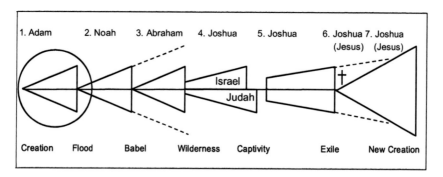

1.1. Start: God Created the Heavens and the Earth (Genesis 1.1–2.4)

In Ancient Near Eastern literary practices the first sentences of the document is also the title of the document. The first sentence of Genesis – 'in the beginning God created the heavens and the earth' – informs its readers that the narrative will begin at the beginning. This beginning is the creation of 'the heavens and the earth'. This phrase is a kind of a 'hendiadys', a Greek word meaning 'one through two'. In the case of Gen. 1.1 the two words 'heavens' and 'earth' are together one all inclusive creative reality. Even so, the phrase heaven and earth might mean different things to different people. For example, to Moses it might be limited to the Nile River Delta of Egypt, the Sinai wilderness, and the sun, moon, and planets, and stars which are visible to the naked eye. On the other hand, to an astro-physicist of the twenty-first century it would include galaxies, nebulae, black holes, and much more never imagined by people in non-technical societies. Though the language of creation has a relevant application to the twenty-first century, its primary meaning also has relevance for pre-technological cultures.

The meaning of the phrase 'heavens and earth' is unambiguous in its biblical context. Moses uses the term four times in his creation narrative. Thus: 1) In the beginning God created the heavens and the earth (1.1), 2) the water laden expanse of the sky is called 'heaven' (1.8), 3) the expanse of the heavens is where the sun, the moon, and the stars are located (1.14-18), and 4) everything which has been created during the six days of creation is summed up by the statement: 'Thus the heavens and the earth were completed, and all their hosts' (2.1). In other words, from first to last (1.1; 2.1), and everything in between (1.8; 14-18) constitutes the heavens and the earth. Thus, in his creation narrative, Moses has defined the phrase, 'heaven and earth' by the narrative strategy of *inclusio* – information given by bracketing.

The strategy of bracketing fully defines what the phrase 'heaven and earth' meant to Moses. Therefore, the heavens and the earth is creation as it is experienced on earth. It includes the creation of light which brings 'day to night' (1.3-5). Therefore, it includes the sun, moon, and the visible stars (1.14-19). In addition, it includes the water-laden atmosphere, and the seas and the dry land. Finally, it describes all the forms of life which populate the seas, the sky, and the land (1.9-30). The actual biblical data (1.1–2.1) makes it clear that the part of the universe which can only be seen through telescopes and so forth is not the purview of the biblical narrative. Therefore, though the magnitude of the universe as we now know it is implicit in the creation narrative, it is not, as such, being described in the narrative.

1.1.1. The creation narrative describes four themes
Looking at the creation narrative from different perspectives reveals the riches of God's handiwork. For example, in comparison to God the creator, human as sub-creator is very limited (compare Ps. 8.1-9). This brief study, however, will focus on just four themes. One, God brings order out of chaos. After having revealed that God created the heavens and the earth (1.1), Moses describes the state of the earth. It was, 'formless and void, and darkness was over the surface of the deep' (1.2). Of necessity, then, God begins to bring order out of chaos; light from darkness (1.3). This is developed in more detail in vv. 14-19. Which describes the function of the sun, the moon and the stars. In addition to creating 'night and day', God

also separated the sky-based water (fog, mist, cloud, rain) from water which lies on the surface of the earth (1.6-8). Next, God caused land, i.e. the continents, to be separated from the oceanic waters (1.9, 10). This land he called 'earth', the second term in the phrase 'heavens and earth' (1.10). Collectively, these creative words transform the undifferentiated 'stuff' or 'matter' of creation into a well-ordered solar system, including a well-ordered earth.

Two, God was the source of life. Once the heavens (solar system) and the earth (the land) have been fittingly structured, God begins to create various forms of life adapted to the suitable environment which he has made. For the dry land, God created vegetation (1.11). He added to creation swarms of living creatures in the waters and birds in the air (1.20-22). Further, he added, 'cattle, creeping things and beasts of the earth after their kind' (1.25). Finally, 'God created man in his own image' (1.27). The creation of the various forms of life is, therefore, suited to their environment (water, air, land) and in a loose hierarchy of life – from simple cellular forms thought to humanity, made in God's image.

Three, God's work of creation was good. After God had created light, he looked at his handiwork, 'and saw that the light was good' (Gen. 1.4). And so it goes on from day to day: the separation of water and land was good (1.10); vegetation was good (1.12); the sun, the moon, and the stars were good (1.18), the creation of life, in its myriad forms was good (1.20, 21), as was, in particular, the creation of wild animals, domesticated animals, and reptiles (1.25). And after God had created humans (1.27), God looked at all that he had made, and saw that it was 'very good' (literally, 'good, good' [1.31]). Thus, the handiwork of the master creator was good from first (day 1) to last (day 6); it was completely good (the sevenfold declaration of goodness). Thematically, this goodness applied to both the ordering of creation, and the life of creation. This goodness was both aesthetically pleasing and morally good. Creation was a series of interdependent, complementary projects – a job in every sense well done.

Four, God's work of creation was complete. David's son, the Preacher, once observed: 'There is an appointed time for everything. And there is a time for every event under heaven' (Eccl. 3.1). He illustrates this by 14 examples, including, 'A time to give birth, and a time to die; a time to weep, and a time to laugh; A time to mourn and a time to dance' (3.2, 4). Nowhere in his list does he observe that there was, at the beginning, 'a time to create, and a time to rest form all the work which he had done'. After the six days of creation God assessed all that he had done and knowing that he had completed what he had done, he simply stopped. The seventh day, as a day of rest is not about 'taking a break', or recouping his energy, or abandoning the project. It is about shifting his activity from 'creating' to 'sustaining' what he had created. (Compare Jesus' observation: 'My Father is working until now and I Myself am working' [Jn 5.16]).

To sum up, the first of the two creation accounts illustrates the following. For example, it presupposes that God (*Elohim*) IS; it does not offer 'proofs' of his existence, though much later the apostle Paul will use creation as a proof of his existence (Rom. 1.20). It also illustrates that creation is God's preferred activity – there was no obligation upon him to create. Further, it illustrates that God creates according to his own divine nature. Thus, God creates light; further on in the Bible we learn that God is light (1 Jn 1.5). God is the source of life; further on in the scriptures we learn that he is the living God (Josh. 3.10). God completes creation; later we learn that creation is completed by redemption (compare the visions of God as creator, and the lamb of God as redeemer, Revelation 4–5), and extended by the creation of a new heaven and a new earth (21.1). For reasons known only to him, God did not create everything at once; he creates day-by-day, systematically, progressively until he had completed what he had set out to make. Finally, the creation account illustrates that God's word is his instrument of creation; that is, his words effect orderliness, life, and goodness.

1.2. The Agents: God Creates Humans (Genesis 2.4-25)

In the first creation account (Gen. 1.1–2.4), God created a suitable environment in which to place humans – the solar system, including the earth itself. Into this environment, as the final, crowning achievement he placed humans, the crowning glory of his good works (1.27-31). This account identifies humans (a.k.a. man, mankind, humankind) to be gendered (male and female). 'Man' (as gen-

or conflict between God and a serpent. It is the story of two antag-
onists – God and the Serpent – with Adam and Eve caught between them.

Moses began his creation narrative (1.1–2.4) by introducing God
without explanation, confident that his readership needed no explanation. Similarly, he introduces his conflict narrative (3.1-24), by
introducing the Serpent with very little explanation, also confident
that his readership needs no explanation. However, as the narrative
proceeds, his readership learns, directly or indirectly, that the Serpent is the craftiest of beasts which God had made (3.1), is a liar
(3.4), an enticer (3.5), and a (four-legged) beast (3.14). But most of
all, Moses' readership recognizes that the Serpent is God's enemy –
the creature attacking its creator (3.1).

This chapter, traditionally described as 'The Fall', is about three
interdependent themes. One, the Serpent accuses God of being a
liar. He asks Eve, 'has God said, "You shall not eat from any tree of
the garden?"' (3.1). She replies in the affirmative, identifying the one
tree of forbidden fruit (3.2, 3), adding the warning, 'you shall surely
die' (3.3b). The Serpent then implies that God is a liar, affirming,
'You surely shall not die' (3.4). This dialogue implies not only that
God is a liar, but that there are no consequences for disobeying
God.

Two, the Serpent accuses God of pettiness (3.5). He entices Eve
with the prospect, 'that in the day you eat from it your eyes will be
opened, and you shall be like God, knowing good and evil' (3.5).
The implication of the Serpent's speech is that God is withholding
good from humanity – being like God, themselves. Ironically, of
course, they are already like God, created in his image. The Serpent
entices them to take more – to cross God-given boundaries. The
result is that Eve was deceived by the 'lust of her eyes', and she and
Adam ate what God had forbidden (3.6). This illustrates the ongoing human vulnerability, specifically, that forbidden fruit is sweetest.

Three, the Serpent forces God to curse humans, the pinnacle of
his creation. Obviously, the Serpent's strategy has been to entice
Adam and Eve to disobey God. This is because the Serpent knows
that God is not a liar. Therefore, should Adam and Eve disobey, the
Serpent knows that God must and will punish them. This punishment is more than simple physical death. It begins with the death of
innocence (3.7). It results in loss of fellowship (3.8). It unleashes a

series of curses: against the Serpent (he will henceforth slither over the ground, and ultimately, a son of Eve with crush him [3.14, 15]). God curses Eve with pain in childbirth and a new relationship with her husband (3.15, 17), and he curses Adam with sweat-inducing toil (3.19). Both Adam and Eve are expelled from the Garden, lest they also eat the fruit of the tree of life and live forever (3.22-24). As time advances, very long lifespans of their descendants (5.1-32) are reduced – first to one hundred twenty years (Gen. 6.3), and later to threescore years and ten (Ps. 90.10).

There is a strange twist in this episode that needs to be noted. This is that the woman was tempted and *deceived* (3.1, 13). Adam, however, *intentionally* disobeyed. This means that Adam (and not Eve) is the fountainhead of human sinfulness (Rom. 5.12). The principle here is that there is a difference between unintended, inadvertent sin and willful sin.

To sum up, as this conflict narrative illustrates, the discrepancy between the goodness of humanity in creation, and their wickedness in society – human sinfulness – is attributable to a paradigmatic, high-handed act of disobedience (3.1-24). There are four parties involved: 1) the tempter, 2) the deceived, 3) the knowing, willful sinner, and 4) nature, the innocent bystander.

The three guilty parties each receive their appropriate and just punishment, but even the innocent party (the ground itself) is tainted by their sinfulness and affected by their punishment. This episode also illustrates that first and foremost, sin is against God the creator, and this has consequences far more serious (2nd death) than sin against humanity. Further, sin is often sociable, i.e. the sinner typically seeks to include others in his/her sinfulness. Finally, at the right time, God triumphs over the Serpent, by the first and second (crushing) advents of Jesus. This means that evil, either individual or empire-wide, can never ultimately triumph over God, no matter what apparent victories evil may win.

1.4. The Spread of Evil: Conflict Between Humans (Genesis 4–5)

When God created humanity, male and female, he commanded, 'Be fruitful and multiply, and fill the earth' (Gen. 1.27). Obedient to this command the children of Adam and Eve and subsequent descendants begin to spread out and populate the earth. However, because of the consequences of Adam's sin (3.12), as the population spreads so sin also spreads. At the time, the primary sin is conflict among humans.

In his narrative strategy, the first thing which Moses reports is a conflict between two of the sons of the man and his wife Eve (Gen. 4.1-8). She names the first son, Cain, and the second son, Abel (4.1-2). Cain was a tiller of the ground, that is, a farmer (compare 3.24) and Abel was a herdsperson, sheep having been subdued (domesticated, 1.29). In the course of time, each one brought an offering to the LORD (4.3). Cain brought an offering of the fruit of the ground (4.3b), and Abel, the herdsperson, brought a firstling of his flock (4.4). Both of these offerings – first-fruit and firstborn – were legitimate offerings, and both would be required of Israel throughout its subsequent history. But, for some unreported reason, God approved Abel's offering and disapproved of Cain's offering. The reason for the approval-disapproval cannot be linked to the fact that one was a blood sacrifice and the other was not. Therefore, God's disapproval of Cain's offering of farm produce must have something to do with Cain's heart attitude. Cain was very angry at God's disapproval, and despite warning from God, rose up and killed Abel (4.5-8). In this way, the narrative illustrates that from the start, Adam's descendants would either honor God, in whose image they were made (1.27), or live like the devil, who was a liar and a murderer from the beginning (3.1-7).

1.4.1. The murder of Abel has an immediate result beyond his actual death (Genesis 4.9-11)

The result of Abel's death is that the very ground has become polluted by Abel's shed blood (4.10). But God had specifically created land = earth, and it was good (1.10). Humankind, however, has now brought God's curse upon the ground (3.17), and their firstborn son has polluted the ground by shedding his brother's blood. This implies that not only must humankind be redeemed (3.16) but that the earth also will be redeemed (Rom. 8.19-22) and, ultimately, be recreated (Rev. 21.1).

The second result of Cain murdering Abel is that he is punished by excommunication or banishment from human society (Gen. 4.12). This not only protects other humans from the possibility of being murdered, but it also protects the ground from further pollution. Cain's banishment from human society also symbolizes his separation from God (4.14). For the murderer, this adds to the alienation from God that Adam introduced into the Creator-creature relationship when, after sinning, Adam and Eve hid from God's presence (3.8-11).

1.4.2. Immense time – generation followed by generation – passes (Genesis 5.1-32)

Wickedness and violence continue, apparently unchecked by banishment (6.5). Mysterious mixed marriage and a preoccupation with doing evil characterize the human population in the time of Noah. Using anthropomorphic language, Moses describes God's reaction to deepening human wickedness as sorrow and grief (6.6). He, therefore, decides, 'to blot out man whom I (God) have created' (6.7). He will do this by sending a massive flood (6.17). This flood will have two purposes: 1) end the violence that is upon the earth (that is, capital punishment will replace banishment [6.13]), and 2) cleanse the earth of its polluted condition. But in the midst of all of this unchecked violence, pollution, and wickedness, there is one person who, 'found favor in the eyes of the LORD' (6.8) – Noah. Because of his righteousness, this one person, and his family, will be rescued from death by drowning, and will be God's agents for a renewed earth, with a fresh start for both the animal population and the human population (6.17-21).

1.5. Judgment upon Wicked Humanity (Genesis 6–8)

Initially, as the examples of Cain and Lamech illustrate (Gen. 4.1-24), God's punishment for violence and murder is banishment. However, as the population grew, 'exile' proved ineffective in curbing this violence. Therefore, in Noah's generation, God brings about judgment upon all humanity. This judgment is not capricious. The punishment fits the crime – the punishment cleanses the ground from its pollution. Neither is it hasty. The history of Adam's sons (Genesis 4) is linked to Noah's generation by a genealogy of ten generations. This is an indefinite period of time, and the Methuselah-like lifespans shows that it is ten very long eras. The Bible contains many examples of God's immediate judgment upon people, such as the episode of Ananias and Sapphira (Acts 5.1-11), but the judgment upon humanity illustrates that God's judgment is sometimes delayed because of God's patience. But though judgment is delayed, God's righteous judgment upon impenitent evil is, ultimately, certain.

After God has commissioned Noah to build an Ark, gathered pairs of all animals, and warned the people about impending divine judgment (6.13-22), God rains down judgment. This watery judgment includes both, 'the fountains of the great deep (which) burst open, and the floodgates of the sky (which) were opened' (7.11). This returns the earth to the water-laden, super-saturated condition of Day 2 of creation (1.6-8), and reverses the process of Day 3, by which dry land appeared (1.9-10). And so, in creation, God caused dry land to appear, and it was good; later, God caused dry land to be replaced by water, and it was appropriate (if not actually good). The judgment by flood waters destroyed every living creature, whose habitation was the land, animals and humans alike. As Moses reported it: 'And all flesh that moved on the earth perished ... Thus he blotted out every living thing that was upon the face of the land' (7.21-23). End of story? What God created on days 3, 5, and 6 is destroyed. But no! God preserved a remnant. Moses reports: 'only Noah was left, together with those that were with him in the Ark' (7.23).

Bible readers know, because the scriptures from Genesis to Revelation illustrate it, that 'God causes all things to work together for good' (Rom. 8.28). This is for God's good, from creation to salvation. Thus, the flood waters of *judgment* upon sinners are at the same time flood waters of *salvation* for the righteous. Compare the 'Pathway through the sea' episode (Exodus 14) and the crucifixion of Jesus (Mark 15). The episode of the flood also illustrates that evil can never ultimately thwart the saving purposes of God. This is true individually and locally and, also, globally. As Bible readers, we have not only read the first chapter in the cycles of turning points (Genesis 1–8), but we have also read the last chapter (Revelation 21, 22).

2

CYCLE TWO: FROM NOAH TO THE TOWER OF BABEL (GENESIS 9.1–11.9)

The following schematic illustrates the place of the Noah cycle of turning points in biblical history and theology. As God's agent of the new start, Noah is the historical bridge between the Adam cycle and the Abraham cycle. Noah, with his family, is the last man of the previous cycle and the first man of the new cycle.

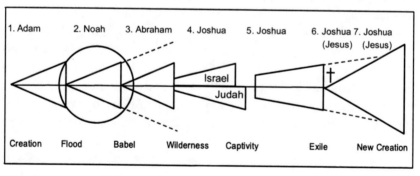

The first cycle of turning points ended in judgment – the total annihilation of humankind by drowning. The sole exception to this fate is Noah and his family, just eight persons. The role of this family is remarkable. Just as Adam and Eve were the progenitors of the human race, so Noah and his family, now for the second time, will become the progenitors of the human race. This cycle is about the following points:

The Agents: Noah and his family, like Adam earlier, are charged to be fruitful and multiply, that is, to be the progenitors of the new human family.

The New Start: a rescued family, the restoration of right worship, and a covenant which God makes with Noah.

The Spread of Humankind: Noah's descendants repopulate the earth, but commit the sin of pantheistic and idolatrous worship, worshipping the creation rather than the creator.

The Judgment: God 'confuses the languages' at Babylon, and disperses the nations over the earth.

2.1. The Agent: Noah, a Second Adam

The Genesis narrative reports very little biographical information about Noah, who is such a key player in the progress of human history. The genealogy of Gen. 5.1-32 informs its readership that Noah is descended from Adam through Lamech (5.28-32), who was introduced in 4.23, 24. Noah will *relieve* humankind from the arduous curse of 'toil' which God had earlier imposed (compare 3.17). He was five hundred years old when he became the father of three sons, namely, Shem, Ham, and Japheth. Uniquely, though before the flood he lived among wicked and violent people (6.5, 13), he found favor in the eyes of the LORD (6.8). Indeed, Noah was a righteous person, blameless in his time (6.9). This and several other tidbits of other information make him comparable to Adam in several significant ways. The chart below demonstrates that Noah is the *alter ego* of Adam.

The chart's comparison of Adam and Noah illustrates many significant, explicit parallels between these two agents of the first two cycles of start/new start. And no other agents (Abraham, Joshua, *et al.*) have these kinds of parallels. Indeed, the parallels between Adam and Noah make each of them to be God's functional (but not ontological) *alter ego* on earth. To understand these conclusions one must keep in mind that Jesus, the agent of the sixth and seventh cycles of new starts, is NOT God's *alter ego* on earth. He is God himself in the flesh (compare Jn 1.1-18) and has a status incomparably and infinitely higher than the highest of humans, such as Adam and Noah.

Aspect	Adam, Agent of the Start	Noah, Agent of New Start
Status	Created in God's image (1.27)	Born with God's image (though tainted by Adam's fall)
Progenitor of humankind	Commanded to be fruitful and multiply and fill the earth (1.28)	Commanded to be fruitful and multiply and fill the earth (9.1)
Ruler of the animal kingdom	Adam will rule over every living thing (1.28)	Noah will rule over every living thing (9.2)
Quality of person-hood	Humans are a 'good' part of God's creation, blameless before God (1.31)	Noah is a 'righteous' person, blameless before God (6.9)
Relationship with Creator	God walked with Adam and Eve (3.8)	Noah walked with God (6.9); right worship (8.20-22)
Vocation	God's assistant gardener (2.8) to cultivate and keep it (2.15)	God's assistant savior (6.13-22; 8.13-19)

2.2. The New Start: Worship, Blessing, and Covenant (Genesis 8.20–9.17)

There are two factors to the new start after the flood: 1) Noah restores right worship; and, 2) on the basis of the restored relationship between God and humankind, God establishes a covenant with Noah. In his flood narrative Moses gives his readership the setting in which Noah will resume right worship (Gen. 8.13-19). He reports: the flood has ended, and, once again, dry land has appeared. Therefore, God commands Noah, who still remains shut up in the Ark, to leave the Ark. He is also to release from the Ark all of the birds, animals, and creeping things which have been saved from the flood. These will breed abundantly and replenish the earth.

In this setting in which life on earth begins to return to normal, the first thing which Noah does is to resume right worship. He builds an altar to the LORD and offers up as a burnt offering one of every clean animal and every clean bird (Gen. 8.20). Moses reports that the LORD is pleased with and accepts Noah's worship (8.21a). Once again, using anthropomorphic language to describe God, the LORD *decides* that he will never again destroy every living thing, as he had done with the flood (8.21b-22).

Once Noah has resumed right worship (Gen. 8.13-19), the LORD establishes several guidelines for life in the new world order (9.1-7). These guidelines or principles are to be blessings for blameless/righteous humanity (9.1a). First, Noah and his sons will be the progenitors of the new, repopulated earth (9.1b). As such, like Adam earlier, Noah will rule/subdue the animal kingdom (9.2). This animal kingdom is, therefore, given as good to humankind (9.3). The LORD gives one restriction only – the blood is to be properly drained from the carcass of the slain animal (9.4). And, finally, the LORD changes the procedure for dealing with murder. Originally, murderers, such as Cain were banished or exiled from human society. But such a penalty did not check human violence (6.13), so after the flood, murderers are to be executed rather than exiled (9.5-7).

The chief blessing which God gives to Noah after the flood is to establish a covenant with him (Gen. 9.8-17). This covenant is not a personal covenant, such as God will later make with Abraham, but is for Noah, his sons, and their descendants (9.8, 9). Of note, this is the first recorded covenant between God and humankind. This covenant is unilateral, that is, God not only takes the initiative, but he also takes the responsibility to make the covenant work (9.8, 9). The covenant is as broad, or as encompassing, as to extend to the animal kingdom (9.10). In the covenant God stipulates that he will never again destroy the earth (globally) by flood waters (9.11). God guarantees the covenant by a sign – the rainbow (9.12-15) which is an earthly echo of God's sovereign, eternal presence (Rev. 4.1-3). Indeed, this covenant is not only unilateral, but it is also an everlasting covenant (Gen. 9.16). To emphasize this dimension, God once again stipulates the rainbow as his sign, guaranteeing the everlasting character of the covenant.

2.3. The Spread of Sin: Noah's Family Repopulates the Earth (Genesis 9.18–10.32)

The human population which survived the flood numbers eight persons. As the narrative unfolds, Moses reports: 'God blessed Noah and said to them, "Be fruitful and multiply; populate the earth abundantly and multiply in it"' (9.7). Therefore, Noah and his sons function as God's sub-creators. Noah's sons are Shem, Ham, and Japheth; and, as Moses will illustrate in detail which follows (10.1-32), 'from these the whole earth was populated' (9.19).

The genealogical record identifies the nations which formed after the flood (Gen. 10.1): the generations of Japheth (10.2-5), the generations of Ham (10.6-20), and the generations of Shem (10.21-31). Thus, the earth was repopulated, 'according to their lands, everyone according to his language, according to their families, into their nations' (10.5, c.f. 10.20, 31). Forming an inclusio with 9.19, Moses concludes his genealogy in 10.32, writing, 'These are the families of the sons of Noah, according to their genealogies, after the flood' (10.32). Left unanswered to this point in the narrative is the question, 'how did these separate languages and nations arise after the flood?'

Moses answers the implied question about the origin of different languages and the scattering of the nations by reporting an historical flashback (Gen. 11.1-9). The setting for this flashback is that the whole earth (= everyone) spoke the same language after the flood (11.1) and settled in the land of Shinar (11.2). Shinar is the Hebrew name for the land of Sumer. The Sumerian civilization is the first great literate civilization in the land more familiarly known to Bible readers as Babylon. This land is the fertile flood plain between the Tigris and Euphrates rivers and is the original setting of the garden of Eden (2.14). The Greeks named this land, Mesopotamia. Here is where the descendants of Noah's sons settled, and from here the LORD scattered them.

Moses' narrative has two foci: 1) city building and 2) false worship (Gen. 11.1-6). City building is the sin of human autonomy. It was first done by Cain (4.17) and is likely the setting for the development of musical instruments and metallurgy (4.21, 22). The problem with city building/dwelling is that it ceases to be theocratic. City dwellers begin to regulate their affairs according to human government. In Shinar, every city-state had its own king. Not only is kingship institutionalized, but it also seeks religious sanction. And in Sumer, every city-state developed its own religious system. Thus, both throne and temple, king and priest, are aspects of developing human autonomy.

The development of false religion, as a complementary aspect of city building, is implicit in the reported desire, 'Come, let us build for ourselves ... a tower whose top will reach into heaven' (11.4). The tower is a ziggurat, an artificial mountain shaped like a step pyramid. Every city-state had one, and though they were built from mud brick, the ruins of many of them have survived. The ziggurat at Ur, Abraham's native city, is the most well-known of the survivors and has been partially restored. The bottom level (of the ziggurat at Babylon) was called 'the foundation platform of heaven and earth'. Three hundred feet above ground level a temple was built as the house of the god, and morning and evening priests would climb up to the temple to perform their duties, in the care and feeding of the gods. Thus, these towers were always associated with false worship. This false worship often included aspects of *astro-pantheism*, that is, the worship of the sun, moon, and/or 'stars' such as Mars and Venus, *polytheism*, which is the worship of many gods, and *idolatry* (images of the deities crafted in wood, stone, and/or metal). And so, after the flood the creatures (Noah's descendants) began to worship gods made after his own image. City-building and false worship provoke God to curse these Mesopotamian city-states for the complementary sins of human autonomy and false worship.

2.4. Judgment

The judgment which brought the first cycle of turning points to an abrupt, universal end was unchecked violence (Gen. 6.13). This bloodshed has, from the time of the murder of Abel, polluted the ground (4.10; 6.11). The flood waters not only brought judgment upon humankind for its wickedness, but it also cleansed the earth itself from its polluted condition. It is a different situation for the judgment of the second cycle of start/new starts in biblical history. The sins which provoked God to judgment are the complementary ones of human autonomy and idolatry. Therefore, the judgment which brings this cycle to an end is of a different nature than the flood. Its purpose is not to cleanse the polluted earth, but to thwart the entrenchment of false worship.

The biblical narrative does not report the origins of false worship after the flood. By the time of the 'tower of Babel' episode, it is deeply entrenched in the civilization of Shinar (= Sumer and Akkad). This false worship is compounded by the human autonomy which is endemic to this civilization. These twin sins see the creature (humanity) worship their creation (idols), rather than worshipping their creator (Gen. 1.27). At the time of the 'tower of Babel' episode, Moses reports, 'the whole earth used the same language and the same words' (11.1). This condition is emphasized in v. 6: 'Behold, they are one people, and they all have the same language'. This condition facilitates human autonomy. Thus, 'nothing which they propose to do will be impossible for them' (11.6b). And so, 1) God confused their language (11.7), and 2) he scattered them abroad over the face of the whole earth (11.9). This judgment was effective, for humankind found themselves unable to understand their neighbor's speech, and they stopped building the city (11.8).

This is the long-lasting, universal condition which summarizes the 'table of nations' which chronologically follows the 'tower of Babel' episode. The record includes the oft-repeated formula: '... the nations were separated into their lands, everyone according to his language ... into their nations' (10.5; compare 10.20, 25, 31). The table of nations concludes with the definitive report: 'These are the families of the sons of Noah ... by their nations; and out of these the nations were separated on the earth after the flood' (10.32).

2.5 Conclusion

The earliest history of humankind (a.k.a. 'ante-diluvium history') is characterized by the origin and spread of evil (Genesis 3–6). However, heedless of the lesson about human accountability to God, Noah's descendants rejected God's theocratic rule and began to practice false worship. As a result, God judged Noah's descendants, confusing their language and scattering the population over the earth. The very long interval from Noah to Babel illustrates the patience, grace, and mercy of God, shown by the lengthy genealogies

(10, 11). Out of this history of human autonomy and false worship God will call a new family to make a new start.

3

CYCLE THREE: FROM ABRAHAM TO ISRAEL'S WILDERNESS WANDERINGS (GENESIS 12– DEUTERONOMY 34)

The circle in the schematic of turning points in biblical history and theology illustrates the place of the Abraham cycle both in relation to the previous Noah cycle (Gen. 9.1–11.9) and the subsequent Joshua cycle (Joshua 1–2; Chronicles 36). Advancing from the Adam and the Noah cycles, the Abraham cycle is set firmly into the written and artefactual history of the ancient near east.

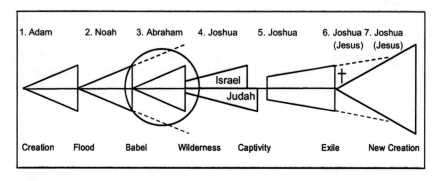

As was observed earlier, the interval from the Adam cycle of turning points to the Noah cycle is an indeterminate era which is several millennia long. Similarly, the interval between the Noah cycle is also an indeterminate period of several millennia. The Abraham cycle advances its readers to the time of the flowering of both the Sumerian civilization and the city of Ur within it (i.e. the second half of the third millennium). In contrast to the primeval Adam cycle, which ended with the annihilation of the descendants of Adam by a global flood, the Noah cycle ended with the confusion of languages and the spread of the nations over the earth. After this judgment, God calls Abraham to separate himself from his native city of Ur, in southeastern Sumer, and with his family, to migrate to a new land (with a different language). The third cycle in human history includes the following emphases:

The Agents of the New Start: Abram and his wife Sarai.

The New Start: the patriarch Terah and his three sons, Abram, Nahor, and Haran.

The Spread of Humankind: Abram's descendants grow to nationhood in Egypt – but will commit the sin of rebellion against the LORD.

The Judgment: The generation of the adults of the exodus will not enter Canaan, the land of promise, but will die off in the wilderness.

3.1. Agents of the New Start

3.1.1. God calls Abraham

The agents of the Adam and the Noah cycles of turning points in biblical history and theology were 'nuclear' families. The same holds true for the agents of the third cycle. They are the married couple, Terah's son Abram and his wife Sarai (whom the LORD renamed as Abraham and Sarah). Abraham is the tenth generation of Noah's descendants through his son Shem (Gen. 11.10-32).

Initially, Terah is a resident of Ur and with his family practiced idolatry (Josh. 24.2; compare Gen. 31.19, 32-35). Terah, however, moves his family from Ur to Haran in Syria – a city where the worship of the goddess, Sin, was also prominent. Abraham's genealogy identifies Abraham as the eldest son of Terah and also as the husband of Sarah, who, ominously, is barren (11.27-30). Now living in Haran, he is called by the LORD to leave the city and journey to the land of Canaan (12.1-5). This relocation of his extended family, which includes his nephew Lot, is probably a challenging move for a man who is, at that time, 75 years old (12.4).

Abraham's move was neither the result of circumstances, nor a mere whim. It was a matter of divine leading. Thus, the LORD said to Abraham, 'Go forth from your country (i.e. Haran) ... to the land which I will show you (i.e. Canaan) (Gen. 12.1). This is the demand that Abraham separate himself from everything he knew and did. Therefore, he must not only move to a new, strange land and culture, but he must also go forth, '... from (his) relatives and father's house' (12.1). Later narratives hint at why such a decisive break is necessary. His younger brother Laban had earlier not only worshipped idols, but continues to do so (31.19). Indeed, Rebekah, Abraham's niece, will steal her father Laban's household gods and bring them with her when she and Jacob move from Haran to Canaan (31.32-35). Though God requires that he separate himself from his native culture, clan, and close relatives, the LORD offers greater compensations.

The LORD will give Abraham compensations which are larger than life. First, these include the promise of the land of Canaan (Gen. 12.7; 13.14-18; 15.18). Second, these compensations include the promise of nationhood – but Sarah cannot bear Abraham even one son (12.2; 15.2-6; 17.1-6) – and personal blessing, and through him, blessings upon the whole world (12.3). No other man in biblical history receives promises of such magnitude. But of greater significance, these promises – whose fulfillment happens across the generations – will only come to fruition through God's intervention in Abraham's life in his old age and as each generation succeeds the next. The fulfillment of these promises presupposes that God will be active in the lives of Abraham's descendants, which include Isaac, Jacob, Joseph, Joshua, David, and Jesus, the Son of God (Lk. 3.23-38). And the amazing thing is that 'Abraham believed in the LORD; and he reckoned it to him as righteousness' (15.6). And so, Abraham looked ahead to the day of fulfillment and not only believed, but he rejoiced in what he saw (Jn 8.56). But all of this is a long way off from the day when Abraham announced to Sarah and his household that they will be moving on from Haran.

3.2. The New Start

There is a specific geography to this new start. It is a city-state named 'Ur of the Chaldees' in the biblical narrative. It sits southeast of Babel/Babylon in the land of Shinar. This is the fertile flood-plain of the Tigris and Euphrates rivers. It is surrounded by other close neighboring city-states such as Erech and Eridu. In Abraham's day, Ur's landscape was dominated by a large ziggurat or temple tower. This was dedicated to the city's patron goddess, Nannar-Sin. The flat horizon in several directions was pierced by the profiles of other ziggurats from Ur's closest city-state neighbors. An agricultural economy which produced surpluses and ready access to adjacent trade routes made Ur a bustling, wealthy city.

There is also a specific culture to this (third) new start. It is the culture of Sumeria and, more specifically, the city-state identified in the Old Testament by the name 'Ur of the Chaldees'. This is the city of Ur in the land of Shinar and not the city of the same name in the land of Syria. Ur of the Chaldees flourished throughout the third millennium and at its height had a population of about 250,000. Fertile soil (until it was ruined by salinization), irrigation, easy access to water ways and trade routes all contributed to its wealth. Temple, throne, and a wealthy class encouraged the development of artisan skills, namely, jewelers, metal workers, textiles, and potters. Temple and throne were also served by highly-trained scribes, whose output is represented by the 100,000 cuneiform documents retrieved by archaeologists from the ruins of the city. As was characteristic of Sumerian civilization everywhere, the religion practiced in Ur was pantheistic (the patron goddess was Sin, the moon goddess), polytheistic (about 300 gods/goddesses dominated the religious landscape), and idolatrous. God's new start after the Tower of Babel episode removes its agents from this civilization, and places them in a new culture and context where they can develop right worship.

3.2.1. The Abrahamic covenant and renewals

The promises which God has made to Abraham at the time of his call are stupendous in their short and long-term implications (Gen. 12.1-4). A husband and wife, still childless, do not grow to nationhood in a lifetime. And neither can they possess the land in a day. In fact, as time advances, instead of being a promised blessing, the land serves up two common curses – famine and warfare (Gen. 12.10–14.24). Therefore, after these things, the LORD appeared to

Abraham to make a covenant with him which will guarantee the fulfillment of the promises.

3.2.1.1. The LORD makes a covenant with Abraham (Genesis 15.1-21)

The raid upon Canaan by a coalition of Mesopotamian kings and the resulting capture of Abraham's nephew, Lot and his household, was, implicitly, very traumatic for Abraham. It seemed to falsify the emphasis on 'blessing', which the earlier promises carried. In addition, it made him aware of his vulnerability as an immigrant and nomad in the land. In this setting, Moses reports, 'After these things the word of the LORD came to Abraham in a vision' (Gen. 15.1).

As the One who both initiates the covenant which he is about to make with Abraham, the LORD gives him a vision of his self-identity (15.1). This revelation of God's self-identity is appropriate for Abraham's life setting. After his war with the kings of Mesopotamia, Abraham has become fearful. The LORD first counsels Abraham, 'Do not fear' (15.1a). The basis of his fearlessness is that the LORD is, 'a shield' to him (15.1b). This means that though Abraham may yet have to fight future battles, as he had earlier fought to rescue Lot, God will continue to give him the victory over his enemies. Complementing this assurance (the LORD is his shield), the LORD informs him that his, 'reward shall be very great' (15.1c). In other words, Abraham does not have to engage in plundering his enemies to enrich himself, for the LORD who had earlier blessed Abraham with riches, 'in livestock, in silver, and in gold' (13.2) will continue to do so.

The promise of great reward is disconcerting to Abraham. It reminds him that he, an old man, approaching the age of 86 years, has no heir for both actual and promised wealth (Gen. 15.2a). He, therefore, asks God to ratify his decision to adopt his slave, Eliezer of Damascus, to be his heir (15.2b-3). At this point, the LORD both rejects Abraham's proposal to adopt Eliezer – 'this man will not be your heir' – and affirms, positively that, 'one who shall come forth from your own body, he shall be your heir' (15.4). As a childless husband with a still childless wife, Abraham, doubtless would have been content with the birth of just one son. But that is not God's way with Abraham. He lavishes on Abraham by promising descendants more numerous than the stars, that is, numerous beyond counting (15.5). In Abraham's circumstances, this promise may have seemed almost laughable. But Abraham did not laugh. Rather, he believed God (15.6). So direct and confident in his trust in God, that God accounted, or reckoned it to him as righteousness. This act of faith created Abraham, not yet the father of a son, to be the father of all those who subsequently will be accounted righteous on the basis of their own belief, faith, trust in God.

The natural corollary to the promise of a son, and, more so, the promise of many descendants is the renewed promise of the land (Gen. 15.7, compare 12.1, 13.12-18). Abraham, who has just had the announcement of a son confirmed (15.5), now asks the LORD to confirm this promise as well (15.8). The LORD, with Abraham's assistance, enters a covenant with him, ratifying it with various sacrifices (15.9-11). But the promise of the land is complicated by a period of exile. Abraham is to 'know for certain that (his descendants) will be strangers in a land that is not theirs, where they will be enslaved and oppressed four hundred years' (15.13).

Nevertheless, Abraham's descendants 'will come out with many possessions' (15.14). The borders of the Promised Land will be 'from the river of Egypt as far as the great river, the river Euphrates' (15.18). These borders define the land of the '-ites', that is, the land of the Kenizzite and the Kadmonite and the Hittite and the Perizzite and the Rephaim and the Amorite and the Girgashite and the Jebusite' (15.19-21).

Observations: In addition to the earlier relationship between God and Abraham that was based solely upon divine promises, the relationship between God and Abraham is now based on a covenant. This covenant not only reiterates the promise of the land (12.1) and identifies its boundaries (15.18-21), but it also specifies that Abraham will have a natural born son (15.4).

Abraham's response is a God-pleasing faith. Like the earlier promises, which extend to worldwide blessings upon a global population (12.3), the covenant is also unilateral and unconditional. In other words, both promise and covenant depend of the power and trustworthiness of the LORD God and not on anything which Abraham brings to the relationship between the two parties.

3.2.1.2. The LORD renews the covenant with Abraham (Genesis 17.1-27)

In Abraham's life, the LORD God covenanted to do for him what no one else on earth could do – give him a son by birth rather than by adoption (Gen. 15.2-4). But the years pass. Abraham was 75 years old when he entered Canaan (12.5). Sarah is barren (11.30). A decade passes. Sarah remains barren, and so she takes the initiative and gives her concubine, Hagar, to Abraham so that he can father a son by her. This strategy is effective and a son is born to Abraham and Sarah by this surrogate woman (16.1-16). In this way, when Abraham is 86 years old, God's earlier promise seems to be fulfilled. But God has a different plan to satisfy Abraham's need for a son.

Thirteen years after Ishmael was born, the LORD again makes one of his periodic appearances to Abraham. Earlier, when God made his covenant with Abraham, he revealed himself as a shield, that is, the protector. To this he adds a new self-revelation, namely, 'I am God Almighty' (17.1). This self-revelation assures Abraham that he alone has the power to do for Abraham what he has promised in the past (12.1-4; 15.1-21), and also what he is now about to promise. The present promises will confirm the earlier promises and also add new dimensions to them. First, God will establish his covenant (17.2a). Second, though Sarah has not yet born a son, God will multiply his descendants exceedingly (15.2a). Third, Abraham will not only be the father of one nation, but nations shall come forth from him. Fourth, God will, therefore, give Abraham a new name – one which will be appropriate to his new status as the father of many forthcoming nations. Henceforth, Abram is named Abraham (17.4, 5). Fifth, befitting his new status, God promises royal descendants, that is, kings shall come forth from him (17.6). Thus, right from the start, God reaffirms the promise of the land of Canaan as the everlasting possession of Abraham's descendants (17.8).

Only someone whose identity is 'God Almighty' could fulfill these promises with their long-term 'everlasting' implications (17.7, 8). In addition, God gives a covenant sign of circumcision (17.9-14). Further, God Almighty will give Abraham a son by Sarah (renamed from Sarai, 17.15-21). Within a year, she will bear the son of promise; and, because of this, she will be the mother of nations and their kings (17.16, 17). By this promise, God rejects Ishmael as the promised son, as he had earlier rejected Eliezer of Damascus (15.4). Nevertheless, God has his own promises of blessing and nationhood for Ishmael (17.20). It is, therefore, ironic that Abraham's two sons will father nations who, down through time, will often engage in bitter warfare against one another.

Abraham is now 99 years old, and has walked with God for at least 24 years. But he has not yet learned what it means for the God whom he follows to be God Almighty. And so, when God, once again, promises that a son will be born to him this strikes him as a preposterous possibility (Gen. 17.17). It is laughable that he, who is approaching the age of 100 years and Sarah, who is 90, will have a son. This news causes him to do this very thing: he laughs (17.17). Later, hearing the same news about bearing Abraham a son, Sarah also laughs (18.12); though when confronted by the LORD about her laughter, she denies it (18.13-15). But the narrative reports, 'Then the LORD took note of Sarah as he had said, and the LORD did for Sarah as he had promised' (21.1). As a result, with Abraham's help, Sarah conceived and bore a son to Abraham in his old age, at the appointed time of which God had spoken to him (21.1). The birth of Isaac is a laughing matter. Abraham and Sarah had earlier laughed in disbelief, but now Sarah, and everyone else who hears the news will laugh with joy (21.6, 7). In this way, Abraham has learned the lesson that the LORD God is God Almighty. In other words, if God has the power to cause Isaac to be born to Abraham and Sarah, who in their old age are as good as dead, then the Almighty has the power to fulfill all of his promises (12.1-4) and his covenants (15.1-21; 17.1-8).

3.2.1.3. Once again, God renews the covenant with Abraham (Genesis 22.1-19)

Abraham's journey toward fatherhood was a 25-year long walk of obedience and faith. It was a road of detours (e.g. the flight to Egypt, Gen. 12.10-20), dangers (14.1-24), and dead ends (16.1-16). But it was also a journey about a personal destination, namely, the birth of Isaac (17.1-22; 21.1-3). Isaac is the focus of this second covenant renewal, as he was earlier the center of the first covenant renewal.

This second covenant renewal follows two episodes in Abraham's life. The first episode is the sending of Hagar and her son away from his household (Gen. 21.8-21). That this is a discreditable act is shown by Abraham's guilty conscience (21.11, 12). It is, however, redeemed by the supernatural care of Hagar and Ishmael

(21.17-21) and God's renewal of his promises about Ishmael's destiny, specifically, that God will make him a great nation (21.18). The second episode is a covenant of peace/peace treaty between Abraham and Abimelech, settling a conflict over water rights (21.22-34). This covenant or treaty has long-term implications for Isaac (compare 26.1-33). The narrative about Abraham next reports that, 'it came about after these things that God tested Abraham' (22.1).

God's testing of Abraham catches many readers by surprise, as it may also have caught him by surprise. There are several reasons for this surprise. One is that this is the first reported test in the narrative to this point; and, two, many readers limit testing to the activity of the devil, as happened in the narrative of 3.1-8. But, surprising or not, the narrative is explicit: 'God tested Abraham', as he will subsequently test Abraham's descendants following their departure from Egypt (Deut. 8.16). God tests his covenant people for two purposes: 1) to humble them, and 2) to show what is in their hearts (8.1-16). From the narrative in Deuteronomy we may infer that the testing of Abraham 'will do (him) good in the end' (8.16).

God's test of Abraham is about his son Isaac. The test is that he is to take his son, now apparently grown to young adulthood, 'to the land of Moriah; and offer him up there as a burnt offering' (Gen. 22.2). The pain and the poignancy of the test is in the double fact that Isaac is Abraham's only son, the one whom he loves (22.1). It also lies in the issue of whether or not God approves of and/or delights in human sacrifices (such as practiced by the Canaanites). Abraham has several options. One is that he can simply ignore the test. Two, he can bargain with God. Three, he can obey. He is caught on the horns of a dilemma. He knows the voice of God, so he cannot pretend that he had simply had a bad dream. Secondly, he has learned that God's relationship with him is unilateral, so he has no choice but to obey. But to obey is to surrender all of the stupendous promises of God – which depend on Isaac. Nevertheless, he has also learned that God is Almighty, and therefore when he takes up the knife to sacrifice his son, God Almighty will still be true to his covenant.

The test is real and not a charade. But God does not want the death of Isaac. He wants to show what is in Abraham's heart. And both parties find faith and obedience still operating in Abraham's

God is responding to the 'groaning' of the harsh treatment which the Israelites are experiencing at the hands of the Egyptians (2.23-25). Hearing their groaning, God 'remembers' his covenant with Abraham, Isaac, and Jacob (2.24). Consequently, he is now giving heed to Israel's cry of suffering (3.8). As a result, God now steps directly down into Israel's history – to deliver Israel from the Egyptians and to bring Israel back to Canaan, a land flowing with milk and honey (3.8). With these words God commissions Moses: 'Therefore, come now and I will send you to Pharaoh, so that you may bring my people, the sons of Israel, out of Egypt' (3.10). Clearly, for the third cycle of turning points in history and theology, Abraham is God's agent as 'Father' and Moses is God's secondary agent as Rescuer or Deliverer.

In God's earlier relationship with Abraham he revealed select and appropriate aspects of his self-identity. For example, when circumstances made Abraham aware of his military vulnerability, God revealed: 'I am a shield to you' (Gen. 15.1). Later, thirteen years after the as yet unfulfilled covenant promise of a son, God reveals himself: 'I am God Almighty' (17.1). Now, when God calls and commissions Moses, he reveals himself, appropriately as 'the God of Abraham, the God of Isaac, and the God of Jacob' (Exod. 3.10) (and everything else [such as the gift of land] which that implies). More importantly, on the threshold of delivering Israel out of Egypt, he reveals his name as their divine Deliverer or Redeemer: I AM WHO I AM (abbreviated as, I AM). In Hebrew this name is the tetragrammaton YHWH (יהוה, which is vocalized as Yahweh). This name is more than merely circumstantial – tied to Israel's deliverance – it is God's memorial name to all generations (3.15). Therefore, it is appropriate that Jesus, the Son of God, also identified himself as the I AM (Jn 8.58; 18.6). And, book-ending God's self-revelation, it closes out Scripture in the complementary forms: 'Alpha and Omega', and the God, 'who is, who was, and who is to come' (Rev. 1.8).

Observation: God progressively reveals himself throughout human history. God's self-revelation is always appropriate for the life-setting in which it was made. This revelation extends to the time of Jesus – who is the full and final revelation of whom God IS.

3.3. The Spread of Sin: Advancing Toward Nationhood

Abraham lived to be 175 years old. Isaac, Jacob, and Joseph had similarly long lifespans. Though they were long-livers, in the nature of the case, none of them ever lived to see Israel's nationhood. But before bringing Abraham's descendants from Egypt back to the land of Canaan, the third new start, in the ongoing cycle of new starts, is given new impetus through the leadership of Moses. There are three phases which combine to give Israel its identity and status as a nation: 1) the deliverance of Israel out of Egypt, 2) the wilderness wanderings, and 3) the Mosaic Covenant. In other words, before Israel is rescued out of Egypt, it is a ragtag group of slaves. During the wilderness phase, Israel begins to develop a cohesive identity; and, finally, at Mt. Sinai God establishes Israel as a unique nation (Exod. 19.5-6).

3.3.1. God's secondary agent, Moses, liberates Israel, and delivers them out of Egypt (Exodus 1–15)

Many Bible readers, when they see/hear the name, Moses, think of him first and foremost as the great Lawgiver. And, indeed, he is God's agent for the giving of the Law. This is often portrayed in religious art in pictures of the imaginary 'Moses' holding the tablets of stone on which God had written the Ten Commandments, which are not only the basic stipulations of the Mosaic covenant, but which were also the foundation of British and American jurisprudence. But the exodus narrative paints a somewhat different picture. In the exodus narrative, Moses is first, if not foremost, Israel's great liberator. This liberation is described by several different English terms: redemption, rescue, deliverance, liberation. In the context of writing about Israel's release from slavery and departure out of Egypt, this discussion will use the terms liberator/redeemer and liberation/redemption synonymously.

When we discussed the third start/new start and Moses as God's sub-agent, who advances the role of Abraham as God's agent, we observed that some anonymous Pharaoh had adopted two strategies to control Israel's population explosion: 1) enslavement of the nation, and 2) the killing of all newborn male babies (Exod. 1.11-22). When God calls and commissions Moses to be his agent of liberation, he explains the consequences of Pharaoh's actions. The LORD said to Moses:

> Then you shall say to Pharaoh, 'Thus says the LORD, Israel is My son, My first-born. So I said to you, "Let My son go ..." But you have refused to let him go. Behold, I will kill your son, your first-born' (Exod. 4.22, 23).

This is the clear and just application of the principle of *lex talionis* (e.g. 'an eye for an eye, a tooth for a tooth'), the principle of just consequences. Therefore, because Pharaoh had instigated the slavery of Israel and the killing/genocide of Israel's newborn male babies, God will enact just judgment against him for this murder.

Pharaoh's fear of Israel and his aggressively hostile actions toward the Israelites, which is matched by God's determination to see justice done, sets up a confrontation between the two parties. Moses and Aaron, his brother, confront Pharaoh: 'Thus says the LORD, the God of Israel, "Let My people go that they may celebrate a feast to Me in the wilderness"' (Exod. 5.1). Arrogantly, Pharaoh responds, 'Who is the LORD, that I should obey his voice to let Israel go?' (5.2a). Ironically, Israel as an enslaved people, was to obey his voice; and, he, Pharaoh and sun-god, is not about to submit to the voice of the LORD – in his mind, clearly an inferior and impotent God. And so, insolently, he continues: 'I do not *know* the LORD, and besides, I will not let Israel go' (5.2b). The LORD accepts Pharaoh's challenge. When Moses turns the Nile River to blood, Pharaoh will *know* that the God of Israel is the LORD (7.17). But, it will take nine plagues (signs and wonders) and the death of the first-born sons of the Egyptians for Pharaoh to *know* the LORD fully.

At the time in Israel's history which we are writing about, Egypt is one of the most powerful nations on earth. Only the Hittites and the Sea Peoples rival Egypt's domination of the eastern Mediterranean world. And, with the support of the priestly caste, Pharaoh is, therefore, one of the most powerful men in the world. Further, Egyptian religion is pantheistic. All of creation, from the Nile River to the sun, is deified. Therefore, the confrontation between Moses and Pharaoh unfolds at both the religious and military levels.

All out war does not begin immediately. First, there is a skirmish at Pharaoh's palace (Exod. 7.9-13). As instructed, Aaron will work a miracle (7.9). He throws down his staff and it becomes a serpent

(7.10). Pharaoh's wise ones duplicate the miracle (7.12a). But Aaron's staff swallowed up their staffs (7.12b). Now, Egyptian iconography from the New Kingdom shows that many (if not all) kings wore a headdress with a coiled cobra (serpent) poised to strike.[1] Therefore, Aaron's miracle about his staff/serpent is a dramatic lesson to the Egyptian ruler that there is a more powerful God in Egypt than he is. 'Yet, Pharaoh's heart was hardened and he did not listen to [Moses and Aaron] as the LORD had said' (7.13). After this preliminary skirmish, the LORD launches a full-scale assault against Pharaoh and the Egyptian kingdom.

The LORD's assault against Pharaoh consists of a series of 'wonders and signs' (Exod. 7.3). Later these wonders and signs are identified as 'diseases' which God put on the Egyptians (15.26). These wonders and signs happen in three groups of three and are followed by a tenth plague, which is the death of all of the firstborn sons of Egypt. The nine plagues/wonders and signs are the LORD's just judgment against Egypt for the years of suffering which their enslavement of Israel brought about. The tenth plague – the death of the firstborn sons – is punishment upon Pharaoh and Egypt for the killing of the Israelite newborn sons. The following chart summarizes this period:

No.	Text	The Signs and Wonders
1	7.14-25	The Nile River is turned to blood
2	8.1-15	The Nile River swarms with frogs
3	8.16-19	The earth produced gnats (lice? mosquitos?) on humans and beasts
4	8.20-32	Swarms of insects throughout the land
5	9.1-7	A severe pestilence kills Egyptian livestock
6	9.8-12	Boils on humans and beasts

[1] Jean-Pierre Isbouts, *The Biblical World: An Illustrated Atlas* (Washington, DC: National Geographic, 2007), pp. 112-13.

No.	Text	The Signs and Wonders
7	9.13-35	An historically unprecedented, very heavy (deadly) hail storm
8	10.1-20	A devastating locust plague
9	10.21-29	The light of the sun is blotted out for three days
10	12.29-36	The LORD strikes all the firstborn in the land of Egypt

Pharaoh's reaction to the LORD and his agents, Moses and Aaron, is one key to understanding the wonders and signs. Sometimes Pharaoh hardened his heart. Other times, he first relented and then hardened his heart. This data portrays a ruler stubborn and yet also vacillating or capricious. But, ultimately, the LORD hardens the heart of this cruel tyrant – guilty of enslaving a nation and murdering a generation of newborn sons. The ten plagues show the LORD to be a just God, punishing Egypt for the suffering they caused God's people and for the murderous way they treated God's people. But, the end result is more than the fact that just judgment is meted out against the Egyptians; it is also that Israel is liberated from her enslavement and expelled from the land of Egypt.

Cumulatively, the oppressive sequence of plagues finally causes Pharaoh to capitulate and expel Israel out of Egypt. At midnight on the appointed day, 'the LORD struck all the first-born in the land of Egypt' (Exod. 12.29). Therefore, just as earlier Israel had cried out in her suffering (2.25-27), so now the Egyptians make a 'great cry' in their time of nation-wide suffering (12.30). As a result, Pharaoh commanded Moses, 'Rise up, get out from among my people, both you and the sons of Israel; and go, worship the LORD' (12.31). Moses had prepared God's people for this time, and so they were already waiting to depart. Their deliverance is called the Passover, and this became one of the mandatory feast days for Israel (12.1-28).

But even after all of this, true to form, this stubborn and capricious Pharaoh once again changes his mind. Equally true to form the LORD hardens Pharaoh's heart, for this perpetrator of genocide against the Israelites had not yet been fully punished for his wickedness (Exod. 14.1-9; compare 4.23). Having been led by the LORD into the wilderness (13.13), Israel finds herself trapped at the Reed Sea, with Pharaoh's elite chariot corps in pursuit (14.9). Moses encourages his frightened, dispirited followers: 'Do not fear. Stand by and see the salvation of the LORD' (14.13). This salvation is certain, for 'the LORD will fight for you' (14.14 [while you keep silent]). The resulting death of Pharaoh, 'honors the LORD' (14.17). The well-known pathway through the sea (14.26-28) becomes the path of rescue for the Israelites and the path of final punishment for Pharaoh and for his charioteers (14.30).

There is only one proper response for Israel to give to the LORD's victory over the Egyptians. In writing his report, Moses observes, 'When Israel saw the great power which the LORD had used against the Egyptians, the people feared the LORD, and they believed in the LORD and in his servant, Moses' (Exod. 14.31). Fearing, that is, reverencing, the LORD, Moses leads Israel in a song of national praise (15.1-18):

> I will sing to the LORD, for he is highly exalted;
> The horse and its rider, he has hurled into the sea.
> The LORD is my strength and song,
> And he has become my salvation;
> This is my God, and I will praise Him;
> My father's God, and I will extol Him.
> The LORD is a warrior;
> The LORD is his name.

Unbelievably, three days later, they begin to sing a new song (Exod. 15.22-26). Leaving the Reed Sea, they entered the wilderness of Shur, where they soon exhausted the supply of water, only to find an oasis, but the water was bitter (15.22, 23). Here, their song of praise at the Reed Sea (15.1-18) is replaced by a chorus of *grumblings*: 'what shall we drink' (15.24). When they exhaust their food supplies a month later, 'the whole congregation of the sons of Israel *grumbled* against Moses and Aaron' (16.2). Soon, at Rephidim, 'the people *quarreled* with Moses', and, '*grumbled* against Moses' (17.2, 3). This ongoing 'chorus' of ingratitude will soon become a settled habit and will ultimately lead to their punishment in the wilderness.

3.3.2. Tests in the wilderness (Exodus 15.22–Numbers 14.45)

Generations earlier than the LORD's deliverance of Abraham's descendants out of Egypt, he promised that Abraham would have a son, and in due time, he would have descendants more numerous than the stars (Gen. 15.4, 5). Abraham believed God (15.6). Later, God would test Abraham's faith, instructing, 'Take now your son, your only son, whom you love, Isaac ... and offer him there as a burnt offering' (22.2). Abraham proceeds to obey this test (22.1), and because of his 'willingness to obey, the LORD not only spared Isaac, but blessed father and son with the renewed promise of many descendants' (22.15-18). Similarly, after seeing God's great power in action at the Reed Sea, God's people 'believed in the LORD' (Exod. 14.31). But, in contrast to Abraham who obeyed when he was tested, Israel consistently *grumbled, complained*, and/or *disobeyed* when God tested them (Exodus 15–Numbers 14). Therefore, in contrast to Abraham who had the blessings of the covenant renewed and extended, Israel's blessing turned into covenant curses.

3.3.2.1. Anticipatory reactions to testing

Israel's grumbling about adversity in the wilderness comes as no surprise to Bible readers who have been reading the exodus narrative sequentially from the beginning through to the end (Exodus 1–40). Twice, before the LORD led Israel into the wilderness, Israel has the opportunity to demonstrate her responses to adversity. First, after Moses had petitioned Pharaoh 'to let Israel go' (Exod. 5.1), he not only refused, but in retaliation he also increased their workload (5.2-18). Having to cope with the increased load of oppression, the Israelites accuse Moses of making things more difficult for the Israelite slaves and themselves (5.19-23). Second, when they find themselves trapped at the Reed Sea, the frightened escapees accuse Moses and wish that they had been left behind in Egypt (14.10-12). These anticipatory reactions illustrate that though the LORD always proves himself to be faithful to Israel, she will repeatedly prove disloyal to the LORD. The narrative's six examples of testing – three before Israel arrives at Mt. Sinai and three after Israel departs from Mt. Sinai – follow a consistent pattern.

3.3.2.2. Patterns of testing in the wilderness

In the two to three months before Israel arrives at Mt. Sinai, where the LORD will make a covenant of nationhood with Abraham's descendants, recently freed from slavery in Egypt, the LORD will test Israel about whether or not she will still, 'believe in the LORD' (Exod. 14.31). The following chart summarizes these three tests, which, in turn, are about water to drink and food to eat:

Pattern	Example 1 Marah (15.22-26)	Example 2 Sin (16.1ff)	Example 3 Massah (17.1-7)
Need	Water was bitter (genuine need)	Food supplies dwindle (genuine need)	No water (genuine need)
Response	Israel grumbled Israel tested God God tested Israel	Israel grumbled Israel tested God They wish to return to the good old days in Egypt	Israel grumbled Israel quarreled with Moses. Israel tested the God
Provision	Put a tree in the water and turned the water 'sweet'	God supplies the need: 1.) Manna 2.) Quails. Note: God's provision becomes God's judgment	Moses is to strike the rock, and water will pour forth
Judgment	Not applicable	Not applicable	Not applicable

The data in the above chart yields several observations. One, an ungrateful attitude can turn quickly into the habit of ingratitude. Two, since God himself leads Israel into those circumstances, it is *his* purpose to test Israel. Three, because their needs are genuine, he always has a provision for them. Four, God's provision, even for meeting the same need, may take different forms.

3.3.3. The LORD makes a covenant of nationhood

Following the third 'test' of Israel in the wilderness, the LORD leads Israel to Mt. Sinai (Exod. 19.1-2). This mountain is also known as the mountain of God, and earlier it was the setting of the 'burning bush' calling and commissioning of Moses (3.1-22). Israel's arrival at Mt. Sinai several months later is 'the sign that it is I (the LORD) who have sent you: when you have brought the people out of

Egypt, you shall worship God at this mountain' (3.12). Mt. Sinai is located in a wilderness which Israel experienced as a 'great and terrible' place (Deut. 1.19). But it is here, in the most inhospitable of places, that God will enter into a covenant with his newly liberated people.

This covenant will establish the nationhood of Israel. It is the second covenant of the third cycle of turning points in biblical history and theology. The first covenant in this cycle is the so-called Abrahamic covenant (Gen. 15.1-21). This is a covenant of 'sonship' (15.4-6), though it also includes the complementary promises of land and nationhood (12.1-2). Now at Mt. Sinai, the mountain of God, God turns the earlier promise of nationhood into a covenant of nationhood. This covenant establishes the essential parameters of the relationship between God and Abraham's descendants.

3.3.3.1. The form of the covenant

The exodus out of Egypt happened no later than the thirteenth century before the coming of Christ (the agent of the sixth cycle of turning points). This gives a date for the so-called Mosaic covenant in the final quarter of the second millennium before Christ. By this time, in the history of the ancient near east, a covenant pattern or form had been developed for international treaties. Scholars identify this form as the 'Hittite Suzerainty Treaty'. Examples of these treaties follow a sixfold pattern: 1) preamble, 2) historical prologue, 3) basic and detailed stipulations, 4) deposition of text, 5) witnesses, and 6) the curses and the blessings. Of course, the subject matter in the Mosaic covenant is unique to the LORD and Israel, his vassal state. Nevertheless, this covenant follows the pattern of late second millennium international suzerainty treaties. The following discussion briefly illustrates both the similarities and differences between Hittite treaties and the Mosaic covenant.

The Mosaic covenant is complex, detailed, and far reaching. The following discussion summarizes the six elements of the second-millennium BCE international treaties as they are to be found in the Mosaic covenant. First, the covenant begins with a **preamble**. The preamble identifies the (two) parties who are entering into the covenantal relationship. These two parties are the LORD and Israel. Moses reports, 'Then God spoke all these words, saying, "I am the LORD your God"' (Exod. 20.1-2). But this is not a treaty between equals (a parity treaty). Rather, it is a treaty between a superior power/party and his vassal (a suzerainty treaty). The LORD, the superior party, is the covenant maker and Israel is his vassal.

Second, the **historical prologue** reports about the previous relationship between the two parties. With stark brevity, the LORD summarizes his immediate past relationship with Israel, saying, 'I am the LORD, your God, who brought you out of the land of Egypt, out of the house of slavery' (Exod. 20.2b). This simple, factual statement of their history implies much more: the flight of Jacob's family to Egypt, their enslavement and genocide at the hands of the Egyptians, the call of Moses, the ten wonders and signs, and the eventual flight of Israel into the wilderness (Exodus 1–18). This, in turn, implies the earlier relationship, which stretches back across the nations to the call of Abraham (Genesis 12–50). Clearly, the two covenant parties are not strangers to each other for they have a long-standing relationship.

Third, the covenant contains an appropriate set of **stipulations**. These are at two levels: basic and detailed. The so-called Decalogue or Ten Commandments are an immediate example of basic stipulations (Exod. 20.3-18). They oversee Israel's relationship to God prohibiting polytheism (many gods), idolatry, swearing oaths, and positively commanding a mandatory Sabbath day of worship (20.3-11). These basic stipulations also oversee or administer basic stipulations at the interpersonal human level. One, the commandment to children to honor their parents rewards obedience 'that your days may be prolonged in the land which the LORD your God gives you' (20.12). The remaining stipulations prohibit murder, adultery, theft, false witness, and covetousness (20.13-17). In general, these basic stipulations prohibit false worship (Nos. 1-4), and unethical conduct (Nos. 5-10). The principles contained in these Ten Commandments are most aptly summed up in the phrase, 'ethical monotheism'. Monotheism is the worship of one God – the LORD, and ethical monotheism is the complementary requirement to live in right relationship with other persons.

The basic stipulations in the Mosaic covenant are supplemented by detailed stipulations. Whereas the basic stipulations typically take the form of direct imperatives, which may be either positive commands or negative prohibitions, the detailed stipulations typically take the form of case laws. The following examples illustrate the difference:

> Basic stipulation: 'You shall not murder' (20.13).
> Detailed stipulation: 'he who strikes a man so that he dies shall surely be put to death' (21.12).

The detailed stipulations regulate the life of the nation living on the land. Nearing the end of his life, Moses exhorts Israel:

> So you shall keep his statutes and his commandments ... that it may go well with you and with your children after you, that you may live long on the land which the LORD your God is giving you for all time (Deut. 4.40).

Fourth, the covenant identifies where the covenant will be **deposited**. The 'tablets of stone' on which the Ten Commandments were engraved, are to be deposited in a special box, which, not surprisingly is named, 'the ark of the testimony' (Exod. 25.19). This box, also known as the ark of the covenant, is the holiest object in Israel's sacrificial system, and therefore is housed in the Holy of Holies in the Tabernacle. The information in the covenant about the deposition of the text is to help keep it secure, and to identify where it can be located. Interestingly, Joshua's covenant renewal, approximately 40 years later, also contains information about the deposition of this document (Josh. 24.26).

Fifth, the covenant identifies the **witnesses**. In the ancient near east, as the example of Esarhaddon's Vassal Treaty illustrates, the covenant parties invoke the gods as witnesses. But, because Israel's God is One, it is not so in its covenants. The Mosaic covenant is witnessed by twelve pillars of stone for the 12 tribes of Israel (Exod. 24.4). A generation later, when Joshua and Israel renew the covenant, it is one stone which is a witness (Josh. 24.26). At this time, Joshua declared 'Behold, this stone shall be for a witness against us, for it has heard all of the words of the LORD which he spoke to us; thus it shall be for a witness against you, lest you deny your God' (24.7). Similarly, though it is not stated in the narrative of the Mosaic covenant, the 12 stone pillars would have had the same function. These memorial stones also functioned as a sign (4.6, 7), and had the Law of Moses written on their surface (8.30-35).

Sixth, the covenant concluded with **the blessings and the curses**. Earlier covenants, such as those made with Noah and Abraham (Gen. 9.8-17; 15.1-21), were both *unilateral* and *unconditional*. The following quotations illustrate the language of unilateral covenants.

> Noahic Covenant: 'Now behold, I Myself (God) do establish My covenant with you, and with your descendants after you ... This is the sign of the covenant (i.e. the rainbow) which I am making between Me and you' (9.9, 12).

> Abrahamic Covenant: 'I am the LORD who brought you out of Ur of the Chaldees, to give you this land to possess it ... On that day, the LORD made a covenant with Abram, saying, "To your descendants I have given this land"' (15.7, 18).

In sharp contrast to these earlier, unilateral covenants, the Mosaic covenant is bilateral and conditional. The following quotations illustrate the language of bilateral covenants.

> Mosaic Covenant: 'Now then, if you will indeed obey My voice and keep My covenant, then you shall be my own possession' (Exod. 19.5).

> 'And Moses recounted to the people all of the words of the LORD' ... and all the people answered and said, All the words which the LORD has spoken we will do!' (24.3).

In unilateral covenants, God takes the initiative and assumes the responsibility to make the covenant work. In bilateral covenants whereas God also takes the initiative, the onus for its success depends upon Israel's obedience. The blessings and the curses reinforce the bilateral and the conditional character of the Mosaic Covenant.

The blessings and the curses are scattered throughout the Exodus and Deuteronomic covenant narratives. Many of them, however, are brought together in Deuteronomy 27–30. The following chart illustrates the conditional language which is associated with a bilateral covenant.

Blessings	**Curses**
If you diligently obey the LORD your God ... all these blessings shall come upon you (28.1-2).	But if you will not obey the LORD ... (then) all these curses shall come upon you and overtake you (28.15).
Blessed shall you be in the city, and blessed shall you be in the country (28.3).	Cursed shall you be in the city and cursed shall you be in the country (28.16).
Blessed shall be your basket and your kneading bowl (28.5).	Cursed shall be your basket and your kneading bowl (28.17).
Blessed shall you be when you come in and blessed shall you be when you go out (28.6).	Cursed shall you be when you come in, and cursed shall you be when you go out (28.19).

Clearly, whether God will bless Israel or whether he will curse Israel depends on Israel – whether she will obey the Law of Moses or whether she will disobey the Law of Moses. Therefore, there are appropriate responsibilities and appropriate consequences which are part and parcel of the bilateral and conditional character of the covenant. Further, the blessings and the curses typically relate to life on the land, which is appropriate for Israel as an agrarian culture (farmers, orchardists, herdspersons). In this regard, obedience yields agricultural abundance and disobedience produces agricultural scarcity. It is not surprising therefore that many of the blessings are directly opposite to each other.

Since the blessings and the curses relate to living on the land, Israel's obedience or her disobedience determines her destiny as a nation. About obedience Moses promises, '(If) you keep his statutes and his commandments, (then) it may go well with you and with your children after you, and that you may live long on the land which the LORD your God is giving you for all time' (Deut. 4.40). On the other hand, Moses warns, 'And it shall come about that as the LORD delighted over you to prosper you, and multiply you, so the LORD will delight over you to make you perish (when you persist in disobeying the LORD) and you shall be torn from the land' (28.63). It is a sobering fact that many generations later when the Babylonians conquered God's people, 'Judah (the southern Israelite kingdom) was led away into exile from its land' (2 Kgs 25.21).

This failure of Israel to keep the Mosaic covenant, which brings about its exile from the land, does not either annul or compromise the unilateral promises of land and nationhood which God gave to Abraham. Paul understood this well writing, 'for the gifts and calling of God are irrevocable' (Rom. 11.29). But, as God announced through Jeremiah the prophet, it would require a new and better kind of covenant than the Mosaic covenant (Jer. 31.31-34; Heb. 8.6-13).

3.4 Judgment: The Exodus Generation Dies in the Wilderness (Numbers 11–Deuteronomy 34)

As we have already observed, when the LORD entered into a covenant with Israel at Mt. Sinai, he reminded them, 'I am the LORD your God, who brought you out of the land of Egypt, out of the house of slavery' (Exod. 20.2). The LORD's self-identification implies all of the recent events of Israel's exodus: 1) God emancipated Israel from slavery by ten awesome signs and wonders of judgment against Egypt (5.1–12.36). He also made a way of escape from the land – the Pathway through the sea (14.1-31). To protect Israel from the military might of Canaan, the LORD led them by a detour route through the wilderness (13.17-22). In the wilderness, God repeatedly watered and fed them (15.22–17.7). At Mt. Sinai itself, the LORD appeared to Israel in fearful theophanic signs (19.16-18); and for many days he revealed his glory (24.12-18). Finally, he entered into a covenant of nationhood with Abraham's descendants, to which Israel declared, 'All that the LORD has spoken we will do, and we will be obedient' (24.7). But throughout all of this time, Israel flirted with ingratitude, which, by the time she departed from Mt. Sinai, had developed into a national, habitual characteristic (Num. 11.1-14, 38).

One of the most shocking attitudes which Israel displays in the early days and weeks of the exodus is ingratitude. God had done so much to emancipate Israel and lead her out of the land. Yet, whenever difficulty and adversity came her way, she invariably 'grumbled' (Exod. 15.24; 16.2; 17.3). Therefore, when the LORD leads Israel on her journey away from Mt. Sinai, Bible readers are not surprised to read, 'Now, the people became like those who complain of adversity, in the hearing of the LORD' (Num. 11.1). The following chart illustrates the pattern of Israel's attitude as she journeys further into the wilderness.

Pattern	Taberah (Num. 11.1-3)	Kibroth Hattavah (Num. 11.4-34)
Need	No need	No need
Response	Habit: they complained	Habit: they complain about lack of variety (v 4-6, 18)
Provision	No provision	The LORD will give them meat for one month (11.18-20; 31-32)
Judgment	Fire (partial judgment)	The LORD's anger burned – some die in the plague

Observation: In these examples, there are no legitimate needs, only desires. Therefore, there was no provision, only judgment. These episodes, which explicitly show that grumbling and complaining have become Israel's dominant attitude, lead to her decisive failure.

It is incredible to contemplate, but Israel's decisive failure is her refusal to follow the LORD's leading into Canaan, the land which had been promised to Abraham at the beginning of this cycle of turning points (Gen. 12.1-2). The episode begins when Moses sends a team of twelve spies – one from each tribe – to reconnoitre the land. From the perspective of these desert dwellers, it proves to be everything that God had promised, 'a land flowing with milk and honey' (Num. 13.27). While the spies are justifiably enthusiastic about the agricultural prosperity of the land, they are intimidated by the inhabitants. They report: 'the people who live in the land are strong and the cities are fortified and very large; and, moreover, we saw the descendants of Anak there' (13.28). One of the spies, Caleb, tries to combat the mood of pessimism which is the 'child of Israel's intimidation'. He urges the people: 'we should, by all means, go up and take possession of it for we shall surely overcome it' (13.30). But the ten dissident spies continued to push their intimidating agenda (13.31-33).

The result of the 'bad report', which the ten spies give, is that, 'the sons of Israel grumbled against Moses and Aaron' (Num. 14.2). They accuse the LORD of wanting them 'to fall by the sword' (14.3).

They encourage one another: 'would it not be better for us to return to Egypt' (14.3b). Joshua and Caleb vainly tried to persuade the people saying 'do not rebel against the LORD; and do not fear the people of the land, for they shall be our prey ... the LORD is with us; do not fear them' (14.9). The glory of the LORD then appears, and through Moses, announces his judgment upon the people:

> Surely, all men who have seen My glory and My signs, which I performed in Egypt and in the wilderness, yet have put Me to the test these ten times and have not listened to My voice, shall by no means see the land which I swore to their fathers, nor shall any of those who spurned Me see it (14.22-23).

But the LORD will also remain true to his covenant with Abraham about the land (Gen. 15.7-21). Therefore, the children of the first generation of the exodus, 'whom you (i.e. Israel) said would become a prey – I will bring them in, and they shall know the land which you have rejected' (14.31).

Psalm 95.7-11 describes this 'loathsome' generation. For 40 years Israel tested God; they hardened their hearts at Meribah and Massah; they repudiated the message of the 'signs' (namely, that God cares and provides). Therefore, God loathed that generation, and he prevented them from entering his rest (the land of promise and covenant). This, of course, is not only a cautionary tale for Israel, but it is also a cautionary tale for the church (Heb. 3.7-19).

Explanation. Note that the fourth cycle begins with a vertical line rather than a point. In the schematic, the point represents a family (e.g. Adam and Eve, Noah, and Abraham). In the fourth cycle, the new start is about a new generation of God's people. Note also that the timeline ends at the Babylonian Captivity and remains broken until the restoration of Judah under the leadership of a second Joshua (the priest). The break in the time line signifies that God's people do not exist as a nation for the 70 years of captivity.

If the *promise* of the land dominates the third cycle of turning points then the *possession* of the land is one of the prominent themes of the fourth cycle of turning points. But, in comparison to the unilateral promises about the land (Gen. 12.2; 15.4; 17.16; 21.1-7; etc.), the issue of the possession of the land is contingent, i.e. it depends on Israel's obedience to the Mosaic covenant (Exod. 24.7; Deut. 4.40). In regards to Israel's possession of the land, the fourth cycle has the following emphases: 1) the conquest and settlement of the land in the time of Joshua, 2) the origin and spread of trib-al/national evil (Judges), 3) the Monarchy (united and divided), and 4) Judgment (the Exile of Israel, the northern Kingdom [722 BCE]; the Exile of Judah, the southern Kingdom [586 BCE]).

4.1. The Agent: Joshua, the Warrior Prophet

Joshua first appears in the exodus narrative in a military role. In the battle against the Amalekites, Joshua functions as the General of Israel's army and Moses functions as the 'Commander in Chief' (Exod. 17.8-14). During the battle between the two enemies when Moses holds up his hands in prayer, Israel prevails over the Amalek-ites, but when he tires and lowers his hands, Amalek prevails (17.11). However, by sunset Joshua had, 'overwhelmed Amalek and his people with the edge of the sword' (17.13). Joshua next appears in a military capacity as one of the twelve spies sent into the land of promise to reconnoitre it. He represents the tribe of Ephraim (Num. 13.8). Along with Caleb, Joshua urges the Israelites to trust that the LORD, 'will bring it into this land (Canaan), and give it to us – a land flowing with milk and honey' (14.8). But the ten other spies give a contradictory report, which intimidates the people. As a result, Israel refuses to enter the land, and, in just judgment, the LORD then denies that generation entry into the land (14.26-35). Further, in the sight of the assembled nation, Moses, at the LORD's command, commissions Joshua to be his successor (27.18-23). Finally, Deuteronomy describes Joshua as 'the son of Nun [who] was filled with the Spirit of wisdom, for Moses had laid his hands on him; and the sons of Israel *listened to him* and did as the LORD had commanded Moses' (Deut. 34.9). These are impressive credentials for Israel's leader-elect.

Deuteronomy ends giving Joshua high praise (34.9). The report, 'and the sons of Israel *listened to him*' (= obeyed him) points back to a prophecy which Moses had earlier given to Israel. The prophecy is that Moses' successor will be a prophet like himself, whom Israel is to listen to, that is, obey (Deut. 18.15). Thus, having been commissioned by Moses, and having been filled with the Spirit of wisdom, Joshua has unparalleled credentials. Following Moses, Joshua will be Israel's next charismatic (i.e. Spirit filled) warrior prophet.

As Israel's second warrior prophet, Joshua, alone in the nation, is best equipped to lead it in the invasion and conquest of the land of Canaan. He is not only experienced in battle (Exod. 17.8-14), but now the LORD, himself, replaces Moses as his 'commander-in-chief' (Josh. 1.1-9). Having earlier been 'filled with the Spirit of wisdom' (Deut. 34.9), Joshua's first act as the 'general' of Israel's army is to send two spies into Canaan in order to reconnoitre the land (Josh. 2.1-24). Next, though it is the season when the Jordan River is at flood level, God makes a pathway through the waters (3.1–4.24), as he had earlier done at the Reed Sea (Exod. 4.26-31). Following this dramatic entry into Canaan, Joshua has a theophanic encounter with 'the captain of the host [army] of the LORD' (Josh. 5.13-15). This echoes Moses' earlier 'burning bush' theophanic encounter with the LORD at Horeb (Exod. 3.1-22). The LORD engages in 'psychological warfare' against the Canaanites ('their hearts melted', Joshua 2.9-11; 5.1). He also announces victory over the fortified city of Jericho: 'see I have given Jericho into your hand with its king and the valiant warriors' (6.2). He makes the same promise about the capture of the city of Ai (8.1). Hearing about these defeats, the king of Jerusalem, Adoni-zedek, forms a coalition of five city-states to fight Israel. But it was in vain, for now, for the third time, the LORD assures Joshua of victory (10.8). Therefore, the LORD confounded this powerful coalition (10.10). He also 'threw large hailstones from heaven on them as far as Azekah' (10.11). As a result of the LORD's intervention, 'there was no day like that before or after it, when the LORD listened to the voice of a man (Joshua); for the LORD fought for Israel' (10.14). Israel also achieves similar results against the powerful Hazor coalition in the north for 'the LORD delivered them into the hand of Israel' (11.8). Thus, the LORD and Joshua prove to be an all-conquering combination. In fact, by the end of the wars of conquest, they had together defeated 31 kings (12.7-24). 'Thus, the land had rest from war' (11.23).

The Abrahamic 'land' theme (Gen. 12.1) and the Joshua 'rest' theme come together early in the book of Joshua. There the LORD renews his promise given earlier to Moses: 'The LORD your God gives you rest, and will give you this land' (Josh. 1.13). This land is identified as extending 'from this wilderness and this Lebanon, even as far as the great river, the river Euphrates, all the land of the Hittites, and as far as the Great Sea toward the setting of the sun' (1.4; compare Gen. 15.18-21). The 'rest' theme in Joshua is nuanced. First, it means rest from Israel's wilderness wanderings (Josh. 1.13). Second, it means rest from the wars of conquest (11.23). Third, it also means the complementary occupation of the land itself (Josh. 13.24). This occupation of the land will be Israel's inheritance tribe by tribe (e.g. 13.7; 23.5).

The land is a good land (13.13). The promise of the land is God's 'words' to Israel and, as Joshua affirms at the end of his life, not one word of God's good words has failed (13.14). But should Israel disobey the LORD, they will forfeit this good land (13.15-16). This threat that Israel might forfeit their rest/land is ominous, but that will not happen until later in Israel's history. In the present, the Israel of Joshua's day enjoyed their threefold rest (from their wanderings, from war, and, positively, their inheritance).

4.2. The New Start: Conquest and Settlement of the Land (Joshua 1–24)

About 800 years after God had promised the land of Canaan to Abraham, the second generation of the exodus is poised to occupy their land. From the start, the land is described in a variety of ways.

It is identified as 'Canaan' after the inhabitants, the Canaanites (Gen. 12.5). But peoples other than the Canaanites also live in this land, whose southern and northern borders extend, 'From the river of Egypt as far as the great river, the river Euphrates' (15.18). This multi-ethnic society includes: 'the Kenite and the Kenizzite and the Kadmonite and the Hittite and the Perrizite and the Rephaim and the Amorite and the Canaanite and the Girgashite and the Jebusite' (15.19-21). The eastern extremity of the land includes the fertile valley of the Jordan River (13.9-13). All of this is the land about which God declared to Abraham: 'I will give it to you and to your descendants forever'.

The 'promised land' is not only multi-ethnic but its peoples are also multi-religious. The dominant religion, as far as the biblical and non-biblical evidence shows, is Canaanite. This religion is pantheistic – all of nature is in various ways deified. It is also polytheistic. The panoply of gods and goddesses is large, and it includes several of special interest to Bible readers, namely, El, the senior god, and Baal and Astarte, two of the many younger gods. Canaanite religion is also idolatrous. This is the worship of idols – both at the sanctuaries and the high places which were scattered throughout the land. Canaanite religion was a fertility religion and cult prostitution was a central preoccupation of the religion. Other features of this religion included human sacrifice and especially sacrifice. For all of these and other reasons when Israel occupies the land, she is to cleanse and purge the land of its Canaanite worship. In other words, in cleansing and purging the land of Canaan of its false worship, Israel is to treat the Canaanite worshipper in the same way that she was to punish the idolater who might arise in Israel – by execution. But one of the saddest, most tragic lessons of Israel's life on the land is that Israel failed to purge the land of false worship.

As we have observed earlier when we looked at the call of Abraham, and the LORD's subsequent covenant with him, God gave him three major promises: land, nationhood, and a son (leading to many descendants) (Gen. 12.1-4; 15.4). These promises are, of course, fulfilled in reverse order: first, Isaac is born (21.1-7); second, God enters into a covenant of nationhood (Exod. 20-24); and third, God gives the land of Canaan to Israel in the time of Joshua (1–24). As the title of this section indicates there are two phases to complete the process of the gift of the land. The first phase is the conquest of the land, reported in Joshua 1–12, and the second phase is that Joshua will apportion the land to the twelve tribes as their permanent inheritance (Joshua 13–24). Joshua is God's agent for both phases.

4.2.1. Joshua and the covenant renewals

By the time of Joshua's leadership of Israel, the nation had been heir to the Abrahamic Covenant (Genesis 15) and its renewals (Gen. 17.22, *et al.)* for many generations. The older Israelites of Joshua's day had also actively participated in the covenant between the LORD and Israel at Mt. Sinai (Exodus), which Moses renewed in the wilderness about 40 years later (Deuteronomy). In addition, shortly after entering the 'promised' land, Joshua led the second generation of the exodus in a renewal of the Mosaic covenant (Josh. 8.30-35). Finally, when Joshua is about to die, he leads the nation in what is now the third renewal of the Mosaic covenant (24.1-28). As Joshua makes the covenant renewal, he affirms, 'but for me and my house, we will serve the LORD' (24.15). Similarly, the nation also affirms, 'we will serve the LORD' (24.21). They stand before the LORD as witnesses against themselves, 'we will obey his voice' (24.24).

They also stand before the memorial stone, which shall be a witness against them, 'lest [they] deny [their] God' (24.27). In the light of their parents' 'grumbling' and 'disobedient' ways, the surprising thing is that the second generation of the exodus, by and large, did indeed obey the LORD. But as the book of Judges will report, such obedience is a rare thing in Israel's history.

4.2.3. The origin and spread of Israel's (tribal) sin

Historically the origin and spread of Israel's sinfulness is a lengthy and convoluted process. It stretches from occupation of the 'promised' land to when Judah is 'torn from the land' (Joshua 24–2 Chronicles 36). It begins with the tribal sins reported in the book of Judges (ca. 1300–1040 BCE), extends to the time of the United Monarchy (1040–920 BC), and finally ends in the exile of Israel to Assyria (722 BC) and of Judah to Babylon (586 BC). As we can see, this is a period of about 600 years and its patterns of tribal and monarchical sinfulness is only alleviated by the brief 'golden age' of the reigns of David and Solomon (1000–920 BC).

4.2.4. The cycles of tribal sins

Before it is united by the reign of Saul, Israel's first king, Israel functions as a loose confederation of quasi-independent states. In this condition, sin quickly develops and spreads. This happens following the death of Joshua and the younger generation of Israelites who followed him into the promised land. The book of Judges explains: 'the people served the LORD all the days of Joshua, and all the days of those who survived Joshua, who had seen all the great work of the LORD which he had done for Israel' (Judg. 2.6). After the death of this generation, however, 'there arose another generation after them who did not know the LORD, nor yet the work which he had done for Israel' (2.10). Lacking the first-hand experience of God which had kept their fathers obedient to the covenant, and by implication also failing to renew the covenant as their fathers had done, this generation turned to the practice of Canaanite idolatry. In the words of Judges, 'the sons of Israel did evil in the sight of the LORD, and served the Baals' (2.11).

The heart of the book of Judges (chapters 2–16) is about the pattern of Israel's sinfulness, and the report of six cycles of Israel's apostasy and judgment. The following chart identifies Israel's sin and gives the first example of this pattern.

Pattern	Example 3.7-11
1. <u>Sin</u>. Israel did the <u>evil</u> (they served the Baals)	3.7 sons of Israel ... served the Baals and Asheroth
2. <u>Servitude</u>. Oppression by a foreign power	3.8 The LORD sold them into the hands of Cushan-Rishathaim (for 8 years)
3. <u>Supplication</u>: Cried out to the LORD (groaned)	3.9 The LORD raised up Othniel, son of Kenaz to deliver them (cried out)
4. <u>Salvation</u> The LORD raised up Judges to deliver Israel	3.10 The Spirit of the LORD came upon Othniel, and thus, he delivered Israel
5. <u>Return to sin</u>	3.11, 12 After 40 years the cycle repeats itself

More briefly, the following chart illustrates the other reported examples:

Pattern	3.12-31	4.1-5.31	6.1-8.32	10.6-16.31	
Sin	3.12 Evil	4.1 Evil	6.1 Evil	10.6 Baal Worship	
Servitude	3.12 Moab	4.2 Hazor	6.1 Midian	10.7 Ammon	
	3.14 18 years	4.3 20 years	6.1 7 years		13.5 Philistines
Supplication	3.15	4.3	6.7	10.10-16	
Salvation	3.15 Ehud	4.4 Deborah 4.6 Barak	6.11 Gideon	11.1 Jephthah	13.24 Samson
Tribe	Benjamin	Naphtali	Manasseh	Manasseh	Dan
Rest	3.30 80 years	5.31 40 years	8.28 40 years		

A survey of the data from Judges yields several important observations. One, God's agents of oppression are various foreign nations including Mesopotamia, Moab, Hazor, Midian, Ammon, and Philistia. This use of foreign nations to chastise God's people foreshadows the prophet Habakkuk's conundrum, 'why are Thou silent when the wicked (nations) swallowed up/Those more righteous than they?' (Hab. 1.13). Two, the tribes of Israel which are being oppressed are Judah, Benjamin, Naphtali, Zebulon, and Manasseh. Three, the (charismatic) warrior judges include Othniel, Deborah, Gideon, Jephthah, and Samson. They are those who have the Spirit/gift of warfare. Four, the narrative in Judges 3–16 hints at other tribes (Issachar) and other judges (Shamgar, Tola, Jair, Ibzan, Elon, and Abdon) being involved in this ongoing cycle of sin→salvation. From the above data, one can conclude that the sons of Israel were very susceptible to the 'evil' of Canaanite religion that the tribes involved are regional and not national, and therefore, are likely to overlap, and that the judges' prowess in warfare is not natural, but is exclusively a gift from God. In this regard, the judges may be classified as charismatic warrior prophets after the earlier example of Joshua.

4.2.5. Light and darkness: impetus toward kingship

Following the report about the six cycles of the pattern, 'sin, servitude, supplication, salvation', and the subsequent 'return to sin' (Judges 2–16), the book of Judges concludes with a series of anecdotes (Judges 17–21). These narratives are further illustrations of the era when Israel 'occupied' the land. These narratives are followed in (canonical) succession by additional information about the days when the judges judged, which is found in the books of Ruth and 1 Samuel.

Judges 17–21 form a sort of appendix to the book which further illustrates the dark days of political, religious, and moral anarchy which characterizes Israel after the death of Joshua. These concluding anecdotes report about: household religion (Judg. 17.1-13), tribal religion with its illegitimate priesthood and forbidden idols (18.1-31), inhospitality, gang rape and murder (19.1-30), and intertribal warfare between the tribes of Israel and the solitary tribe of Benjamin (20.1-48). This is clearly the time when 'everyone did what was right in his own eyes' (17.6; 21.25). But in contrast, if they had done what was 'right in God's eyes', they would not have violated the prohibitions in the Mosaic covenant against polytheism, idolatry, adultery (rape), murder, covetousness, *et al.* (Exod. 20.2-17). The blame for Israel's anarchy is that at this time 'there was no king in Israel' (17.6; 18.1; 19.1; 21.25). This wistful refrain, which laments the lack of a central government, identifies the longing for a king.

The dark days of anarchy in the days when the judges judged seem to be the whole story. But it is not so. The episodes in the book of Ruth are a beacon of light into the dark night of the nation. The book is about a Judean family who migrate to Moab when the land is under the curse of drought (compare Deuteronomy 18). The main characters in the book are the two women, Naomi and her daughter-in-law Ruth the Moabitess, both of whom are widowed. This much beloved and well-known story does not need to be retold here. Suffice it to observe that when God lifts the curse from the land of Judah and begins to bless it again, Naomi, accompanied by Ruth, returns to her native city Bethlehem. God's providential care is at the forefront of the narrative. At the forefront of this care is the decision of a near kinsman, Boaz, to redeem that is to marry Ruth. So when everything in the lives of these women seems to be about loss, God is working through a series of 'happenstances' to bring blessing and fruitfulness – marriage between Ruth and Boaz and the birth of a son – into their lives. But there is a long-term significance to this narrative. This is that Obed, the son who is born to Boaz and Ruth, 'is the father of Jesse, the father of David' (Ruth 4.17). This son will be God's agent to establish the future dynastic kingship for Israel (1 Sam. 16.1-13; 2 Sam. 7.16). The birth of Obed (grandfather of David) is the light at the end of the tunnel.

But before David is born and is given kingship, God must establish Israel's king-maker. This king-maker proves to be a certain Samuel who will be born to an Ephraimite couple, Elkanah and Hannah (1 Sam. 1.1-20). Like so many notable women of Old Testament times, Hannah is barren, but in answer to her prayers, the LORD enables her to conceive and bare a son, Samuel. This birth happens as the era of the judges draws toward its close, and in fact, Samuel will be the last of the judges. At this time, Eli is the priest who serves at the Sanctuary/Tabernacle. His one notable fault is that he cannot control his sons who 'were worthless men; they did not know the LORD' (2.12); that is, they were greedy and sexually immoral (2.13-17). In their place, the boy Samuel will grow up to become Eli's successor as priest (2.35), and though he does not yet know the LORD, he will become the LORD's prophet to Israel (3.20), and judge (7.15), and Israel's king-maker (8.1-20). In fact, he will be the one to anoint Israel's first two kings: Saul (9.15-17; 10.1-14) and David, son of Jesse (16.1-13). Metaphorically, in the days when darkness and chaos covered the land, God said, 'Let there be light', and Boaz and Ruth, Hannah and Samuel, and, finally, David, shone his light onto God's people. God said, 'Let there be light', and David was anointed to kingship.

4.3. The Monarchy: United and Divided (1 Samuel–2 Chronicles)

The 'Occupation Era' of the Judges was not to be the permanent political plan for Israel. Bible readers will remember that from the beginning of the third cycle of turning points, God covenanted with Abraham that 'Kings shall come forth from you' (Gen. 17.6).

In the time of Jacob, Abraham's grandson, the promise of kingship is narrowed to the tribe of Judah (49.10).

By the time of Moses, kingship still had not yet been implemented, but nevertheless, it is encoded in the Mosaic covenant (Deut. 17.14-20). After Israel had conquered Canaan, the land was divided to Israel on a tribal basis, and the result is that tribal loyalties gradually became paramount. While the tribes were united by their common history, there was no central government to give this loose tribal confederation a national identity. However, tribal vulnerability to foreign oppressors and the internal lawlessness and false worship eroded tribal loyalties, and in part, replaced them with a somewhat wistful longing for a king (Judg. 17.6; 21.25).

There are two immediate factors prompting Israel's demand for a king in the latter days of Samuel's judgeship. The one factor is external and the other is internal. The external factor is the invasion by the Sea Peoples of the eastern Mediterranean seaboard, and their Viking-like raids and occupation of the agriculturally rich plain of Sharon. Incidentally, these Sea Peoples are named in the Bible as Philistines, and their lasting legacy is the name Palestine for the land of Canaan. The Philistines are an 'iron' age culture whereas the Israelites at this time are still a bronze age culture. This gave the Philistines decisive advantages over the Israelites in the areas of agricultural implements (e.g. the plowshare) and weaponry. Taking full advantage of their military superiority from the time of Samson onwards, they regularly encroached upon the western slopes of the Judean Hills (Judg. 13–16). Once in an attack against the Israelites, they even captured the Ark of the Covenant (1 Samuel 4–6), and it was this event that led in part to the demand for a king (who would have a trained and armed standing army).

The demand for a king is also precipitated by internal factors. These relate to the wicked conduct of Samuel's sons. When he was old, Samuel appoints his sons to succeed him as judges. In other words, he turns the function of the judge into a hereditary office. However, unlike their remarkable father, who functioned as a godly priest, prophet, and judge, Samuel's sons were guilty of a bundle of wicked activities. They are worthless men as Eli's sons had been a generation earlier (2.12). The biblical narrative reports, 'they turned aside after dishonest gain and took bribes and perverted justice'

(8.3). This wicked activity precipitated a crisis, and, 'all the elders of Israel gathered together and came to Samuel at Ramah' (8.4). The narrative implies that the elders have an agreed upon agenda. They observe, 'Behold, you have grown old' (8.5a), which implies that Samuel's judgment can no longer be trusted. They criticize him because his sons are unworthy to be judges (8.5b). And finally, they announce their agenda: 'Now appoint a king for us to judge us like all the nations' (8.5c). Clearly, in their perspective, a king is a national, hereditary judge.

The elders' demand for a king, not surprisingly, displeases Samuel. From his perspective, his rule as judge is being criticized. He is right. The elders have lost confidence in his leadership. But God who promised that Abraham's sons would include kingship instructs Samuel: 'Listen to the voice of the people in all that they say to you' (1 Sam. 8.7). What is wrong with the people's demand is their attitude and their timing. The attitude of the people is wrong: it is like the attitude of the first generation of the exodus, whom God punished in the wilderness (8.7, 8). This attitude includes the rejection of God as their king, and therefore, substitutes a person for their deliverer and judge. Because kingship itself is from God, there are upsides to having a king (namely, a central government). But the history of kingship will show that because they are too impatient by one generation (since kingship in God's announced plan is to be from the tribe of Judah [Gen. 49.10]), there are numerous penalties which will accrue to Israel during the reign of Saul, Israel's first king. Therefore, the Israel of Samuel's generation will have to take the bad with the good.

Because of both the external factors (the Philistine menace) and the internal factors (the wicked conduct of Samuel's sons), the LORD will add one final portfolio to his service. In addition to being Israel's prophet, priest, and judge (i.e. Israel's non-hereditary king), Samuel will end his days as Israel's unique king-maker. It is in his role as king-maker that Samuel will challenge the nation to obey the LORD and to warn them against disobeying the voice of the LORD (1 Sam. 12.11-25). After Samuel has anointed Saul, he addresses the assembled nation. This address uses the conditional, 'If … then …' language of the Mosaic covenant (Deut. 24.1, 15). Thus:

If you will fear the LORD and serve Him, and listen to his voice and not rebel against the command of the LORD, then both you and also the king who reigns over you will follow the LORD your God. And if you will not listen to the voice of the LORD, but rebel against the command of the LORD, then the hand of the LORD will be against you as it was against your fathers (1 Sam. 12.14, 15).

This is a self-explanatory exhortation, but Samuel solemnizes it in their presence with an enacted curse. The Mosaic covenant is about long life on the land. Therefore, it is natural that many of the blessings and curses relate to agricultural scarcity. The assembly at which Saul is presented to the nation as king is happening at harvest time (blessing) (12.17). Samuel challenges the assembled nation:

Even now, take your stand and see the thing which the LORD will do before your eyes (12.16).

Answering Samuel's prayer, the LORD sent thunder and rain that day (which destroyed the harvest); and all the people greatly feared the LORD and Samuel (12.18).

The enacted curse; the destruction of the harvest caused the people to be afraid. Samuel allays their fears (12.20). However, he presses home the lesson of the enacted curse; namely, 'if you still do wickedly, both you and your kingdom will be swept away' (12.25). The entire history of the Monarchy, both United and Divided, is about this issue of Kingship as either blessing or cursing (1 Samuel 12–2 Chronicles 36). Finally, God's long-suffering patience is exhausted, and, 'Judah was led away into exile from its land' (2 Kgs 25.21).

4.3.1. Saul, David, and Solomon: the united monarchy

The era of the United Monarchy (ca. 1040–920 BCE) is a time of unprecedented and wholesale transformation. For example, by the end of Solomon's reign, she will have become a power player in international trade and commerce. Many benefits accrue to Israel at this time, but, as Samuel reminds Israel, there will be a heavy price to pay. He identifies this cost as, 'the procedure of the King' (1 Sam. 8.11). Israel's kings will:

- Conscript their sons to serve in a standing army,

- Conscript some of their sons to work his fields and others to manufacture weapons for warfare,
- Conscript their daughters to become perfumers, cooks, and bakers,
- Confiscate the best of their fields, vineyards, and olive groves, and
- Levy taxes at the same level as their tithe to the LORD (8.11-17).

In other words, the kings will take Israel's sons and daughters and their male and female servants to use for his own work (8.16). Samuel warns them that they will find this cost of kingship to be unexpectedly oppressive (8.18). However, their 'occupation era' experiences have been so bad that they are adamant: 'No, but there shall be a king over us ... that our king may judge us, and fight our battles' (8.19, 20). Contrary to Samuel's warning, the united monarchy under Saul, David, and Solomon, surprisingly will be the Golden Age in the history of the nation, but in the end, Samuel was right: 'you will cry out in that day because of your king whom you have chosen' (8.18).

The Golden Age of the united monarchy in Israel lasted for three generations – the reigns of Saul, David, and Solomon (1 Sam. 9.1-1 Kgs 11.43). This golden age happens at the time when there is a power vacuum in the lands of the ancient near east. Though Israel does have troublesome neighbors, such as Philistia and Moab, the great powers including Egypt and Assyria are relatively weak and quiescent. As a result of this power vacuum Saul, David, and Solomon advance Israel from being a weak confederation of quasi-independent tribes to being a relative powerhouse. These first three kings to rule over Israel have widely different personalities and backgrounds. Nevertheless, they also have much in common.

4.3.1.1. Saul is Israel's first king (1 Samuel 9.1–31.13)

Saul is a son of Kish of the tribe of Benjamin (9.1-2). In Samuel's role as Israel's king-maker, he anoints Saul to be king (10.1). When Samuel anointed Saul, 'the Spirit of God came upon him mightily, so that he prophesied' (10.10). As Israel's first king, Saul is successor to the judges. Like many of them, such as Othniel, he is a charismatic warrior (Judg. 3.10; 1 Sam. 11.6). Thus, his royal role is to deliver Israel from foreign oppressors (9.16). Saul's great achievement is to transform a village and tribal society into a united nation; making it better able to resist the Philistine menace.

But in spite of all of the promise for good resulting from Saul's kingship, there is a dark and tragic side to Saul. Just seven days after Samuel anoints Saul to be king, he disobeys and wrongfully performs priestly duties reserved for Samuel (1 Sam. 1.1; 13.8-13). Soon Saul will commit a second act of disobedience by failing to destroy the Amalekites, as commanded (15.1-35). When Samuel confronts him about his disobedience, Saul excuses himself. In the first instance, he complains that Samuel was late in arriving and the people were getting restless. 'So', he tells Samuel, 'I forced myself and offered the burnt offering' (13.12). On the second occasion, he protests: 'I did obey the voice of the LORD' (15.20). In his defense, he claims that the people spared the best of the spoils to devote to the LORD in sacrifice. To this, Samuel gives his now classic reply:

> Has the LORD as much delight in burnt offerings and sacrifices as in obeying the voice of the LORD? Behold, to obey is better than sacrifice, and to heed than the fat of rams (1 Sam. 15.22).

By seeking to justify his repetitive disobedience, Saul, the LORD's anointed, cuts himself off from grace and forgiveness. In this way, he loses the kingdom. Samuel announces the divine judgment: 'Your kingdom shall not endure. The LORD has sought out for himself a man after his own heart and the LORD has appointed him ruler over his people, because you have not kept what the LORD has commanded you' (13.14). Subsequent events identify David to be Saul's successor (16.1-14).

4.3.1.2. David is Israel's second king (1 Samuel 16.1–1 Kings 2.11)

David is the youngest of the eight sons of Jesse the Bethlehemite (16.11). He is also a direct descendant of Ruth and Boaz (Ruth 4.18-22). Samuel, who had earlier anointed Saul to be king (1 Sam. 10.1), will as Israel's king-maker also anoint David to be Israel's next king (16.13). Paralleling the experience of Saul, when Samuel anointed David, 'the Spirit of the LORD came mightily upon David from that day forward' (16.13; compare 2 Sam. 23.2). The LORD's gift of the Spirit to David authenticates him as the true successor to

Saul. This is further confirmed by the fact that having come mightily upon David, 'the Spirit of the LORD departed from Saul (16.14).

David is a worthy successor to Saul. His single combat with Goliath, the Philistine giant, illustrates his courage (1 Samuel 17). His refusal to take advantage of his opportunities to slay Saul, the LORD's anointed, illustrates his loyalty (24.1-7; 20.6-12). When David learns of Saul's tragic death, he responds with genuine sorrow (2 Sam. 1.11, 12). His remarkable kindness is evident in his treatment of Mephibosheth, Jonathan's son and Saul's grandson (2 Samuel 9).

David's achievements match his noble character. David's achievements include completing the process of unification and centralization begun by Saul. During his 40 years, he reunites the twelve tribes under the monarchy. He captures the Jebusite city of Jerusalem and makes it both the royal city and the central sanctuary. As a charismatic warrior, like Saul and the judges before him, he defeats the Philistines (2 Samuel 5, 6). But of greater significance, he extends Israel's borders to include all of the land which, 1,000 years earlier, God had promised to Abraham (2 Samuel 8; compare Gen. 15.18-21). The plunder, tribute, and the control of the trade routes from these territorial gains enrich the royal treasury and will later finance the building of the Temple. Despite David's remarkable achievements, his reputation is forever tainted by two acts of great wickedness.

When David is king, he commits two vicious sins. First, he commits adultery with Bathsheba, the wife of his neighbor, Uriah the Hittite. Second, when he learns that Bathsheba is pregnant, he seeks to cover his tracks by having Uriah murdered (2 Samuel 11). Just as royal status could not earlier excuse Saul's sins, so now neither can it excuse David's evil. Initially, his sins may have been hidden from the nation, but they were not hidden from the LORD. Therefore, he sends his prophet Nathan to David to confront him about his guilt. David differs from Saul, however, in that unlike his predecessor, he does not attempt to justify his wickedness, but openly confesses, 'I have sinned against the LORD' (12.13). David's confession elicits grace and results in forgiveness. Nevertheless, though he is forgiven, both he and his family will suffer short and long-term consequences of his wickedness. However, in God's mercy a second son will be born to David and Bathsheba about whom the text witnesses: 'Now the LORD loved him' (2 Sam. 12.24). In God's sovereign election and grace this son, Solomon, will become Israel's next king, and the final king of the era of the United Monarchy.

4.3.1.3. Solomon is Israel's third king (1 Kings 1.1–11.43)

Solomon is the son of David and Bathsheba (2 Samuel 12) and, being David's son, will inherit the throne. Zadok and Nathan, priest and prophet respectively, anoint Solomon to be David's successor (1 Kgs 1.34). When Samuel anointed Saul, and then David to be kings over Israel, the Spirit came mightily upon each man and they became Spirit-empowered warrior kings. But 40 to 80 years later, Israel needs another kind of king – a wise administrator. As the LORD's anointed, 'the wisdom [of the Spirit of God] was in him to administer justice' (3.28).

Solomon's great achievement is to build the Temple for the LORD in Jerusalem (1 Kings 6–8). Earlier, David had established the city as the royal city and sanctuary for the Ark of the Covenant, but because he was a man of war, he had been forbidden to build the Temple. Because Solomon is a man of peace, the LORD gives him the privilege of building the LORD's house (2 Sam. 7.13). However, the illustrious splendor of Solomon's reign is tarnished by apostasy. He marries foreign princesses in violation of the Law, and allows them to turn his heart away from wholehearted devotion to the LORD (1 Kgs 11.1-8). In other words, he worships the gods of his wives in addition to worshipping the LORD. Angered by Solomon's compromised worship, the LORD decrees judgment. This is that with the exception of one tribe, the LORD will wrest the kingdom out of the hand of his son and will give it to another. He will also raise up adversaries against Solomon because of his sin: Hadad the Edomite, Rezon of Damascus, and Jeroboam the son of Nebat, who will become the future king of Israel in the Divided Monarchy (11.9-40). These judgments reverse David's earlier success in consolidating the union of the twelve tribes, and in enlarging the covenantal borders. In effect, what David achieved for Israel, Solomon lost through his sinfulness.

The following chart summarizes the character of Israel's kings of the United Monarchy, and identifies their achievements and their judgments:

Pattern	King Saul	King David	King Solomon
Character	A choice, handsome man (1 Sam. 9.2), humble (15.17)	A man after God's heart (1 Sam. 13.14), courageous (17.34f), loyal (24.6-7)	The LORD loved Solomon (2 Sam. 12.24), Solomon loved the LORD (1 Kgs 3.3)
Achievement	United the Twelve tribes	Establishes Jerusalem (2 Sam. 5.6-10), establishes the covenantal boundaries (2 Sam. 8.1-18)	Builds the Temple (1 Kgs 6-8)
Sin	Disobedience (1 Sam. 13.13; 15.19-24)	Adultery (2 Sam. 11.4), murder (2 Sam. 11.17)	Apostasy (1 Kgs 11.4)
Response	Blames Samuel (1 Sam. 13.11), blames the people (1 Sam. 15.21)	Confesses sin (2 Sam. 12.13)	
Judgment	The kingdom is taken from Saul and will be given to David (1 Sam. 13.14)	David is forgiven (12.14), nevertheless, 1) sword in David's house, 2) his wives will be raped, 3) the child will die (2 Sam. 12.1-24)	The kingdom will be divided during the reign of his son (1 Kgs 11.9-13)

4.3.2. The Davidic covenant (2 Samuel 7.1-29)

Immediately after Saul's death only the tribe of Judah anoints David to be their king (2 Sam. 2.1-4); the northern tribes of Israel remain loyal to Saul's household, anointing Saul's son Ishbosheth to be their king (2.8-11). This division resulted in a long war between Israel and Judah (3.1a). The result of this conflict is that 'David grew steadily stronger, but the house of Saul grew weaker continually' (3.1b). Therefore, in the end, Israel's leaders also anointed David to be their king (5.1-4). David ruled over Judah for seven years and over Judah and Israel together for another 33 years. Altogether, like Saul earlier, he reigned forty years (5.5).

Early in David's reign, he achieved two great accomplishments: 1) he captured the Jebusite city of Jerusalem and made it the royal city (2 Sam. 5.6-10), and 2) he brought the Ark of the Covenant from Baale-Judah to Jerusalem (6.1-19). These achievements are the setting for the making of the Davidic Covenant (7.1-28). This covenant of kingship will be the second and final development and extension of the Abrahamic Covenant (compare Gen. 17.6).

In its historical and narrative content, the LORD's covenant with David arises from the 'house' theme. Briefly stated, David, former shepherd boy and long-time refugee from Saul, now lives in his own *house* (2 Sam. 7.1). He apparently feels guilty about this because the LORD's dwelling place is still the Tabernacle, a portable sanctuary (7.2). Therefore, he proposes to build a permanent *house* (Temple) for the LORD. The prophet Nathan without consulting the LORD endorses David's proposal (7.5). The LORD, however, forbids this and in turn promises to build a *house* for David (7.11). This house will be David's royal dynasty. It is in this context that the LORD enters into a covenant of kingship with David.

This second and final development of the Abrahamic covenant (the Mosaic covenant is the first) has three fundamental commitments. One, the LORD reaffirms the gift of the land (2 Sam. 7.10). Two, in contrast to Saul's kingship, the LORD will make David's kingship hereditary or dynastic (7.12). Three, the LORD will establish a father-son relationship between himself and David's descendants (7.14). The father-son relationship is not about deifying the king. It is the language of adoption such as when Israel is identified as God's son, his first-born (Exod. 4.22). The father-son relationship implies God's care and protection (compare Ps. 2.7), and because God is righteous and just, it also includes divine punishment should the king act wickedly (2 Sam. 7.14).

The father-son relationship is one of the most distinctive features of the Davidic covenant, yet at the same time it is to be found in four covenants: the Abrahamic, Mosaic, Davidic, and Jesuanic. From the first to the fourth covenants there is a narrowing of the 'sonship' theme. The Abrahamic covenant promises blessing upon 'all the families of the earth' (Gen. 12.2); the mosaic covenant narrows this to the nation of Israel (Exod. 4.22); the Davidic covenant, to one man, who is the unique, literal son of God (Lk. 1.32-35; Jn 1.18). The following schematic illustrates the narrowing of the father-son relationship which God establishes in successive covenants:

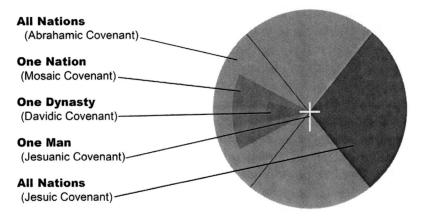

All Nations
(Abrahamic Covenant)

One Nation
(Mosaic Covenant)

One Dynasty
(Davidic Covenant)

One Man
(Jesuanic Covenant)

All Nations
(Jesuic Covenant)

The 'covenantal circle' illustrates the centuries-long process by which the father-son relationship is narrowed. As the covenants advance across time, it funnels from 'all the families of the earth' to one person. But what a person! This son, born in a humble cattle stall, is not only King David's direct descendent, but he is also David's lord (Mk 12.35-37; Ps. 110.1). Even before he is anointed to be king, he is the redeemer son, who like Moses and Israel was called out of Egypt (Mt. 2.15; Hos. 11.1). Finally, this son is also Abraham's promised seed through whom all the families of the earth would be blessed (Gal. 3.16; Gen. 12.2; 22.18). As the above schematic illustrates, the weight of David's dynasty, the weight of Israel's redemption, and indeed the weight of the world rests on the shoulders of just one man, but oh what shoulders! In him the three earlier covenants are not only fulfilled, but are extended to include all of the families of the earth. In this way the covenantal circle, begun with Abraham (Genesis 12, 13, 17, 22), in Jesus has come full circle. Hallelujah, the Son of God omnipotent reigns.

4.4. The Nation Divides: Marching to Judgment

The monarchy is a failed experiment, humanly speaking. The twelve tribes of Israel are united under one king (in succession) for just three generations, that is, about 120 years. At this time, Israel's advancement and progress toward nationhood is spectacular, as any comparison between Israel at the beginning of Saul's reign and the conclusion of Solomon's reign shows. But each king not only contributes to Israel's advancement, but also contributes factors leading to its dissolution. Solomon, guilty of religious compromise, perhaps contributes the most to the dividing of the nation. The division of the twelve tribes into the Northern Kingdom, which retains the name Israel, and the Southern Kingdom, also known as Judah, takes place early in the reign of Rehoboam, Solomon's son (1 Kgs 12.1-24).

4.4.1. Rehoboam and the dividing of the kingdom (1 Kings 12.1-24)

After the death of Solomon, all Israel gathers at Shechem to ratify Solomon's son, Rehoboam, to be their king (1 Kgs 12.1). Apparently, the nation as a whole comes to the meeting intending to negotiate a lighter 'taxation/forced labor' load. They complain to Rehoboam, 'your father (Solomon) made our yoke hard' (12.4a). Since the costly Temple and Palace are now complete they demand of Rehoboam, 'therefore lighten the hard service of your father and his heavy yoke which he put on us' (12.4b). If Rehoboam is prudent in meeting this demand, they assure him, 'we will serve you' (12.4c). Their commitment to serve Rehoboam implies that if he decides imprudently, they will not accept him as their king.

In the light of their historical circumstances, the demand that the economic burden of kingship be lightened is reasonable. But Rehoboam does not see this. Rather, he consults the elders who have earlier served as Solomon's counselors. They advise the obvious response: 'If you will be a servant to the people today, will serve them, grant their petition and speak good words to them, then they will be your servants forever' (1 Kgs 12.6). But stupidly, Rehoboam forsakes their counsel and instead followed the contrary counsel of his young friends.

Therefore, he 'answered the people harshly ... saying, "my father made your yoke heavy, but I will add to your yoke ... I will discipline you with scorpions"' (12.14). Rehoboam's unwise and arrogant reply, 'is a turn of events from the LORD' to fulfill the prophecy of Abijah the Shilonite about the dividing of the kingdom (11.11, 31).

Hearing the arrogant threats of Rehoboam, the Israelites reject him as their king. The rallying cry of Israel the ten northern tribes is:

> We have no inheritance in the son of Jesse;
> To your tents, Oh Israel!
> Now look after your own house, David (12.16).

History is full of examples of this kind of royal arrogance and its unintended consequences (compare Marie Antoinette's infamous, 'let them eat cake', repudiation of the French people's request for bread). She lost her head; Rehoboam lost 10/12 of his kingdom. The ultimate, long-term result is that Israel remained in rebellion from this day (ca. 920 BCE) until the all-conquering Assyrians sent the nation into exile in 722 BCE (2 Kgs 17.1-18).

4.4.1.1. The sin of Jeroboam leads to judgment

The dividing of the kingdom of Saul, David, and Solomon into the two kingdoms of Israel and Judah was permanent. The chronicler of this history initially observes, 'so Israel has been in rebellion against the house of David to this day' (1 Kgs 12.19). After Assyria has defeated Israel and captured its capital city, Samaria, this historical situation continues: 'so Israel was carried away into exile from their own land to Assyria until this day' (2 Kgs 17.23). And so, for many generations adding up to 200 years (920–722 BCE) while Judah was ruled by the house of David, Israel was ruled by 19 kings representing nine royal households or dynasties. The first of these kings is Jeroboam the son of Nebat.

4.4.1.2. Jeroboam: the prototypical evil king in Israel

Jeroboam is the first king to rule over the rebellious tribes of Israel. He is first introduced into the narrative during the reign of Solomon. He is identified as the son of Nebat, an Ephraimite who was a servant of the king (1 Kgs 11.26). Along with Hadad the Edomite and Rezon of Damascus (11.14-23), Jeroboam was one of the LORD's adversaries whom he raised up against Solomon (11.26). He is characterized as 'a valiant warrior' and as being 'industrious', and Solomon had appointed him in charge of all of the forced labor of the house of Joseph (Ephraim and Manasseh) (11.27-28). One day, when Jeroboam has left Jerusalem, he is found by the prophet, Ahijah the Shilonite (11.29). At this time, on behalf of the LORD, Ahijah appoints/calls Jeroboam to rule over the ten tribes of Israel (11.30-32). His call to kingship is, however, conditional:

> If you listen to all that I (the LORD) command you and walk in My ways and *do what is right* (italics added) in My sight ... as My servant David did, then I will be with you and build you an enduring house as I built for David, and I will give Israel to you (11.38).

While Jeroboam may have been a valiant warrior, he will prove to be a frightened, insecure king, and this motivated him to devise a new, innovative religion for Israel to follow (12.26-33). By doing this, God's chosen ruler for Israel, in contrast to David, did evil causing Israel to sin.

In spite of the fact that through his prophet, Ahijah, the LORD had called Jeroboam to be the king of the ten tribes, and despite the fact that these tribes had rejected Rehoboam as their king and had made Jeroboam their king he was afraid that when the Israelites worshipped the LORD in Jerusalem they would rebel against him and return to the house of David (1 Kgs 2.25-33). Therefore, Jeroboam devised a new religion to protect himself from this potential problem. In inventing a new religion, Jeroboam faces two challenges: 1) his innovations would have to *appeal* to the majority of Israelites, and 2) these innovations had to be similar to the religion practiced at Solomon's Temple so as not to alienate the more traditionally-minded Israelites. In order to meet these challenges, Jeroboam put into effect three innovations. One, he established two centers of worship in Israel: Dan in the north and Bethel in the south. A golden calf of his making was placed in each center as 'their gods that bought them up from the land of Egypt' (12.28). Two, he established a non-Levitical priesthood (12.31); and three, he changed the religious calendar for the celebration of feasts, such as the feast of Tabernacles (12.32-33). These religious innovations produced a false religion, which became Jeroboam's legacy of sin/evil in Israel.

To many Bible readers, some of Jeroboam's legacy may seem relatively harmless. For example, the two golden calves need not be idols, but could simply function as visual focal points for faith. Fur-

'Golden Calf' episode in the wilderness when the people imposed their wish for deviant religious practices upon Aaron, the High Priest (Exod. 32.1-10). Two, it is easier to perpetuate false religion than to repent and return to true religion; and three, once people have practiced false religion, they typically fall into a downward spiral of wickedness – e.g. cult prostitution and child sacrifice. For the above reasons, the LORD finally sends irrevocable judgment upon Israel (since none of her kings departed from the sin of Jeroboam).

4.5. The LORD Judges Israel (2 Kings 17.1-18)

Israel's existence as a nation ends at the hands of the Assyrian Empire. The end comes during the reign of a certain king, Hoshea, who rules Israel as a tributary nation to Assyria (2 Kgs 17.1).

But like every Israelite king before him, 'he did evil in the sight of the LORD' (see chart above). But in unspecified ways, he was not as evil as some of his predecessors (17.2a). In spite of this, judgment looms on the horizon in the person of Shalmanezer V, King of Assyria. In spite of the Assyrian menace, Hoshea turns to Egypt – a broken reed – for military help. Because of this, Shalmanezer 'invaded the whole land and went up to Samaria and besieged it for three years' (17.5). Therefore, in the end, the new king of Assyria, Sargon II 'captured Samaria and carried Israel away into exile to Assyria' (17.6). Thus ends the woeful tale of Israel, which at this point ceases to exist.

What kind of a God will destroy a nation which He, himself, had earlier redeemed, which he had created by covenant, to whom he had given a land of their own, and to whom he had given a king? Answer: a God more powerful than the nations, a God who keeps his promises, a God of love and mercy, a patient and long-suffering God, BUT FINALLY A GOD OF JUSTICE AND RIGHTEOUSNESS. The Assyrian captivity shatters the false belief that the love and mercy and patience of God always triumphs over justice and righteousness, but the writer shows that this belief is presumptuous.

The exile of captive Israel to Assyria is a stunning, devastating blow. Israel is abandoned, if not actively betrayed by its gods, the two golden calves set up in Dan and Bethel. Conversely, the LORD, the God whom Israel has spurned is (providentially) the active agent in Israel's defeat. The 'exile' narrative is followed immediately by the historical and theological explanation of Israel's exile.

Israel has been exiled because she has spurned her God, the LORD, her redeemer (2 Kgs 17.7). This repudiation of the LORD is matched by Israel turning to/worshipping the gods of the nations. This is compounded by the fact that she also worshipped the gods of her apostate kings beginning with Jeroboam (17.8). In this apostate condition, the Israelites worshipped at the high places which they had built (17.9), and worst of all, they worshipped idols (17.12).

Finally, to the sin of idolatry, they added the sins of child sacrifice and magic (17.17). In these ways, rather than being 'a light to the nations' (Isa. 42.6; 49.6), 'they sold themselves to doing evil in the sight of the LORD, provoking Him' (17.17). So, Israel's sins were not done innocently, or inadvertently; they are 'sins of a high hand'.

The LORD had instructed Israel about true worship and false worship in the basic stipulations of the Mosaic covenant. He had commanded: 'You shall have no other gods before Me', and 'You shall not make for yourself an idol … you shall not worship them or serve them' (Exod. 20.6). When Aaron subsequently made the golden calf in the wilderness, he declared, 'This is your god, Oh Israel, who brought you up from the land of Egypt' (32.4). But there is only one God – the LORD (Deut. 6.4), and he is a jealous God (Exod. 20.5), and in judgment upon this sin he declared, 'whoever has sinned against me, I will blot out of My book (Exod. 32.33). But when Jeroboam mimicked the golden calf episode (1 Kgs 12.25-30), the LORD, gracious and merciful, did not immediately judge Israel. But the wicked reign of Ahab illustrates that Israel's evil went from bad to worse. And yet, the LORD continues to warn Israel through his prophets, saying, 'turn from your evil ways and keep My commandments' (2 Kgs 17.13). However, in spite of the LORD's longsuffering grace, 'Israel did not listen', 'they rejected his covenant', 'they forsook all the commandments of the LORD' (17.14-16). The inevitable result/outcome of Israel's persistent apostasy is that 'the LORD was very angry with Israel, and removed them from his sight' (17.18). 'So Israel was carried away into exile from their own land to Assyria until this day' (17.23).

4.5.1. The LORD judges Judah (2 Kings 24.10–25.30)

Two Hundred years before the exile of Israel to Assyria, the twelve-tribe kingdom became divided: the ten-tribe kingdom of Israel in the north and the two-tribe kingdom of Judah to the south. From first to last, the ten-tribe kingdom of Israel accepted and then followed the false religion which Jeroboam had instituted. But the story of Judah is somewhat different. In part, this difference can be attributed to a different model of kingship in Judah. David, rather than Jeroboam, is this model. In contrast to Jeroboam, who models 'evil' kingship in Israel, David models 'right' kingship in Judah. The kingdom of Judah had other advantages which Israel did not have: the holy city, Solomon's Temple, and the Levitical priesthood. As a result, though the history of Judah parallels the history of Israel in significant ways, its history has the advantage of David's model of right kingship.

As mentioned above, David, Saul's successor to the throne of Israel, is the model for 'right' kingship in Judah. David's model is activated as early as Solomon's reign, and continues in effect until she, like ten-tribe Israel, is torn from the land by the Babylonians (587/586 BCE). At the beginning of Solomon's reign, the LORD promises 'if you walk in My ways, keeping My statutes and commandments, as your father, David, had walked, then I will prolong your days' (1 Kgs 3.14). After Solomon had completed building his two great projects, the Temple and the royal palace, the LORD renews his promise of blessing: 'if you will walk before Me as your father, David, walked, in integrity of heart, and uprightness ... then I will establish the throne of your kingdom over Israel forever' (9.4-5). This promise of blessing, however, is balanced by the complementary warning of cursing – for disobedience, Israel will be swept from the land (9.6-9). Sadly, when Solomon was old, 'his heart was not wholly devoted to the LORD his God, as the heart of David had been' for his foreign wives 'had turned his heart away after other gods' (11.4). The immediate consequence of Solomon's sin is two-fold: 1) the LORD raised up adversaries against him, and 2) the kingdom will be divided during the reign of his son into ten-tribe Israel and two-tribe Judah (11.9-40).

Rehoboam, Solomon's son is not directly compared to David in the assessment of his reign. Nevertheless, it is implied in the report,

'Judah did evil in the sight of the LORD' (1 Kgs 14.22). Of Abijah, Rehoboam's son, it is reported, 'his heart was not wholly devoted to the LORD his God, like the heart of his father, David' (15.3). In contrast, Asa, Abijah's son 'did what was right in the sight of the LORD' (15.11). And in this way, the reports about Judah's history advances. When they are compared to David, many kings who reigned over Judah, like Solomon and Abijah, did not do what was right in the sight of the LORD. Other kings, like Asa, did right in the sight of the LORD. Two of these kings are Hezekiah and Josiah. During the fateful reign of Hoshea in Israel (2 Kgs 17.1-6), the 25-year-old Hezekiah became king over Judah (18.1-2). The narrative reports, 'he did right in the sight of the LORD, according to all that his father, David, had done' (18.3). Similarly, following the wicked reigns of Manasseh (55 years) and Amon (2 years; 21.1-26), Josiah, the great grandson of Hezekiah, 'did right in the sight of the LORD and walked in all the ways of his father, David' (22.2). These observations about the 'walk' of the kings of Judah illustrate the parable of the two roads (Mt. 7.13-14). Many kings of Judah travel the broad road, which is the way leading to Judah's subsequent destruction; conversely, kings like Hezekiah and Josiah, travel the narrow road, which is the path of righteousness.

In contrast to Hezekiah and Josiah, who each did right in the sight of the LORD, as their father David had done, Manasseh, who is Hezekiah's son, and in turn, the grandfather of Josiah walked the broad way which leads to destruction. Concerning him, the narrative reports, 'and he did evil in the sight of the LORD' (2 Kgs 21.22). But Manasseh is not judged according to David's pattern of right kingship. Rather, his evil is compared to 'the abominations of the nations whom the LORD dispossessed before the sons of Israel' (21.2b). Manasseh earned this evaluation because he reversed his father's religious reforms (18.4-8). Hezekiah had put an end to Judah's programmatic sins; namely, polytheism, idolatry, magic, cult prostitution, and child sacrifice. Manasseh, however, reintroduced these programmatic evils – even desecrating the Temple, itself (21.3-7). The result is that, 'Manasseh seduced them (Judah) to do evil more than the nations whom the LORD destroyed before the sons of Israel' (21.9). Compared to the evil done by Manasseh, Jer-

5

CYCLE FIVE: FROM JOSHUA AND ZERUBBABEL TO THE JEWISH REVOLT

Each of the four earlier cycles of turning points in biblical history and theology ended in acts of divine judgment: the flood, the tower of Babel episode, Israel's wilderness wanderings, and the exile of ten-tribe Israel and two-tribe Judah. At the end of each of the first three cycles of turning points, God calls and commissions agents who will initiate the new start in the ongoing history of humanity (Noah), or the history of God's uniquely chosen people (Abraham and Joshua, the son of Nun). The fourth cycle has one difference to this pattern. After the judgment wreaked on the temple, Jerusalem, and Judah, there is no agent of a new start waiting in the wings. As nations, Israel and Judah have been destroyed; but there are no called and commissioned agents in place to initiate a new start in the covenantal history of Abraham's descendants. There is only judgment. Israel is like a valley strewn with the bones of decayed carcasses. As time passes, the question which God poses is, 'Son of Man, can these bones live?' (Ezek. 37.3). 'Man', even if he is a Spirit-inspired prophet like Ezekiel, has no answer. And this is how Israel's condition exists – for the generation of the Babylonian conquest of Judah, and the next generation – a gap of 70 years. In the following schematic, the circle places the next new start in the fifth cycle of turning points in this historical context.

The fifth cycle is unique in two ways. One, the new start only begins after a gap of 70 years, and two, judgment does not fall on unbelieving Israel (the Jewish war) until 70 years after the agent of the new start (Joshua = Jesus) has been born.

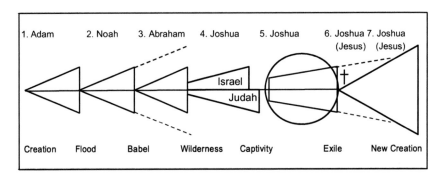

5.1. Mind the (Captivity) Gap

At the beginning of the fourth cycle, God calls and commissions Joshua, the son of Nun, to be his agent of salvation for the second generation of the exodus. Interestingly, after a gap of 70 years in the national history of Israel, God will call another Joshua to be one of several agents of the salvation of 'captive/exiled' Israel. The two-generation gap between Exile and Restoration speaks to the finality of judgment upon Judah, but also it prepares the remnant people for the salvation that is the restoration of the exiled captives back to the land. The remnant theme is embedded in the conditional nature of the Mosaic covenant. The blessings of the covenant are about a long and (agriculturally) prosperous life on the land (Deut. 28.1-14). On the other hand, the covenant curses are about agricultural scarcity and ultimately, the exile of God's people (28.15–30.6). When Israel finds herself scattered among all the nations – as it does after the LORD's judgments upon both ten-tribe Israel and Judah – she is to 'return to the LORD (their) God and obey Him' (30.1-2). This obedience of 'heart' and 'soul' will be the basis upon which the LORD will restore his people from captivity. This restoration is not the reward for 'works righteousness' but is motivated by the LORD's compassion (30.3). This restoration of Israel back to the land extends even to those outcasts 'at the ends of the earth' (30.4). Once the scattered captives have been brought back to the land of their fathers, the LORD will prosper them and multiply them even more than he prospered their fathers (30.5). In fact, spiritually, they will be a new creation: 'the LORD your God will circumcise your heart and the heart of your descendants, to love the LORD your God with all your heart and with all your soul, in order that you may live' (30.6).

The 70-year gap between judgment and restoration begins the transition from the 'curse' of exile to the 'blessing' of renewal – that is from national death. The prophet Jeremiah has a vision which illustrates the nature of national judgment and the preservation of a remnant (Jer. 24.1-10). It happens after Nebuchadnezzar had the King Jehoiachin and other prominent Judeans exiled to Babylon (24.1). At this time, the LORD showed the prophet two baskets of figs. One basket is filled with very good figs; the other is filled with rotten, inedible figs (24.2-3). What might this vision mean? The Bible reader does not have to speculate for the LORD interprets the imagery (24.4). On the one hand, the basket of good figs represents the captives of Judah, such as those whom the LORD regards as good whom the LORD has sent into Babylon (24.5). These are the ones upon whom the LORD will set his eyes with favor, and therefore whom he will bring back to the land, having given them a new heart (24.6-7).

On the other hand, Zedekiah, who replaced the exiled King Jehoiachin, is identified to be the basket of bad figs (24.8). The LORD will abandon all those who remain in Jerusalem and Judah, 'as a reproach and a proverb, a taunt and a curse in all places where I (the LORD) will scatter them' (24.9). They will be cursed by the sword, the famine, and the pestilence (Deut. 28.15–29.29) 'until they are destroyed from the land' (24.10). This vision is a shocking reversal of expectations. These presume that those who are sent into captivity are the basket of bad figs; that those who remain in Jerusalem and Judah are the basket of good figs. But in a startling twist he regards as good those whom he sends into captivity.

The 70-year captivity gap is not simply a 'vacant' time to be endured. Jeremiah describes this captivity gap this way: 'the whole land shall be a desolation and a horror … Jerusalem and the cities of Judah (made) a ruin, a horror, a hissing, and a curse' (25.11, 18). In contrast, the LORD speaks to the exiles through his prophet:

… build houses and live in them;
Plant gardens and eat their produce.

mon. For example, they were both the LORD's shepherd – a commonplace term for kingship; they were both the LORD's anointed (called and consecrated) to serve Judah. Thus, each king established (or re-established) Jerusalem as the city of David, and each king financed/rebuilt the Temple in Jerusalem. No other king in biblical history is so like David. Therefore, all in all, by royal title, by calling, and by achievement, the Bible identifies Cyrus, this king of Persia, as the Gentile David-like agent for the new start of the fifth cycle.

5.2.2. Zerubbabel and Joshua: return of exiles
Zerubbabel and Joshua are two other primary agents for the return of the Israelite exiles from Assyria and Babylon (Ezra 2.2). The prophet Haggai identifies Zerubbabel as the son of Shealtiel and Joshua (alternate spelling of the name Jeshua) as the son of Jehozadak, the high priest (Hag. 1.12). Thus, these two leaders are the royal and priestly agents of the new start for the fifth cycle of turning points. But they do not serve alone. They are but the lead agents of a team consisting of either eleven or twelve elders (Ezra 2.2; Neh. 7.7). Though Joshua and Zerubbabel are God's primary agents, they and the elders, as a twelve-member team, represent the whole house of Israel, as it is being restored and rebuilt.

The task of relocating the exiles of the Assyrian and Babylonian captivities back to Jerusalem and to the land is a monumental one. It includes bringing back the 'sacred' temple vessels, which 70 years earlier Nebuchadnezzar had taken from the temple in Jerusalem. These temple vessels number 5,400 articles of gold and silver (Ezra 1.7-11). In addition, the exiles, 'whose spirit God had stirred to go up and rebuild the house of the LORD', numbered 42,360 persons (1.6; 2.64), besides their servants, who numbered 7,337 persons (2.45). When the seventh month came the returned exiles began the task of rebuilding.

5.2.3. Haggai and Zechariah: rebuilding the temple
After the Babylonians had conquered Judah, the land lay desolate. But it was not always like this. It was a good, agriculturally prosperous land. Moses described it this way:

> ... a land of brooks of water, of fountains and springs flowing forth in valleys and hills; a land of wheat and barley, of vines and fig trees and pomegranates; a land of olive oil and honey; a

land where you shall eat food without scarcity ... a land whose stones are iron and out of whose hills you can dig copper (Deut. 8.7-9).

Clearly, the land which God had much earlier promised to Abraham (Gen. 12.1-2) and which Israel conquered in the time of Joshua, has been for Israel a land of blessing (Deut. 28.1-14). This blessing not only applies to the land itself, but it also applied to human habitation.

When Israel conquered Canaan, God gave to them, 'great and splendid cities which you did not build, and houses full of good things which you did not fill, and hewn cisterns which you did not dig, vineyards and olive trees which you did not plant' (Deut. 6.10-11). So, when Israel returned to the land it was now a land under curse (Deut. 28.15-68). Thus, the great and splendid cities which the Israelites had not built now lie devastated, and the houses which they had not built are now empty of all the good things with which they had filled them, and the hewn cisterns which they had not dug are now filled with rubble, and the vines and the olive trees which they had not planted are now uprooted. The task facing those exiles who have now returned to their 'promised' land is to rebuild their houses out of the heaps of rubble in which they lie, to clear and replaster their cisterns, to replant wheat and barley, and grape vines and olive trees. In addition, city walls must be rebuilt, and the altar and temple must be rebuilt. To Joshua, Zerubbabel, and the other leaders, rebuilding a nation devastated by war must have seemed to be a hopeless task. And, probably for a variety of reasons, they faltered and focused on building their own houses rather than rebuilding the house of the LORD. And so, God called two prophets to be his agents of refocused priorities and encouragement. The two prophets are Haggai and Zechariah.

In their capacity as God's spokesmen, Haggai and Zechariah are secondary agents for the fifth new start of turning points. Their messages to the returned exiles are recorded in the canonical books which bear their names. In the historical literature, i.e. the book of Ezra, they are reported to prophesy as if they were a tandem team. They prophesy in the second year of Darius, King of Persia (Ezra 4.24). This is 520 BCE, slightly less than 20 years after Cyrus's edict encouraging the Jewish exiles to return to Judah and to rebuild Jerusalem and its temple.

Though the foundation for the temple had soon been laid, no further progress had been made. Now, in the reign of Darius, who had recently come to the throne, the LORD sends Haggai and Zechariah who 'prophesied to the Jews who were in Judah and Jerusalem, in the name of the God of Israel, who was over them' (5.1). At this point, the Ezra narrative simply presupposes the prophecies which are recorded in their canonical writings. Somewhat laconically, Ezra immediately reports that Zerubbabel and Joshua, 'arose and began to rebuild the house of God which is in Jerusalem' (5.2a), adding the cryptic observation, 'and the prophets of God were with them supporting them' (5.2b).

National sanctuaries are not built in a day. Solomon's temple, for example, took seven years to complete (1 Kgs 6.38). Similarly, it will take five years to build Israel's second temple (520–515 BCE). Credit for successfully completing this project goes to the two prophets: 'and the elders of the Jews were successful in building through the prophesying of Haggai the prophet and Zechariah the son of Iddo' (Ezra 6.14a). Credit is also attributed to 'the command of the God of Israel, and the decree of Cyrus, Darius, and Artaxerxes, King or Persia' (6.14b). Having completed the project, worship is restored, 'as it is written in the book of Moses' (6.18). The dedication of the temple brings together the sons of Israel, the priests, the Levites, and the rest of the exiles (6.16). The dedication includes the sacrifice of 100 bulls, 200 rams, and 400 lambs (as peace offerings, 6.17). This is a far cry from the magnitude of offerings – 22,000 oxen and 120,000 sheep – when all Israel gathered to dedicate Solomon's temple (1 Kgs 8.63). But, obviously, post-exilic Jewry is both fewer in number and also much poorer than Israel was during its 'golden age' in the time of David and Solomon. In addition to the peace offerings, as a sin offering for 'all Israel', they offered twelve male goats, 'corresponding to the number of the tribes of Israel' (6.17). Of particular note is the fact that, once again, God's people act as one united 'twelve-tribe' Israel. Clearly, few prophets enjoyed success equal to that of Haggai and Zechariah, secondary agents for the new start.

Haggai prophesies with single-minded purpose, namely, to motivate the returned exiles to complete the building of the second temple (Hag. 1.1–2.23). Zechariah's prophecies complement Haggai's, but they have a much broader focus. In the context of this study one prophecy, in particular, demands our interest. This is the prophecy that Joshua, the Branch, will build the temple (Zech. 6.9-15). In this prophecy, the LORD instructs Zechariah to crown Joshua, the son of Jehozadak, the high priest (6.11), and to prophesy that he, the Branch, will build the temple of the LORD (6.12). On first reading, this seems to be a simple, straight-forward prophecy. But on second reading, it becomes somewhat enigmatic, for priests are not crowned, nor are they named the Branch. Thus, the prophecy also points to someone other than Joshua – One whose name is both Joshua (Greek: Jesus) and the Branch, who is a descendant of David, and who will rebuild the temple (Jn 2.19). Only one man meets these criteria – Jesus of Nazareth.

5.2.4. Ezra and Nehemiah: renewing the covenant and rebuilding Jerusalem

The first and topmost priorities of the returned exiles were to rebuild the altar and to rebuild the temple. The first of these tasks – rebuilding the altar – was done in 539/38 BCE, and the second task – rebuilding the temple – was finally completed in 515 BCE. Once these two projects were completed, Israel could then turn to other projects. These include the obligation to renew the Mosaic covenant of nationhood and the need to rebuild and to repopulate the city of Jerusalem. Ezra, the scribe, and Nehemiah, the cupbearer, will give effective leadership to these projects.

5.2.4.1. Ezra renews the covenant of nationhood

Ezra's family was not among those exiles who returned to Jerusalem and Judah in 539/38 BCE on the basis of Cyrus's leadership (Ezra 1.1-4). Ezra's leadership, as one of the secondary agents for the new start of the fifth cycle of turning points, will be needed much later. Ezra, typically identified as 'the scribe', is also a direct, though remote, descendant of Aaron, the high priest (7.1-5). As a priest-scribe, Ezra is 'skilled in the law of Moses' (7.6). In fact, he 'had set his heart to study the law of the LORD, and to practice it, and to teach his statutes and ordinances in Israel' (7.10). Not surprisingly, the narrative reports, 'the hand of the LORD his God was upon him' (7.6). Enjoying the LORD's favor, he requests of the king, namely Artaxerxes, permission to return from Babylon back to Jerusalem. Artaxerxes grants his request, and about five months later with 'the good hand of his God (still) upon him', he arrived in Jerusalem (7.9). He arrived with a letter in hand from Artaxerxes granting him wide-ranging administrative authority (7.11-25). He also arrived bringing with him gifts of silver and gold both from the king and from the exiles who have continued to live in Babylon (7.16-20), and the authority to tax the inhabitants of the land (7.21-23). More importantly, he is given the right to teach anyone who is ignorant of the laws of the God of Israel (i.e. the covenant) (7.25). Thus, Ezra is uniquely the agent of covenant renewal.

Before Ezra can lead Israel in covenant renewal, he must first journey from Babylon to Judah (Ezra 7.7-9). But he does not travel alone. Like Zerubbabel and Joshua before him, he will lead a large contingent of exiles back to their homeland (8.1-20). Before they leave Babylon, Ezra assembled the exiles for prayer for their safety, fasting, and repentance (8.21), because he was ashamed to ask the king for protection for their journey (8.22). Priests and Levites are recruited, sanctified, and made custodians of the silver and gold which they will carry with them (8.24-30). Five months later, the returnee exiles arrive at Jerusalem, and they 'offered burnt offering to the God of Israel, 12 bulls for all Israel, 96 rams, 77 lambs, 12 male goats for a sin offering' (8.35; compare 6.17). Finally, Ezra delivers the king's edict to his officials (satraps and governors), who, perhaps grudgingly, 'supported the people and the house of God' (8.36).

After Ezra arrived at Jerusalem, he quickly learns about a serious problem in the Jewish community (Ezra 9.1). The problem is that many Israelite men are taking wives from among their Gentile neighbors (9.2). This, of course, is not a racial issue; it is a spiritual issue. It is an extension of the 'Solomon Syndrome' – marrying foreign wives, which typically causes religious compromise (if not actual apostasy). The problem is made more serious by the fact that some leaders of the people are setting a bad example (9.3). Ezra investigates the reports and finds that they are accurate. This causes him great grief and consternation (9.4-15). His concern is that this sin will finally provoke God to destroy his people, even leaving them without a remnant (9.15).

Ezra is well-positioned to deal with the problem of mixed marriages. The biblical narrative has already reported his spiritual credentials (high priestly heritage and commitment to the law, i.e. the Mosaic covenant [Ezra 7.1-10]). The narrative has also reported that he is the Persian King's special agent (7.11-25). Because of these religious and political credentials, the post-Exilic community turns to him, confessing 'we have been unfaithful to our God' (10.2). They propose '[to] make a covenant with our God to put away all [foreign] wives and their children' (10.3a). This drastic action is to be done 'according to the law' = Mosaic covenant (10.3b). This is a heart-wrenching matter, and the people, therefore challenge Ezra '[to] be courageous and act' (10.4). Ezra responds by requiring that the people bind themselves to act according to the law/covenant (10.5). But separating themselves from their foreign wives and their children is a complicated process, so they establish a procedure to facilitate their commitments (10.9-17). And there the matter stands for another dozen years until another leader, Nehemiah the son of Hacaliah, returns from Persia to the Promised Land.

5.2.4.2. Ezra and Nehemiah renew the covenant of nationhood

As early as the time of Cyrus, King of Persia, the LORD had 'stirred (up many captive exiles) to go up and rebuild the house of the LORD which is in Jerusalem' (Ezra 1.7). As we have observed, Joshua and Zerubbabel are God's agents for what became the first mass migration of captive Israelites back to their homeland (2.1-70). Eighty or so years after, Ezra, priest and scribe, is God's sub-agent for a second, though smaller migration of exiles back to Judah (8.1-36). After another twelve years have passed, another prominent Israelite, still living in Persia, will lead a third group of exiles back to Judah (Neh. 2.11). This sub-agent is Nehemiah the son of Hacaliah, who is cupbearer to the King, Artaxerxes, and newly appointed governor of God's people in Judah (1.1, 11; 8.9). Ezra, his older contemporary, is a scholar by temperament (Ezra 7.10), but Nehemiah is a man of action and resolve (2.12-20). Therefore, Ezra is well positioned to lead the remnant in covenant renewal, and Nehemiah is well suited to lead the nation in rebuilding the still deso-

late city and its walls (2.11). The strengths of each agent come together to lead the restored remnant in covenant renewal.

This covenant renewal happens when the people assemble to
celebrate the Feast of Booths/Tabernacles and the Day of Atonement (Neh. 8.14, 18). Each day of the Feast from early morning
until midday, Ezra publicly reads the book of the Law of Moses
(8.3-4). Because much of the population had grown up speaking
Aramaic rather than Hebrew, the elders 'explained the law to the
people ... translating to give the sense so that they understood the
reading' (8.7-8). Learning about the Feast of Booths from Ezra's
reading of the law, the people celebrate the Feast for the first time
since Joshua and Israel had celebrated it (8.17, 18). Not only do they
joyfully celebrate Booths but they confess their sins (celebrate
Atonement? [9.1-38]), acknowledging, 'Thou [LORD] art just in all
that has come upon us; for Thou hast dealt faithfully, but we have
acted wickedly' (9.33). They make their covenant agreement in writing and Nehemiah the Governor and other nobles sign it (9.38–
10.27). The assembly also joins with their leaders, committing themselves 'to keep and to observe all the commandments of God our
LORD, and his ordinances and his statutes' (10.29). They also affirm
that they will provide all that the Temple might require to function
properly (10.32-39). This is a new day, a fresh start in Israel's history.

In addition to working with Ezra to bring about this renewal of
the Mosaic covenant, Nehemiah leads the nation in several other
projects. The first of these was the rebuilding of the walls of Jerusalem (Neh. 2.17–4.23), a massive project, but nevertheless, one
which was completed in 52 days (6.15). Nehemiah and other leaders
are also involved in the repopulating of the city of Jerusalem.
Those outside the city 'cast lots to bring one out of ten to live in
Jerusalem ... while nine-tenths remained in the other cities' (11.1).
As time passes, Nehemiah becomes involved in other issues, such as
the presence of foreigners (13.1-3), improper use of some rooms in
the Temple (13.4-9), neglect of the Levites (13.10-14), violations of
the Sabbath 'rest' laws (13.15-22), and mixed marriages (13.23-29).
Having vigorously dealt with these issues Nehemiah reports, 'Thus
I purified them (the people) from everything foreign and appointed
duties for the priests and the Levites, each in his task, and I ar-

ranged for the supply of wood at appointed times and for the first fruits' (13.30-31).

We have now observed that as God's agent and as agent of the Persian King, Artaxerxes, Nehemiah is an important leader of Israelites in the land of Judah. Either alone, or in partnership with Ezra, he accomplishes great things for the LORD and his people, Israel. No one can take this away from him. But the reports which chronicle his deeds also introduce a new, jarring refrain into the narrative. With variants, this refrain appears four times, as follows:

> Nehemiah 5.19 – Remember me, O my God, for good, according to all that I have done for this people.

> Nehemiah 13.14 – Remember me for this (care for the Levites), O my God, and do not blot out my loyal deeds, which I have performed for the house of my God and its services.

> Nehemiah 13.22 – For this also (sanctifying the Sabbath), remember me, O my God, and have compassion on me according to the greatness of Thy lovingkindness.

> Nehemiah 13.31 – Remember me, O my God, for good.

This refrain is jarring because it petitions God to bless/reward him for the works which he has performed according to what is written in the book of Moses. It is bad enough that Nehemiah is infected with the expectation that his God will reward him on the principle of works/righteousness, but the tragic, unintended consequence will infect various Jewish pietistic renewal movements, such as the Essenes and the Pharisees.

5.3. The Spread of Sin

After a century of restoration activity, Nehemiah's righteousness by law keeping brings the fifth new start to an end. At this point, the biblical record of the fifth cycle of turning points also comes to an end, but, of course, the history of post-exilic Judaism does not end. It continues unreported. Nevertheless, some aspects of this history are hinted at in certain prophetic narratives. For example, Malachi describes the rapid descent into false worship after the time of Nehemiah. Earlier, from the era from the Judges to the Babylonian captivity, many prophets condemned the programmatic evils of pantheism, polytheism, idolatry, and child sacrifice. In contrast, Malachi condemns a new kind of false worship. This is the mean-spirited hypocrisy by which the Israelites now despise God, offering up 'the lame, the halt, and the blind' in place of the best of the firstborn and the first fruits.

This 'robbing' of God is a negative prelude to the note of hope on which the fifth cycle of turning points ends. Malachi prophesies about a special, unique messenger who will in the future announce the coming of the LORD to Israel:

> Behold, I am going to send My messenger, and he will clear the way before Me. And the LORD whom you seek, will suddenly come to his Temple; and the messenger of the covenant, in whom you delight, behold, he is coming, says the LORD of Hosts (Mal. 3.1).

This messenger will be 'like a refiner's fire and like fuller's soap' (3.2). The result will be that 'the offering of Judah and Jerusalem will be pleasing to the LORD, as in the days of old and in former times' (3.4). In light of this, those who fear the LORD's name, 'the sun of righteousness' will arise with healing in its wings (4.2). In response to these promises, God's people are to 'remember the law of Moses, My servant ... lest I (the LORD) come and smite the land with a curse' (4.4-6).

5.4. Judgment

The Mosaic Covenant had set before Israel a blessing and a curse, that is, 'life and prosperity, and death and adversity' (Deut. 30.15). Ultimately, persistent disobedience to the law of Moses will cause the LORD to tear Israel from the land (28.63). Earlier, the fourth cycle of turning points in biblical history and theology ended in God's ultimate judgments – the Assyrian captivity for ten-tribe Israel (722 BCE), and the Babylonian captivity for two-tribe Judah (586 BCE) (2 Kgs 17.1-6; 25.21). In spite of the fact that after the captivities of Israel and Judah God had reunited the twelve tribes and had restored this remnant back to the land of Judah, and in his providence had restored the altar, the Temple and the city of Jerusalem, and renewed the covenant, at the end of the fifth cycle, history will repeat itself. In 70 CE the Roman army will destroy the altar, the Temple, the city of Jerusalem, and scatter the captive Jews throughout the far-flung Roman Empire. But, in one of the strangest silences in all of biblical history, this catastrophic judgment is nowhere actually described in the scriptures.

Rather, the future focus of biblical history and theology turns to the new start of the sixth cycle of turning points. In order to inaugurate this new cycle, God will, now for the third time, raise up a new leader by the name of Joshua (Greek, Jesus) who will be his primary agent of the new start for the sixth cycle of turning points.

PART 2

NEW TESTAMENT THEOLOGY

TRANSITION AND INTRODUCTION

The narrative about the fifth cycle of turning points in historical and biblical theology ended abruptly after reporting the lengthy process of effecting the fifth new start: rebuilding the altar, temple, city, and resettling many exiled Jews in their homeland. To be sure, there are hints in prophetic writings, such as Daniel, about the history which will follow the new start. Also, the prophet, Malachi, has shown that very quickly Israel's worship will demean God rather than honor Him. The Hebrew Bible has shown that the creator of the heavens and the earth, and the redeemer of humankind is a just and righteous judge. It has also shown that this same God is equally gracious and merciful. Therefore, it does not surprise the Bible reader that Malachi ends on a strong note of gracious and merciful restoration – a messenger of the covenant, who is identified as the prophet Elijah (Mal. 4.5), who will clear the way before the LORD (3.1).

But the sixth cycle of turning points will not be just a new repetition of the previous cycles. It will be a change so radical that the old covenant is made obsolete and will be replaced by a new covenant (Heb. 8.6-13).

This radical change in covenants is explicit in the two parts which make up the Christian Bible – the Old Testament or Covenant and the New Testament or Covenant. In the Old Covenant, God spoke to the fathers (i.e. the house of Israel) through the prophets in 'many portions and in many ways' (Heb. 1.1). But in the last days, which is the era of the sixth cycle of turning points, God has spoken in his Son (1.2). This radical change in covenant, from the old to the new is matched by an appropriate change in history and culture. For example, the fifth cycle of turning points is associated with the Persians, which has ended Babylonian control of the Ancient Near East and which controls the Near East from India to Egypt. Therefore, from the perspective centered on Judah and Jerusalem, the geographic orientation is eastward. This means that post-exilic Judaism has two centers: Jerusalem and Babylonia. The exile, itself, has also effected a change in the language spoken by God's people, Aramaic rather than Hebrew. In Jerusalem, itself, the Temple has been rebuilt and is once again the focus of Israel's religious life. Finally, the priesthood has succeeded the monarchy as Israel's political/administrative leaders. When the sixth cycle begins, i.e. the new covenant is inaugurated, these factors are all different.

When the narratives of the New Covenant begin (Matthew, Mark, Luke, and John), the Roman Empire, having displaced the Greek empires, controls the eastern Mediterranean world. As a result, there is now a strong geographic orientation to the West – i.e. Europe. This westward orientation, directed by the Holy Spirit, means that the so-called missionary journeys of Paul have an increasingly westward orientation. Indeed, Spain is Paul's ultimate destination. Furthermore, God's people are now also dispersed westward, and they often speak Greek, rather than Hebrew and/or Aramaic. The Second Temple, rebuilt by Herod, still stands proudly in Jerusalem, but Israel's religious life is focused on the Jewish synagogue, with its emphasis on prayer and the scriptures. Finally, the priesthood has given way to the scribes and the Pharisees in popular religious influence. These highlighted differences have repositioned Judaism from its place in the history and culture of the Ancient Near East to the history and classical culture of the so-called Western Civilization.

This orientation toward Western Civilization happens according to God's providential plan and purpose which plays out during the sixth cycle of turning points. One of the foremost prophets of the early days of this cycle expresses it this way:

> But when the fullness of time came, God sent forth his Son, born of a woman, born under the Law, in order that he might redeem those who are under the Law, that we might receive the adoption as sons. And because you are sons, God has set forth the Spirit of his Son into our hearts, crying, 'Abba! Father!' (Gal. 4.4-6).

Interpreters typically identify a cluster of factors which make up the 'fullness of time' about which Paul writes. These include, but are not limited to, 1) the pervasive penetration of Hellenistic culture throughout the Mediterranean world, 2) the complementary widespread use of a 'common' Greek language, 3) Roman roads and Roman peace, and 4) growing Jewish longing for the long-promised Messiah. These then are important factors which give to *this* sixth cycle of turning points such dramatic and momentous changes. The world has never been the same since.

The new start to the previous cycles always follows a dramatic act of judgment upon a wicked population. Thus, the new start with Noah follows world-wide judgment by flood waters; the new start with Abraham follows the Babel incident; with Joshua the son of Nun, judgment in the wilderness; and with Joshua and Zerubbabel, 70 years after the Babylonian captivity. The sixth new start does not follow this pattern. This time God establishes the new start approximately 70 years before judgment – in the form of the Jewish War against Rome – falls upon the Jews. Thus, the new start to the sixth turning point and the judgment which ends the fifth cycle overlap by about two generations. The following schematic highlights this unique relationship between the two cycles of turning points:

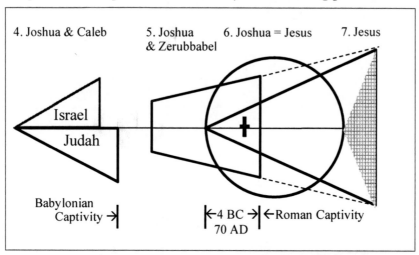

This illustration is an abbreviation of the schematic illustrating the seven cycles of turning points in biblical history and theology. The circle spotlights the overlap by 70 years of the sixth new start and the judgment which brings the fifth cycle of turning points to its terrible conclusion in the Jewish War of 70 CE.

The time span between the new start of the sixth cycle of turning points and the seventh cycle cannot now be known, for the simple reason that it has not yet been concluded by the second coming of God's agent: Joshua = Jesus. Though the length of the sixth cycle is not yet known, the interpreter can name the era which the cycle spans. It is called the 'last days' (Acts 2.17; compare 1 Pet. 1.20; Heb. 1.2). In other words, *human history from the first coming of Jesus to his second coming is the last days*. The first coming of Jesus inaugurates the last days, which continues as history advances until Jesus comes a second time to consummate the last days. Many Bible readers believe that the present time is much closer to the consummation of the last days than it is to its inauguration two millennia ago. Clearly, because Jesus both inaugurates and consummates the last days – the sixth cycle of turning points – his role as God's agent in human history is, and will remain, unprecedented.

6

CYCLE SIX: THE NEW COVENANT

Earlier in biblical history God, the LORD, entered into covenants with various persons and people groups. These covenants include those made with Noah, Abraham, secondary covenants with Moses and David, and covenant renewals with Joshua the son of Nun, and Ezra-Nehemiah. Several of these characters/families were agents of the new starts to the sequence of turning points in biblical history and theology. John the Baptist and Jesus of Nazareth are the two primary agents of the sixth cycle of turning points

6.1. Agents of the New Start: John and Jesus

John the Baptist and Joshua/Jesus of Nazareth are the two primary agents of the sixth cycle of turning points. Each person is a Spirit-filled prophet, but they are not equal. They differ in status. John is 'the prophet of the Most High' (Lk. 1.76), whereas Jesus is, 'the Son of the Most High', that is, he is 'the Son of God' (1.32, 35). The two prophets also differ in function. John is the promised messenger who announces the coming of the LORD (Isa. 40.3; Mal. 4.5); whereas Jesus is the 'Savior who is Christ the Lord'. The fact that Jesus is superior to John in no way diminishes John as a primary agent of the new start.

6.1.1. John the Baptist

In his Gospel, Luke the Evangelist answers the implied question, Who is John? According to Luke, John fulfills several announcements and/or prophecies. For example, the angel Gabriel announces that the aged couple, Zacharias and Elizabeth, though presently childless will give birth to/bear a son (Lk. 1.13). As Malachi earlier prophesied, this son will have a Spirit-filled, Elijah-like ministry (1.15-17). This means that Zacharias' son will be called the prophet of the Most High (1.76). Luke also reports Jesus' estimation of John. Jesus affirms that John truly ministers as a prophet (7.27). High praise, indeed! However, Jesus asserts that humanly speaking, John is the greatest prophet; but, nevertheless, speaking spiritually, those born into the Kingdom of God are greater (7.28). On another occasion, Jesus asserts that John is a dividing point in salvation history, that is, the Law and the Prophets extended up to, but did not include John; since then, however, including John the Gospel of the Kingdom is preached (16.16; compare 3.18). From what Luke reports, the biblically informed reader will recognize that John has a unique place on the honor rule of the prophets, from Samuel and his successors onwards.

John's prophetic ministry stirred national interest. It is set in the context of both Roman and Jewish history – in the time of Tiberius Caesar, Pontius Pilate, Herod the Tetrarch, etc. (Lk. 3.1-2). John's ministry is about 'a baptism of repentance for the forgiveness of sins' (3.3). Further, John identifies himself to be 'the one who prepares the way for the coming of the LORD' (3.4, 5; compare Isa. 40.3-5). For those who do not repent John's message is the way of judgment (by fire 3.15-17). In addition, he prophesies about a successor who will baptize God's people in the Holy Spirit and fire (3.16, 17). Luke summarizes his report about John's preaching, concluding 'so with many other exhortations also he preached the *gospel* (italics added) to the people' (3.18). This prophetic ministry about repentance and forgiveness = salvation and/or judgment upon the stubbornly impenitent is not only powerfully appealing but also a puzzlement.

As the prophet who, himself, fulfills earlier prophesies from Isaiah to Malachi, John's Spirit-filled ministry provokes much speculation – might he be the long-awaited Messiah (Lk. 3.15). John firmly denies this Messianic attribution, but even after his death, his reputation flourishes. Herod the Tetrarch, John's executioner, hears that John continues to be reputed to be 'risen from the dead, and by some Elijah (compare Mal. 4.5; Lk. 1.15-17), and by others that he is one of the other prophets of old' (9.7-9). So closely are the lives and the ministries of John the prophet of the Most High and Jesus the son of the Most High intertwined that the same crowds who speculated about John later speculate that Jesus is 'John the Baptist, ... Elijah, ... [or] one of the prophets of old' (9.18-19). But the crowds get it wrong both times: John is not the Messiah/Christ (3.15) and Jesus is not John the Baptist (9.19).

Overall, and in detail, Luke portrays John to be a powerful but enigmatic prophet. His birth is an answer to prayer (Lk. 1.13), and he is commissioned to be a Spirit-filled, end-times, Elijah-like prophet (1.15-17). He is the evangelist who first preaches the gospel = good news about salvation (3.18). But most of all, he is the messenger who prepares the way of the LORD, that is Christ, the Spirit-baptizer (3.4, 16). And so, Jesus got it right. John, this agent of the new start of the sixth cycle of turning points, is uniquely the greatest of ones born to women – greater than Noah, greater than Abraham, than Joshua, and all other primary and secondary agents of every previous turning point. Though John is the greatest of God's 'new-start' agents, there is, paradoxically a greater agent in biblical history and theology. This is another Joshua (Hebrew) = Jesus (Greek) who is uniquely, paradoxically greater than the greatest.

6.1.2. Jesus of Nazareth

As has been observed (above), Jesus esteems John, because of his prophet/messenger role, to be the greatest. But, of course, as the one who *effects* salvation, Jesus, himself, is greater than John, who announces the LORD's salvation. So, just as we earlier asked and answered the questions, who is John? I will now answer the question, who is Jesus? The answer to the questions comes from a survey of the gospels according to Matthew and Luke.

6.1.2.1. Jesus' identity according to Matthew

According to the evidence which Matthew reports, Jesus is the direct though remote descendant of two of God's earlier covenant agents. Looking backward in time, Jesus is the son of David, the son of Abraham (Mt. 1.1). Matthew next traces Jesus' family tree (1.2-17). He divides his report of Jesus' ancestry into three distinct, symmetrical units: 1) from Abraham to David (14 generations), 2) from David to the Babylonian Captivity (14 generations), and 3) from the Babylonian Captivity to the birth of the Christ = Messiah = the Anointed One. This genealogical record signifies three identifying facts. One, Jesus is the heir to the Abrahamic promises and covenant (Genesis 12, 15). Two, Jesus is the direct heir of Judah, which is the tribe from which Israel's future kings will come (Gen. 49.8-12). Three, more specifically, Jesus is the heir to the Davidic covenant and subsequently, the dynastic lineage through Solomon (2 Samuel 7; 1 Kgs 1.38-40). Therefore, as the history of Israel advances from the Abraham cycle of turning points, through the Davidic covenant (fourth cycle), the restoration from the Babylonian Captivity (fifth cycle), and ultimately to the Christ, Joshua/Jesus is the extension of the earlier covenants and agent of the sixth cycle of turning points. Therefore, the identity of Jesus arises from more than his individual personhood; it is shaped by the key turning points in Israel's history.

Jesus' identity is, however, not only shaped by Israel's salvation history, it is clarified by the several titles which Matthew reports about this Joshua/Jesus, who is the son of David, the son of Abraham. Thus, the names/titles for Jesus arise out of his genealogy and are appropriate to it. For example, Joseph's and Mary's son is to be named Joshua/Jesus, which signifies that God will save his people from their sins (Mt. 1.22). Further, fulfilling prophecy, Jesus is also named Immanuel, that is, 'God with us' (1.23; compare Isa. 7.14). After Jesus' birth, three Magi arrive at Jerusalem, seeking out the infant, 'King of the Jews' (2.2). Herod, the reigning monarch understands that this title identifies the Christ/Messiah (21.3; compare 1.16). Again, fulfilling prophecy, Jesus is born to be a ruler (*hēgoumenos*) and shepherd (*poimēn*) his people (2.6; compare Mic. 5.2). Matthew also applies a prophecy of Hosea – 'out of Egypt have I called My [God's] son' (2.15; compare Hos. 11.1; Exod. 4.22). By any human standard, these names – God saves, God with us, God's son – and titles – Christ, King of the Jews, and Shepherd – would never be given to a baby born into the household of an artisan (Joseph was a carpenter). Therefore, the only possible explanation is the whole reality of the incarnation, that is the 'virginal conception', a.k.a., the virgin birth of Jesus (1.18-25). Matthew observes that the doctrine of the 'virginal conception' fulfills many prophecies.

The following table illustrates Matthew's prophecy/fulfillment theme:

Text	Fulfillment Formula	Prophecy
Mt. 1.22 Isa. 7.14	That which was spoken of by the prophet might be fulfilled	The virgin shall be with child
Mt. 2.5 Mic. 5.2	For so it has been written by the prophet	(The Christ) has to be born in Bethlehem of Judea
Mt. 2.15 Hos. 11.1	That which was spoken by the LORD through the prophet might be fulfilled	Out of Egypt did I call my Son
Mt. 2.17 Jer. 31.35	Then that which was spoken through Jeremiah the prophet was fulfilled	A voice was heard in Ramah Weeping and great mourning

Other prophecy/fulfillment texts can be found in Mt. 3.3; 4.14; etc. By using this narrative strategy, Matthew emphasizes the actual, explicit continuity between earlier cycles of turning points in biblical history theology and the present.

6.1.2.2. Jesus' identity according to Luke

As is Matthew's gospel, so also in Luke's gospel, both John the Baptist and Jesus are the two primary agents of the sixth cycle of new starts. Luke's narrative complements that of Matthew. For Luke, the births of John and Jesus signal that the 'last days' have begun. In the Hebrew Bible, the fifth cycle of turning points (agents: Joshua and Zerubbabel) concludes with the Malachi prophecies. These are followed by several generations of the perceived cessation of prophecy (Tos. Sota 8.5). Against this background, Luke reports an outburst of renewed prophecy upon various righteous and devout persons. For example:

- The first agent of the sixth new start, John the Baptist, will be filled with the Spirit from birth (Lk. 1.15-17).
- Elizabeth, John's mother, is filled with the Spirit, resulting in praise-prophecy (1.14).
- Similarly, John's father, Zacharias, is filled with the Spirit and prophesies (1.67).
- Finally, an aged worshipper, Simeon, is led by the Spirit and prophesies (2.25-27).

Individually and cumulatively, these experiences of the Spirit, who inspires prophecy, signals that the 'last days' (i.e. the sixth cycle of turning points) have begun. This interpretation of Luke's narrative (1.5–2.41) is confirmed by the fact that this outburst of prophecy is an initial fulfillment of Joel's prophecy about the outpouring of the Spirit in the last days upon sons and daughters, young men and old, and even upon male and female bondslaves (compare Acts 2.17-18; Joel 2.28-32). As the last days have begun, the two greatest agents in the history of God's people are born: John the Baptist and Jesus of Nazareth (1.76; 1.32-35). Both of these agents owe their births to divine intervention, but Jesus is immeasurably greater because the Son of God is superior to any and every prophet (compare, for example, Heb. 1.1-2).

Luke identifies Mary's baby son by name and title. Her baby is to be named Joshua/Jesus (because of everything which this name implies) (Lk. 1.35). Further, on the night when he is born, angels identify Jesus by the titles Savior, Christ, and LORD (2.11). In an earlier age, the titles are used to identify Israel's God. Further, all three titles are variously ascribed to Greco-Roman kings and emperors. Here they are attributed to a baby boy, born to artisan class parents (i.e. Joseph is a carpenter). This is presumptuous, blasphemous, and/or seditious for any baby, except for the unique baby who truly fully is the God who saves his people from their sins.

Luke's genealogy of Jesus reinforces the uniqueness of this baby. It begins with the enigmatic, mysterious statement that Jesus is 'supposedly *the son* of Joseph' (3.23). This genealogy concludes, identifying Jesus to be 'the *son* of Adam, the *son* of God' (3.38). These concluding names in the genealogy clearly, emphatically identify the 'dual nature' of Jesus. He is at once both human and God. This is the result of his virgin birth (the miracle of conception effected by the overshadowing power of the Holy Spirit, compare 1.35). Incidentally, it must be observed that all Christological heresies are distortions of these two symbiotic realities. On the one hand, there are those heresies which emphasize Jesus' humanity at the expense of his deity; on the other hand, there are those heresies which emphasize his deity at the expense of his humanity.

Luke not only reports that Jesus is identified as Savior and LORD, but that he is the Christ. This title can be confusing because of the two languages by which the Bible was written. In the Hebrew Bible, the word for 'anointed one' is *Mashiach* (anglicized as Messiah), and in the Greek Bible (Septuagint, New Testament) the word is *Christos*. Therefore, Jesus is the 'anointed one' = Messiah = Christ. Both the Hebrew term (Messiah) and the Greek term (Christ) identify Jesus as the anointed one, that is, dedicated, consecrated, and/or commissioned to be God's servant. Jesus' anointing happens when Jesus is baptized by John the Baptist (Lk. 3.21, 22). At that time, Luke reports, while Jesus is praying, 'heaven was opened, and the Holy Spirit descended upon him in bodily form like a dove, and a voice came out of heaven, "Thou art My beloved Son, in Thee I am well-pleased"' (3.21, 22). As Luke reports it, the two signs of Jesus' anointing are the descent of the Spirit and the explanatory voice from heaven. This anointing commissions Jesus to preach the gospel, that is, the good news of God's salvation (4.18, 19). This anointing identifies Jesus as God's consecrated or commissioned prophet (4.24), after the pattern of Isaiah (4.18, 19), and two charismatic prophets, Elijah and Elisha (4.25-27), and the many rejected prophets throughout Israel's history (e.g. 4.28-30).

6.2. The New Start According to the Gospels

The four gospels do much more than briefly identify the two remarkable prophets, John the Baptist and Jesus of Nazareth. Each, in its own way gives an extensive record of the three years of Jesus' public ministry. The four gospels are identified by two groupings: 1) the synoptic gospels (Matthew, Mark, and Luke) – so classified because they give a distinctive but nevertheless, common viewpoint of Jesus, and 2) autoptic – the unique viewpoint of the gospel according to the apostle John. The following discussion of the new start, of which John and Jesus are the primary agents will therefore survey the new start according to this twofold classification: 1) Synoptic gospels, and 2) John's gospel. I will discuss the synoptic gospels according to the order in which they are presumed to have been written: Mark, Matthew, and Luke.

6.2.1. The new start according to the Synoptic Gospels

The data about Jesus' life and ministry is immense. At 16 chapters, Mark's gospel is longer than most books within the collection of books in the New Testament, but Matthew and Luke are the two longest books in the New Testament canon. Therefore, the discussion of the new start according to the synoptic gospels is necessarily selective and indeed, truncated. It will focus on one title per gospel by which Jesus is identified and one other prominent theme for each gospel. The following table summarizes this approach.

Gospel	Titular Theme	Secondary Theme(s)
Mark	Jesus is Son of Man	Four Portraits: Teacher, Prophet, Messiah, King
Matthew	Jesus is Son of David	Kingdom of God
Luke	Jesus is Son of God	Jesus is Prophet, Savior, salvation, to save

These gospels contain a common core, which makes up about 90% of Mark's gospel, and is also common to the lengthier gospels of Matthew and Luke. Each gospel writer supplements this core in a variety of ways. These two facts – common core and unique supplementation – mean that each gospel is unique in itself and yet complementary to the other synoptic gospels.

6.2.1.1. The new start according to Mark

In the prologue to Luke's gospel, he informs Theophilus, his patron, that many gospels have been written earlier than his own. Mark's gospel may not have been the earliest gospel to have been written, but it is the earliest of the three synoptic gospels and was known and used by Matthew and Luke when they wrote their own gospels. Mark's gospel is therefore the key to understanding the gospels according to Matthew and Luke.

Mark identifies his narrative about Jesus to be the 'gospel,' that is, to be 'good news' (Mk 1.1), and he identifies Jesus to be the Messiah/the Christ, the Son of God. But the Jesus about whom he writes insists that the characters in Mark's story about him do not speak about him in this way (1.41, etc.). Rather, Jesus consistently refers to himself as 'the Son of Man' (2.10, etc.). At a time in Israel's history when God's people are becoming increasingly susceptible to Messianic excitement, the self-designation 'Son of Man' is politically neutral, and will hide the speaker from the prying ears of the Roman rulers. But it is more. The term is a puzzle or conundrum. It causes people to puzzle out Jesus' identity, and soon they are asking questions like, 'Why does this man speak this way?' and, 'who, then, is this, that even the wind and the sea obey Him?' (2.7; 4.41). This term, which is, at one and the same time, both revealing and hiding, is rooted in the Hebrew Bible.

Perhaps the earliest use of the term is found in a psalm of David (Psalm 8). Comparing the glory of God's creation – the heavens – to the smallness of man, David expresses his wonderment: 'What is man ... and the Son of man, that Thou [the LORD] dost care for him?' (8.4). Later in biblical history, the LORD will address the prophet, Ezekiel, as 'Son of man' (Ezek. 2.1, etc.). But the background to Jesus' use of the term as a self-designation most likely echoes the Son of man text in Daniel 7. As one element in a dramatic vision Daniel sees '... with the clouds of heaven, One like a Son of Man was coming. And he came up to the Ancient of Days, and was presented before Him' (7.13). This human-like person was given 'dominion ... glory and a kingdom ... which will not pass away ... which will not be destroyed' (7.14). Since these verses are quoted in the New Testament and explicitly applied to Jesus (Rev. 1.6, 10; compare Mk 14.15), there can be no doubt that Dan. 7.13, 14 is both the source of Jesus' Son of Man designation and also his complementary teaching about the Kingdom of God – a subject which dominates his teaching from first to last.

Against this background Jesus, the Christ, the Son of God (Mk 1.1), regularly identifies himself to be the Danielic 'Son of Man'. For example, early in his ministry, certain scribes charge him with blasphemy for forgiving sins, something which, in their theology, God alone can do (2.7). Jesus defends his action, asserting 'in order that you may know that the Son of Man has authority on earth to forgive sins', he said to the paralytic, '... rise, take up your pallet and go home' (2.10, 11). In a later episode, the Pharisees accost Jesus, saying, 'See here, why are they (Jesus' disciples) doing what is not lawful on the Sabbath?' (2.24). Jesus deflects this implied accusation, stating that the Son of Man – and neither the Pharisaic traditions nor the Mosaic covenant – is LORD even of the Sabbath' (2.28). As Jesus' ministry begins to draw to a close, he warns his followers: '... the Son of Man must suffer many things and be rejected by the elders and the chief priests and the scribes, and be killed, and after three days, rise again' (8.31; compare 9.31; 10.33). After Jesus and his three disciples, Peter, James, and John, descend from the so-called Mount of Transfiguration, he orders them, 'not to relate to anyone what they had seen, until the Son of Man should rise from the dead' (9.9). Concerning his substitutionary Passover death, Jesus teaches, 'for even the Son of Man did not come to be served, but to serve, and to give his life a ransom for many' (10.45). At his trial before the Jewish Council, Jesus prophesies in the words of Daniel that the Son of Man will come 'riding on the clouds' (13.26; compare Dan. 7.13). Finally, at the Passover, one of his disciples betrays the Son of Man (14.21, 41).

Mark brackets Jesus' ministry by identifying him from first to last to be the Son of God (Mk 1.11; 15.39). But mysteriously, in Mark's narrative, the Son of God is also, first and foremost, the Son of Man, the son of Mary (2.10; 6.3). Enigmatically, though Jesus is fully human, he has God-like authority (2.10, 28), a redemptive substitutionary death (10.45), and God-like mobility (13.26, 14.62). Because his death is redemptive, substitutionary, he is also betrayed; he suffers; he is killed; he rises from the dead, and he will return to earth riding on the clouds of glory (14.21, 41; 8.31; 9.12, 31; 10.33; 13.26; 14.42). Clearly, in all of human history, Jesus is unique – mysteriously and fully human, yet, at the same time, fully divine. Note that Matthew and Luke, who write later than Mark does, explain the mystery of Jesus' two natures by prefacing their narratives about Jesus with birth-accounts (Mt. 1.18–2.12; Lk. 1.5–2.42).

6.2.1.1.1. Mark's four portraits of Jesus
Right from the start of his narrative, Mark demonstrates that Jesus, in comparison to his contemporaries, has a qualitatively superior ministry. For example, Jesus' teaching is superior to that of the scribes and the Pharisees because of its authority (Mk 1.21, 22). Jesus' authority extends to the casting out of demons (1.23-28). He also has the power to heal all kinds of diseases and afflictions (1.29-34). His superiority is also evident in his authority to forgive sins (2.1-12). He (and not Moses) is LORD of the Sabbath. He also controls nature, the wind and the waves (4.35-41). Among the most dramatic of his miracles is that he raises the dead (5.35-42). He also feeds a multitude of five thousand from a supply of five loaves and two fish (6.30-44).

Apart from some echoes from some Old Testament narratives, such as Moses feeding Israel with manna in the wilderness (Exodus

16), Jesus' teaching and actions are unique and unprecedented. Not surprisingly, this evokes a variety of responses: amazement (1.22, 27; 2.12, etc.), opposition (2.7; 3.6, 21, 3), and puzzlement (1.27; 2.7, 18, 23). His disciples ask the ultimate question about Jesus' identity: 'Who then is this, that even the wind and the sea obey Him?' (4.41). Mark answers these and other questions about him by giving his readership four portraits of Jesus.

Mark portrays Jesus to be: teacher (Mark 1.21–4.41), prophet (5.1–7.37), Messiah or Christ (8.1–9.50), and, finally, the (rejected) King of the Jews (10.1–16.20). With some overlapping, these portraits are sequential; that is, Jesus began his ministry as a teacher, and though he begins to function as a prophet, he never ceases to function as a teacher. The sequence of these portraits is given on the principle of 'progressive revelation'. The portraits advance from the function that is best known in contemporary Jewish culture – teacher – to that which is least known, namely, Jesus is the King of the Jews. Though these portraits are progressive, each one is introduced by Mark's report that Jesus performs two miracles, namely, 1) Jesus casts out demons, and 2) Jesus heals the sick (e.g. 1.23-28; 1.29-34).

One, Mark portrays Jesus as teacher (Mk 1.21–4.41). This is primarily the role of the synagogue, though the teacher, himself, often trains his disciples on an itinerant or walk-about strategy. Jesus' ministry follows his commissioning by John the Baptist (1.11). The accompanying descent of the dove from heaven signifies that God is empowering Jesus (1.10), and the accompanying voice from heaven signifies that God approves of his son (1.11). As an itinerant teacher, Jesus' ministry begins in the synagogues of Galilee (1.21, 22). It includes functions such as casting out demons and healing the sick (1.23-34). Jesus' teaching ministry also includes forgiving sins (2.1-12). Typical of a first century Jewish Rabbi (teacher), Jesus calls and commissions a group of (young?) men to be his disciples (3.13-19). Finally, Jesus characteristically taught in parables (4.1-31). Though Jesus is recognized to function in some ways like a typical Galilean rabbi, his disciples slowly begin to understand that he is more than, and greater than a teacher. Having experienced Jesus' control of the wind and the waves, they ask, 'who then is this, that even the wind and the sea obey Him?' (4.41). The partial answer to this question is that Jesus is more than a teacher; he is a prophet.

Two, Mark portrays Jesus as prophet (Mk 5.1–7.37). As Mark's narrative about Jesus advances, Jesus begins to function as a prophet. This advance is signaled by a sequence of three miracles: 1) Jesus casts out the demons, 'Legion', 2) he heals a sick woman (5.1-34), and 3) he raises Jairus' daughter from the dead (5.1-43). The first two miracles are programmatic indicators that Jesus is advancing his self-revelation beyond that of teacher (compare 1.23-34), and the third miracle identifies his new status as prophet. Thus, when Jesus raises Jairus' daughter from the dead, he functions like one of the prophets of old, namely, Elijah, who raised the widow's son from the dead (1 Kgs 17.17-24). Next, in Nazareth, his hometown, Jesus identifies himself to be a rejected prophet like many earlier prophets to Israel (2 Kgs 17.7-25). Following this, Jesus multiplies a boy's lunch, so that this meager supply feeds a crowd of five thousand hungry men, first as Moses and later as Elijah and Elisha had also done (Exodus 16; 1 Kings 17; 2 Kings 4). Clearly, in ways like his prophetic predecessors, particularly Moses, Elijah, and Elisha, Jesus extends and develops his prophetic ministry to God's people in Galilee and beyond (Lebanon, Syria). But even this progress – from teacher to prophet – is inadequate to reveal the full status of Jesus and his ministry. The third portrait continues to advance and elevate Jesus' own self-revelation.

Three, Mark portrays Jesus to be the Messiah/Christ (Mk 8.1–9.50). As was mentioned earlier, 'Messiah/Christ' are the untranslated Hebrew and Greek words, both of which mean 'Anointed One'. In Israel's history, priests, kings, and prophets were anointed to office. Therefore, in Jesus' progressive self-revelation, the one who has revealed himself to be a prophet (Mk 6.1-6), will next reveal himself to be the LORD's 'Anointed One' (Messiah/Christ). As Jesus' ministry advances he has earned the widespread, popular reputation that he is a prophet. Consider the following:

> … people were saying John the Baptist has risen from the dead … But others were saying, he is Elijah. And others were saying, he is a prophet, like one of the prophets of old (6.14) … [Jesus questioned his disciples] 'Who do people say that I am?' And

they told Him, 'John the Baptist, others Elijah, others again, one of the prophets' (8.27, 28).

But, though Jesus is rightly reputed to be a prophet, he is more than a prophet. In this context, Peter affirms that Jesus is the Messiah = Christ = Anointed One (8.28). Significantly, Peter's confession that Jesus is the Christ is soon followed by the 'transfiguration' (9.1-8). For the transfiguration to happen, Jesus takes his inner circle of disciples, namely, Peter, James, and John, up on a high mountain (perhaps Mt. Hermon). There, with snow-covered mountain packs behind Him, Jesus is transfigured, that is, metamorphosed. In other words, he *radiated* divine glory – in contrast to Moses who had *reflected* divine glory. In this dramatic scene, Elijah and Moses, the two greatest of Jesus' charismatic predecessors, appeared. At the same time a 'cloud' (of his Presence) overshadowed them, and God affirmed Jesus to be his Anointed One, his Son. But if Jesus is more than a prophet, what is his anointed function to be? The answer to this implied question is found in Mark's fourth and final portrait. He is the King of the Jews.

Four, Mark portrays Jesus to be the King of the Jews (Mk 10.1–16.25). David is the founder/progenitor of Israel's dynastic kingship (2 Samuel 7). His kingship is uniquely associated with Jerusalem, the Jebusite city which David and his companions captured (2 Sam. 5.6-10). But initially, Jesus' ministry has been associated with Galilee, where he ministered as teacher, prophet, and anointed one. For Jesus to reveal himself as anointed king, he must necessarily relocate to Jerusalem. Mark reports this relocation in some detail (Mk 10.1–11.11). This is the Passover season, and Jesus journeys from Galilee to Jericho, and on to Jerusalem in company with his disciples and other Jewish pilgrims.

As the actual Passover day approaches, Jesus is arrested and put on trial (Mk 14.61-64). The High Priest challenges Him, asking, 'Are you the Christ, the Son of the Blessed One?' (14.61; compare 8.29). Jesus affirms, 'I am' (14.62). His answer is considered to be 'blasphemy' (14.63, 64); and because of this 'blasphemy', Jesus is sentenced to death (14.64). Mark reports that in addition to being rejected by the Jewish leaders, Jesus is also rejected by the Passover throng. Pilate, the Roman governor, offers to release the 'King of the Jews' (15.9). But the crowd will have none of it. Earlier in the week, Jesus had turned his back on the crowd, and now they turn their back on him (compare 11.11). And so, they insist that Pilate 'crucify' the 'King of the Jews' (15.12, 13).

Mark reports that Jesus' crucifixion mocks his anointed kingship (Mk 15.16-39). The soldiers mock Jesus as King. They dressed him in purple, symbolizing royal status (15.17a). They crown Him, but with a crown of thorns (15.17b). Next, they acclaim Him, 'Hail, King of the Jews' (15.18). Finally, they affix to the cross the charge against, which reads, 'The King of the Jews' (15.26). Adding insult to injury, the chief priests mock, 'Let this Christ, the King of Israel, now come down from the cross' (15.32). Ironically, an anonymous Roman Centurion (Cornelius?, Acts 10.1-48) recognizes what the mockers could not see, observing, 'Truly this man was a son of [a] God' (15.39).

And so, one fateful Passover festival in Jerusalem, the one who earlier had shown himself to be: 1) teacher, 2) prophet, and 3) anointed one, dies in the royal city as the (rejected) King of the Jews – giving his life as a ransom for many (compare Mk 10.45).

6.2.1.2. The new start according to Matthew

Mark's gospel appears to have been the earliest of the so-called synoptic gospels, namely, Mark, Matthew, and Luke. Turning from Mark's gospel to Matthew's gospel, the alert Bible reader can readily observe that it serves as the core of Matthew's gospel, which, he, in turn supplemented with a block of Jesus' teaching which he has in common with Luke's gospel, and to which he also added his own unique material. In brief, this introduces the synoptic problem – specifically, the literary, the historical, and the theological interdependence of these three gospels. To a large extent, however, *by studying each gospel independently, and, therefore, on its own merits*, there is a broad enough consensus about the problem that it can be set aside. The Gospel of Matthew has the distinction of being the lengthiest book in the New Testament. The following discussion will focus on just two of the primary and secondary themes which are to be found in the gospel. These are the gospel's 'Son of David' and 'Kingdom of Heaven/God' themes. These two themes both complement Mark's 'Son of Man' and 'Four portraits' themes and do their part to add to the richness of the gospels' story about Jesus.

6.2.1.2.1. *Matthew's Son of David theme*

Matthew begins his gospel with a straightforward statement of its general subject. He writes, 'The book of the genealogy of Jesus Christ, the son of David, the son of Abraham' (Mt. 1.1). This immediately connects Jesus to two of Israel's greatest agents, and the covenants which God had established between himself and them. Abraham is the starting point in Matthew's genealogy of Jesus and David is a decisive point in the genealogy (1.2, 6). The genealogy extends down through time to the present, that is, 'to Joseph the husband of Mary, by whom was born Jesus, who is called Christ (Anointed One)' (1.16). In regards to Jesus' link to Israel's covenant history, the important fact is that Joseph is a 'son of David' (1.20). Thus, before he begins to write the actual story of Jesus, beginning with his birth (1.18), Matthew has identified Jesus as the direct (though remote [28 generations, 1.17]), legitimate heir to David's throne. This identifies Jesus as the Anointed King of the Jews.

Matthew's identification of Jesus as the son of David = King of the Jews is highly improbable for a baby who will soon be born to artisan class parents (Joseph is a carpenter or stone mason). But mysterious wise ones (magi) from the east will travel to Jerusalem to pay him homage (Mt. 2.2). At a time when a certain Edomite named Herod rules as king over Judea on behalf of Rome, it is also dangerous; and, warned about the danger by an angel, Joseph flees with his family to Egypt (2.13-17). After Herod dies, Joseph will establish his young, still vulnerable family, in Nazareth in Galilee (2.19-23).

Against this background, Matthew uses the 'Son of David' title four times to identify Jesus as a healer and/or exorcist. On one occasion, after Jesus has raised a young girl from the dead and as he passes along the road two blind beggars accost him, imploring, 'Have mercy on us, son of David' (Mt. 9.27). Later, Jesus heals a man who is blind and dumb, with the result that the multitudes are amazed, and speculate, 'This man cannot be the son of David, can he?' (12.23). Eventually, Jesus will travel into the Lebanon, and there a Canaanite mother begs Jesus for help for her demon-possessed daughter, imploring, 'Have mercy on me, O LORD, Son of David' (15.22). Finally, as Jesus passes through Jericho en route to Jerusalem where within the week he will be crucified; once again, two blind men beg for his help, pleading, 'Have mercy on us, Son of David' (20.30). These texts are surprising for the Davidic narratives do not portray Israel's first dynastic king to have a healing ministry. But here, Jesus, King David's descendant, heals and casts out demons. Apparently, this is because as the Spirit-anointed royal servant, healing expresses his merciful and just reign (12.18-21).

In addition to his merciful reign as Son of David, on one occasion Jesus must defend his disciples for having violated traditional Sabbath work laws (Mt. 12.1-8). Jesus' challenges their accusers, the Pharisees, asking (rhetorically), 'Have you not read what David did ... how he entered the house of God, and they (David and his companions) ate the consecrated bread, which was not lawful for him to eat' (12.3, 4). Here, Jesus is defending his disciples on the principle of historical precedent; that is, David did not incur guilt for violating a law about 'ritual'. This, then, is an example of the human condition: 'like Father (David) like son (Jesus)'.

The final three 'Son of David' texts relate to Jesus' final Passover week in Jerusalem (Matthew 21-22). During Jesus' triumphal entry into Jerusalem, the Passover pilgrims, fired by Messianic fervor, exclaim, 'Hosanna to the Son of David' (21.9). Joining the adults, crowds of children also exclaim, 'Hosanna to the Son David' (21.15). Day after day, Jesus will speak to the crowds who gather on the Temple mount. Speaking about himself on one of these occasions, he applies the messianic text (Psalm 110) to himself, insisting that the LORD's 'Christ' (Messiah) is the Son of David (22.14, 15).

Clearly, Matthew's gospel interpreted on its own terms presents Jesus as the Son of David, heir to the royal throne. This conclusion is reinforced by the identity of Jesus as the 'King of the Jews'. Thus, the Magi had enquired at Herod's court, 'Where is he who has been born King of the Jews?' (Mt. 2.2). At his appearance before the Roman governor, Pilate confronts Jesus, demanding, 'Are you the King of the Jews?' (27.11). In reply, Jesus affirms, 'It is as you say'. Finally, Pilate permits the execution of Jesus as, 'The King of the Jews' (27.27). Thus, Matthew reports that the One born to be king – and is revered as King of the Jews – dies in Jerusalem – David's City – the ignominious death of the *rejected* King of the Jews.

6.2.1.2.2. Matthew's Kingdom of Heaven/God theme
Another of Matthew's special emphases is the Kingdom of Heaven theme for the term, 'Kingdom of Heaven', appears 32 times in his gospel. This term, Kingdom of Heaven, is Matthew's preferred way for the parallel term, Kingdom of God, which is regularly found in Mark's and Luke's gospels. This theme, which is the primary subject of Jesus' ministry, is the natural complement to Matthew's portrait of Jesus as the Son of David, that is, the King of the Jews. As reported by Matthew, the Kingdom of Heaven theme has two temporal emphases. These are that the Kingdom of Heaven is a present reality, and also that it is a future reality.

First, in Matthew's witness to Jesus, the Kingdom of Heaven is a present reality. Its arrival is announced by John and Jesus, the two primary agents of the new start. John the Baptist preaches, 'Repent, for the Kingdom of Heaven is at hand' (Mt. 3.2). In his own turn, Jesus preaches the identical message, namely, 'Repent, for the Kingdom of Heaven is at hand' (4.17). Jesus also teaches, 'Blessed are the poor in spirit, for theirs is the Kingdom of Heaven' (5.2).

Bracketing the beatitudes, Jesus concludes his teaching, announcing, 'Blessed are those who have been persecuted for righteousness' sake, for theirs is the Kingdom of Heaven' (5.20). So important is the subject of Heaven's rule that Jesus teaches his disciples, 'unless your righteousness surpasses that of the scribes and Pharisees, you shall not enter the Kingdom of Heaven' (5.20). Indeed, the first petition in prayer that the disciples are to make is, 'Father in heaven ... Your kingdom come' (6.9). See, additionally, Mt. 11.11-13; 12.22-28; 13.11, 16-17, *et al.*)

Second, in Matthew's witness to Jesus, the Kingdom is also a future reality. In other words, the present reality may be either, a) the immediate future, or b) the distant future. Jesus taught that the Kingdom may be an immediate reality. This teaching immediately follows Peter's confession at Caesarea Philippi: 'You are the Christ, the Son of the living God' (Mt. 16.16). In this context, Jesus assures his disciples: 'some of those who are standing here shall not taste death until they see the Son of Man coming in his Kingdom' (16.28). This is an oblique announcement of Jesus' 'transfiguration' six days later (17.1-8). Jesus also taught that there is a distant dimension to the Kingdom of Heaven. For example, on the one hand,

Gentile believers shall participate in the future Messianic banquet; on the other hand, unrepentant Jews will be rejected (8.10-12). At the end of the age, the 'tares' will be separated out of the Kingdom and cast into a furnace (13.39-42; compare 13.49, 50). Similarly, in some of the last teaching which Jesus gave before his crucifixion, the 'sheep' of the parable inherit the Kingdom, but the 'goats' are excluded from the Kingdom (25.31-41).

To sum up, John and Jesus are the primary agents announcing the Kingdom. To them, heaven's rule is experienced in repentance and forgiveness, and in this life bestows blessings, even, or especially, on the disenfranchised, such as the poor and the persecuted. Heaven's Kingdom is expressed in submission to God the Father's will, and is a matter of the kind of righteous living which issues forth from transformed attitudes. The dividing between those who repent and those who do not extends throughout history to the end of the age. Those who have lived according to God's rule are blessed; those who have continued to live in a state of impenitence are excluded from God's eternal blessing.

6.2.1.3. The new start according to Luke

In canonical order, the Gospel According to Luke, following Mark and Matthew, is the last of the gospels to be written. Like Matthew, Luke also incorporates the 600 or so verses from Mark's gospel into his gospel. In addition, he incorporates the approximately 200 verses of Jesus' teachings which Matthew includes, but which are not found in Mark's gospel. Finally, Luke has additional information which is exclusive to his own gospel. The implication of this inter-relatedness between the gospels is that in terms of message there is *one* gospel; but in terms of form, there are many gospels, each of which has unique emphases. As a reminder, one of Mark's distinctive titular themes is that Jesus is the Son of Man (see above discussion), and one of Matthew's distinctive titular themes is that Jesus is the Son of David (see above). Similarly, Luke's Jesus as the Son of God title contributes to the distinctive character of his gospel.

6.2.1.3.1. Luke's Son of God theme

Whereas Mark's gospel puts special emphasis on the title Son of Man, and Matthew puts special emphasis on Jesus as Son of David, Luke puts special emphasis on Jesus as Son of God. Thus, Luke's genealogy of Jesus traces his ancestry from Joseph all the way back to, 'the *son* of Canaan, the *son* of Enosh, the *son* of Seth, the *son* of Adam, the *son* of God' (Lk. 3.38). Luke's 'Son of God' theme gives a distinctive meaning to four key points/events in the life of Jesus: his conception, anointing, recommissioning, and resurrection-ascension.

Luke reports that Jesus is God's son at his conception. The angel Gabriel announces to Mary, 'you will conceive in your womb ... and (He) will be called Son of the Most High' (Lk. 1.31, 32). Mary, a virgin, asks, 'how can this be?' (1.34). Gabriel explains, 'the power of the Most High will overshadow you; and for that reason, the Holy Offspring shall be called the Son of God' (1.35). Now, the alert Bible reader will remember that earlier in Israel's history, the nation (Exod. 4.22; Hos. 11.1) and her king (2 Sam. 7.14; Ps. 2.7) were identified as the Son of God. But in these cases, this is the language of adoption. In contrast, Jesus is the Son of God through the miracle of the the virgin birth.

Luke also reports that Jesus is identified as God's Son at his anointing (Lk. 3.21, 22). His anointing happens at the time when Jesus is baptized in the Jordan River by the prophet John. At that time, 'the Holy Spirit descended upon him in bodily form like a dove, and a voice came out of heaven, "You are My beloved Son, in You I am well-pleased"' (3.21, 22). The visible descent of the Spirit is the sign that God is commissioning Jesus; God's voice is the announcement of God's approval of his Son. The Heavenly Father's approbation of Jesus is expressed in the language of a psalm, 'You are my Son' (Ps. 2.7), and the Prophets: 'In you I am well-pleased' (Isa. 42.1). Thus, Jesus is the Father's well-pleasing Servant King. This anointing by the Spirit commissions Jesus to preach the gospel/good news of God's favor toward his disenfranchised people (4.18-21).

Further, Luke reports the episode when Jesus is recommissioned for ministry away from Galilee – on the road to Jerusalem (Lk. 9.51). This recommissioning takes place when Jesus is transfigured (9.28-36). The Jesus who prayed when he was baptized/anointed (3.21) is also found to be praying when he is transfigured (9.29). As Jesus is transfigured, 'the appearance of his face became different, and his clothing became white and gleaming' (9.29). Moses and Elijah prepare Jesus for the new aspect of his ministry, namely, his departure. This departure is, literally, his exodus from Jerusalem (9.31; compare Acts 1.9-11). In this dramatic context God, now for the second time, identifies Jesus to be his Son (9.35; compare 3.22 [Ps. 2.7; Isa. 42.1]). But now, God also identifies his Son to be the 'prophet like Moses' of the Law (Deut. 18.15). In these ways, Jesus is God's incomparable Son fulfilling the aspirations of the Psalms (2.7), the Prophets (Isa. 42.1), and the Law (Deut. 18.15).

Finally, Luke reports that Jesus is identified as God's Son at his resurrection-ascension. On Paul's first Evangelistic Tour, Paul is given the opportunity to address the synagogue crowd at Pisidian Antioch (Acts 13.14-43). Having canvassed Israel's 'salvation history', he begins to witness about Jesus – his death, his resurrection, and his ascension (13.28-37). About Jesus, Paul declares: 'he [God] raised up Jesus, as it is also written in the second Psalm, "You are My Son, today I have begotten You"' (13.33). In the light of Luke's earlier reports about Jesus' resurrection (Luke 24.1-24) and, forty days later, his ascension (Acts 1.9-11), the 'raising up' about which Paul speaks can only be a specific reference to the resurrection-ascension of Jesus.

To sum up, Luke reports that Jesus is the Heavenly Father's Son from first (his virgin birth) to last (his ascension). This identity is made to Mary in Galilee, to Jesus at the Jordan River, to Jesus on the Mount of Transfiguration, and to Jesus in Jerusalem, ascending from the Mount of Olives. His divine Sonship is affirmed when he is commissioned to 'preach the gospel' (Lk. 4.18), when he is re-commissioned for his 'exodus' from Jerusalem (9.32), and when, having completed the tasks for which he has been commissioned, the Father God exalts him to his right hand (Acts 2.33). In this distinctive portrait about Jesus, Luke's 'Son of God' theme adds a necessary emphasis to Mark's 'Son of Man' and Matthew's 'Son of David' themes.

6.2.1.3.2 *Luke's Jesus as anointed prophet theme*

The angel Gabriel, who announces to Mary that she will conceive and give birth to the 'Son of the Most High' also informs her that the Lord God, 'will give him the throne of his father, David, and he will reign over the house of Jacob forever' (Lk. 1.32, 33). But heirs to a throne do not become kings at birth. And so it will be with

Mary's son, Jesus. At about age thirty, he is anointed to be King by the descent of the Holy Spirit upon him (3.21, 22; Ps. 2.7). About three years later, he is welcomed into Jerusalem by Passover festival crowds who exclaim, 'Blessed is the King who comes in the name of the Lord' (19.38; compare Ps. 118.36).

However, Jesus refuses the implied 'insurrectionist' role expected of this 'king', and about a week later, he is crucified as the (rejected) King of the Jews (23.38). To everyone's surprise, his death is not the end of the story; 40 days later, Jesus ascends into heaven, and is enthroned at the Lord's right hand (Acts 2.34; Ps. 110.1). This means that Jesus' public ministry is not that of a royal, but it is that of a Spirit-anointed, Spiritful, Spirit-led, and Spirit-empowered prophet (3.21, 22; 4.1, 14, 18). Thus, the baby who is born to be king is first and foremost an anointed prophet.

Luke's report of the inaugural events, which begin with his baptism by John, are programmatic for his entire public ministry. Jesus' public ministry begins with his baptismal 'anointing' (Lk. 3.21, 22; 4.18). It includes his inaugural 'test' for which he is 'full of the Holy Spirit' and 'led about by the Spirit' (4.1). Remaining a well-pleasing Son (3.22), Jesus ministers throughout Galilee in the power of the Spirit (4.14). At this point, Jesus will begin to minister as a prophet. The prophet Isaiah establishes his agenda for ministry to the poor and other disenfranchised persons (4.16-21). The charismatic prophets, Elijah and Elisha, are early models for his own Spirit-empowered charismatic ministry (4.25-27). His rejection by his own townspeople anticipates his own rejection, for, in the end, he will die in Jerusalem as the rejected royal prophet. In retrospect, two of his own disciples recognize that Jesus' entire ministry has been that of 'a prophet mighty in deed and word and all the people … [but] the chief priests and rulers offered him up to the sentence of death, and crucified Him' (24.19, 20).

The religious and aristocratic leaders may have rejected Jesus, but the evidence shows that the common people, i.e. the people of the land, often receive Jesus as a prophet. Thus, Jesus not only identifies himself to be a prophet (e.g. Lk. 4.24; 13.33), but others do as well. For example, two texts report that others presume Jesus to be a prophet (7.39; 22.64). In addition, two texts report that Jesus is reputed to be a prophet (9.8, 19). Another two texts report that the people and/or the disciples identify Jesus to be a prophet (7.16; 24.19).

In spite of the clear, pervasive evidence that Jesus claims to be a prophet and also that many other people identify him to be a prophet, there are Bible interpreters who deny this. For example, one scholar recently wrote, 'Luke does not want Jesus to be called a prophet or to be presented as one'.[2] This denial is motivated by the desire to protect Jesus in his roles as Lord and Christ. But it is both misguided and unnecessary to deny the one role – prophet – to safeguard the other, complementary vocational roles. Jesus is prophet, Lord and Christ, and much more – including, 'Savior'.

6.2.1.3.3. Luke's savior, salvation, and to save theme

Jesus' prophetic, public ministry is centered around the Sea of Galilee (e.g. Capernaum, Bethsaida, the Decapolis, Tiberius, *et al.*), but he will die in Jerusalem as the rejected royal prophet (Lk. 13.33-35; 23.38). The 'rejected' prophet and King themes are negative aspects of his death. But, arising out of his rejection, Jesus' death achieves positive results, specifically, God's salvation. Luke's 'savior, salvation, to save' theme is complex and is the focal point of all of the other primary and secondary themes in Luke's theology.

Luke introduces the multi-faceted 'salvation' theme into his gospel when he writes about the births of John and Jesus, the two primary agents of the new starts of the sixth cycle of turning points. For example, Mary worships the Lord as 'God, my Savior' (Lk. 1.47). About three months later, when his promised son has been born, Zacharias is filled with the Spirit, who, in this case, inspires prophetic worship. This prophetic praise is directed to the Lord God of Israel. God is worshipped because he has raised up a horn of salvation (1.69), because he effects salvation from Israel's enemies (1.71), and because he gives salvation by the forgiveness of sins (1.77). Several months later, Mary and Joseph bring their baby son, Jesus, to the Temple to be dedicated. There, they meet an aged prophet, a certain Simeon, who breaks forth in Spirit-inspired praise (2.25-27), because he has now seen Jesus, the (infant) agent of

---

[2] Joseph Verheyden, 'Calling Jesus a Prophet, as Seen by Luke', in J. Verheyden, K. Zamfir, and T. Nicklas (eds.), *Prophets and Prophecy in Jewish and Early Christian Literature* (Tübingen: Mohr Siebeck, 2010), pp. 177-210 (p. 204).

God's salvation (2.3). A generation later, Zacharias' son, John the Baptist, preaches prophetically about the salvation of God (3.6). This data illustrates that the births of John and Jesus renew God's salvation plan, not only for Israel (as prophesied by Zacharias), but also for the nations (as prophesied by Simeon [1.71; 2.30-32]).

Not only does Luke's narrative identify God as Savior, but it also identifies Jesus as Savior. Mary is to name her son Jesus. Implicit in this name is the meaning, 'God saves' (Lk. 1.30; compare Mt. 1.21). At his birth, angels announce to shepherds that Jesus is, 'a Savior, who is Christ the Lord' (2.11). True to his name, as an adult, Jesus functions as a Savior. For example, on one occasion, Jesus forgives the sins of a penitent woman, declaring, 'your faith has saved you' (7.48-50). Later, while he is enroute to Jerusalem, Jesus has to defend his mission to sinners (15.1, 2). He does so giving three parables to his critics. In the parables, Jesus is the shepherd seeking a lost sheep (15.3-7); he is the woman searching for her lost coin (15.8-10); and he is the father waiting for his lost son to return (15.11-32). Finally, passing through Jericho, Jesus encounters a publican, who is not only on the margins of the crowd, but who is also on the margins of Jewish society. He is 'lost', but Jesus 'finds' him and publicly declares, 'today, salvation has come to this house [of Zacchaeus]' (19.9). Having brought salvation to this one 'sinner who repents', Jesus declares that he came for this very purpose – 'to seek and to save that which was lost' (19.10). On the principle of inclusio (from first to last), Jesus functions as a Savior (2.11; 19.10). This confirms that he is, indeed, 'Lord and Christ' (2.11; Acts 2.36).

6.3. Conclusion

The synoptic Evangelists, namely Mark, Matthew, and Luke, have written lengthy reports about John the Baptist and Jesus of Nazareth. These men are the two primary agents of the new start for the sixth cycle of turning points in biblical history and theology. Their narratives contain a common core, which give them a common perspective. But their gospels also contain distinctive, overlapping emphases which give significance to each gospel narrative. This chapter has discussed the synoptic gospels as follows:

Gospel	Titular Theme	Secondary Theme(s)
Mark	Jesus is Son of Man	Four Portraits: Teacher, Prophet, Messiah, King
Matthew	Jesus is Son of David	Kingdom of God
Luke	Jesus is Son of God	Jesus is Prophet, Savior, salvation, to save

Despite their lengths, and their ranges of primary, secondary, and tertiary themes, the synoptic Evangelists do not give their readership the full story. There is one further Evangelist, the apostle John, who writes a later, distinctive narrative that not only presupposes the synoptic gospels but which adds significant theological insight into the man who is Jesus.

7

CYCLE SIX, CONTINUED: THE NEW START ACCORDING TO JOHN THE EVANGELIST

Biblically speaking, in regards to message, there is only one gospel. This is the good news that God has once acted decisively in human history through his Son to effect the salvation that it has always been his nature to give. As the most well-known verse in the Bible reports, 'For God so loved the world that he gave his only begotten Son, that whoever believes in him should not perish, but have eternal life' (Jn 3.16). Though the message is one, it is such good news that it soon breaks forth in a chorus of many written reports (Lk. 1.1). Four of these stand out as a Gospel quartet, namely, Mark, Matthew, Luke, and John. God's Good News concerts have two parts: 1) a trio (Mark, Matthew, and Luke), and 2) a soloist (John). John's solo part has its own distinctive historical and theological emphases, which complement the earlier trio of synoptic 'Harmonaires'. For example, one central theme of the synoptic gospels is, 'the Kingdom of God'. In comparison, the equivalent theme of John's gospel is 'eternal life'. Thus, John writes his singular gospel, '… that you may believe that Jesus is the Christ, the Son of God; and that believing, you may have life in his name' (Jn 20.31).

7.1. Agents of the New Start: John and Jesus

As John the Evangelist (to distinguish him from John the Baptist) sets reed to papyrus, that is, pen to paper, he immediately identifies the two primary agents for the new start of the sixth cycle of turning points in biblical history and theology. These are John the Baptist and Jesus of Nazareth, as first identified in the synoptic gospels. Though John and Jesus are the primary agents of the sixth new start, they do not have the same rank. John is inferior to Jesus as a 'prophet of the Most High' is inferior to Jesus, who is the 'Son of the Most High' (Lk. 1.35; 1.76), or as the 'man sent from God' is inferior to God's only begotten Son (Jn 1.6, 18). John the Baptist witnessed to the superiority of Jesus' rank, insisting, 'This was he of whom I said, "he who comes after me has a higher rank that I, for he existed before me"' (1.15; compare 3.30).

7.2. John the Baptist

John's ministry was populist; it stirred crowds of the common people. It was pietist; it addressed the human condition – sinfulness – on an individual basis. It was also radical; it called God's people to repent for the forgiveness of their sins. All of this is consistent with the portrait of the Baptist which the Evangelist paints. For example, John the Baptist is apostle-like. He is sent (*apostellō*) from God (Jn 1.6). He is disciple-like. In other words, John the Baptist is a witness about the Light (1.7), about the Word (1.15), about the Lamb of God (1.29), who is the Spirit-anointed one (1.33, 41), who is also the Son of God (1.34). To be the announcer of such a One, inevitably, not only stirs interest, but it also stirs puzzlement and speculation about the identities of the announcer and the One whom he heralds.

Not only do the common people flock to John the Baptist, but the leaders of the Jews in Jerusalem send messengers – priests and Levites – to him on a fact-finding mission. They ask him, 'Who are you?' (Jn 1.19). In reply, John insisted, 'I am not the Christ' (1.20). In this way, John deflects possible Messianic speculation about his mission. So, they ask him, 'what then? Are you Elijah?' (1.21). This question asks if John fulfills the prophesies about the coming of an 'end-times' or eschatological Elijah (1.21; Mal. 4.5). He also denies this speculation, insisting, 'I am not' (1.21). Next, they ask, 'are you *the* prophet?' (like Moses, Deut. 18.15). Again, he negates the speculation: 'No' (1.21). Stuck with a quandary, the team of priests and Levites finally ask, 'Who are you, so that we may give an answer to those who sent us? What do you say about yourself?' (1.22). Finally, John identifies himself, 'I am the voice of one crying in the wilderness, "Make straight the way of the Lord"' (1.23). 'But why are you baptizing', the Pharisees want to know (1.24). Because, John replies (in effect), I am merely a water baptizer, but the one who is the Christ, Elijah, and the Prophet, he it is who will baptize in the Holy Spirit (1.25-28). Indisputably, in John's mind, his role as messenger prophet is subordinate to that of the One who will follow him.

7.3. Jesus Christ

John the Evangelist's gospel does not have an infancy narrative such as Matthew's and Luke's gospels have. But the Evangelist's prologue to his gospel (Jn 1.1-18), and also to his first epistle (1 Jn 1.1-4), serve a similar function. Both introduce one who is not only extra-historical, but who is also God in the flesh.

John 1.1-18	**1 John 1.1-4**
In the beginning …	What was from the beginning
Was the Word … in him was life	the word of life
The light shines in the darkness	the life was manifested

John's emphasis in his two prologues is that the eternal Word, who was from the beginning, is identifiable in history. Thus, the eternal Word is a certain Joshua = Jesus, God's Son (1 Jn 1.3). The Son's blood was shed to cleanse God's people from all their sin (1.7). He also 'appeared' to destroy the works of the devil (3.7). In other words, the Father sent his Son to be the savior of the world (4.14).

God's Son, who is the eternal Word, is identifiable to the senses. The Evangelist writes about, 'what our hands have handled' (1 Jn 1.1). He insists that his gospel is about, 'what we have seen' (1.2), and 'what we have heard' (1.3). This insistence on the physicality of Jesus illustrates that, like Matthew and Luke, John also has an 'incarnation' Christology.

Not everyone acknowledges Jesus as God's Son, the Christ (i.e. the anointed One). John identifies other, self-appointed teachers as 'antichrists' (i.e. those who, in fact, are 'against' Christ). These teachers are liars, and their biggest lie is that they deny the Son

(2.22). Their motive is to deceive those who have believed, put their trust in John's teaching about Jesus (2.26). These 'antichrist' teachers claim to be inspired by the Spirit, but they are false prophets (4.1). They are false prophets because they deny that Jesus *Christ* (italics added) has come in the flesh (4.2). This denial is the spirit of the antichrist (4.3). Though these false prophets claim to be inspired by the Spirit, they are from the world, motivated by the lust of the flesh, the lust of the eyes, and the pride of life (4.4; compare 2.16). In summary, the antichrists of John's day are agents of the 'spirit of error', and their error, to deny that Jesus Christ is the Savior of the world, is the sin that leads to death (5.16).

In contrast to these 'antichrist' false prophets, John is the agent inspired by the 'spirit of truth', and by implication is a true prophet. As he begins his letter, he affirms, 'what we have seen and heard we proclaim' (1 Jn 1.3). Further along, John implicitly claims to be 'anointed' (2.27). This 'anointing' (Spirit-inspired proclamation) teaches his audience and is true and is not a lie (2.27). This means that he has the Spirit of God, and anointed by the Spirit, confesses that Jesus Christ has come in the flesh (4.2). Therefore, for John, the truthfulness of what he proclaims validates that he is the prophetic agent of Jesus Christ. Assuredly, the truth about Jesus is the best and most necessary antidote to error about Jesus, whether this error is in the church or in the world. In John the Evangelist's gospel, there are many primary themes identifying Jesus, but perhaps, the most unique of these themes is that Jesus is the 'I am'.

7.3.1. Jesus is the 'I Am'

Each of the four Evangelists, Mark, Matthew, Luke, and John, has his own distinctive emphases by which to describe Jesus. For example, Mark's distinctive emphasis is that Jesus is the Son of Man; Matthew's is that Jesus is the Son of David; Luke's Jesus is the Son of God; and John's distinctive emphasis is that Jesus is the 'I am'. Through John's gospel, Jesus often identifies himself to be the 'I am'. He does this in two ways: 1) 'I am' sentences, and 2) absolute 'I am' sayings.

As reported seven times in John's gospel, Jesus affirms his identity by using 'I am' declarations with a predicate (object). Taking the first one as an example, Jesus solemnly declares, 'I am the bread of life' (Jn 6.35, *et al.*). The grammar of the Greek sentence behind this

English translation contains two additions not required by Greek syntax: 1) the pronoun '*ego*' (English: 'I'), and 2) the definite article '*ho*' (English: 'the') which goes with the object.

These two additions make the statement emphatic. Therefore, when Jesus says, 'I am the bread of life'; he is actually declaring, 'I [and only I] am the [only] bread of life'. The same emphatic emphasis extends to the other 'I am' sentences. Altogether, John reports that Jesus makes seven of these emphatic declarations about his identity.

Seven times Jesus emphatically declares: 'I am the bread of life' (Jn 6.35); 'I am the light of the world' (8.12); 'I am the door of the sheepfold' (10.7-9); 'I am the good shepherd' (10.11-14); 'I am the resurrection and the life' (11.25); 'I am the way, the truth, and the life' (14.6); and 'I am the true vine' (15.1-5). Each of these 'I am' declarations has its own context. For example, the 'bread of life' declaration is given at the Passover season (6.4), with all of the festivals, exodus, wilderness, and manna connotations. Also, the 'light of the world' declaration is given during the feast of Tabernacles, when the Temple is celebrated as the light of Jerusalem. Jesus' Jewish audience would recognize the earlier biblical heritage in the metaphors which give the 'I am' sentences evocative meanings. When Jesus identifies himself as the 'door of the sheepfold', he is using a metaphor about the safety of the shepherd's sheep; similarly, the 'good shepherd' declaration has obvious, both with royal and divine, shepherd imagery. Several of the 'I am' declarations are also explanations of Jesus' miracles. For example, Jesus associates the healing of a blind man with his self-revelation that he is the light of the world (9.1-12). More dramatically, the raising of Lazarus from the dead is living proof that Jesus is the resurrection and the life (11.25, 38-44). A full exposition of the 'I am' sentences lies outside the scope of this study. It is sufficient to observe that John reports about seven of these sayings in order to illustrate something of the fullness of Jesus' self-revelation.

In addition to reporting Jesus' revelatory 'I am' declarations, John also reports Jesus uttering several absolute 'I am' sayings. These are 'I am' sayings without an object, such as '... the bread of life'. '... the light of the world'. The Hebrew Bible is the background to this distinctive name, most particularly to be found in

God's revelation of his name, 'I AM WHO I AM' and more briefly, 'I AM' (Exod. 3.14-16). This name appears in English translations of the Hebrew text as either Yahweh or LORD. Implicit in God's revelation of his name to Moses, and hence to Israel is that he is Creator, LORD of History, and Redeemer (Isa. 41.4; 45.18). Thus, for Jesus to identify himself by the name 'I am' in the absolute, he is identifying something about his Oneness with God his Father. Therefore, he can claim, 'I manifested Thy name ...' (Jn 17.6, 11, 12; compare 17.22).

The absolute 'I am' sayings are found in widely scattered texts, such as, 'I am, who is speaking to you' (Jn 4.26), 'I am, do not fear' (6.20). Accepting or rejecting Jesus' identity as the 'I am' is a matter of life and death for Jesus asserts, 'You will die in your sins unless you believe that "I am"' (8.24). He also asserts, 'when you crucify the Son of Man, then you will know that "I am"' (8.28). Jesus' enemies, the Jewish leaders, clearly understand the significance of Jesus' claim to be the 'I am' of God's ancient self-revelation. On one occasion, Jesus solemnly affirms, 'Truly, truly, I say to you, before Abraham was born, I AM' (8.58). To his audience, this self-identification is blasphemous, and they picked up stones to throw at him (i.e. execute Him, 8.59). At the end of the gospel story, Jewish leaders backed by a Roman cohort – 600 soldiers – come to Gethsemane, a place of prayer, to arrest Jesus. Having submitted himself to doing his Father's will, Jesus asks, 'whom do you seek?' (18.4). The reply, 'Jesus the Nazarene' (18.5). The Evangelist reports, 'when therefore he said to them, "I am", they drew back, and fell to the ground' (18.6). In these absolute 'I am' sayings, Jesus is appropriating the name of Israel's Redeemer God (Exod. 3.16), and, in some cases, at least, is claiming deity (Jn 8.58) and shows the power of deity (18.6). Also, as the Evangelist narrates the story of Jesus, he reports that Jesus performs seven signs: miracles with a message, which complement the 'I am' sayings.

7.3.2. Jesus performs seven signs

All of the gospels report that Jesus performs many miracles. These are done in a variety of locations: Galilee, the Lebanon, the Decapolis, Samaria, and Jerusalem. The beneficiaries of the miracles include Jews, Samaritans, and Gentiles; and children, women, and men; the rich and the poor. The miracles are of all kinds – casting out demons, curing fevers, hemorrhages, and leprosy, raising the dead, calming storms on the Sea of Galilee, and multiplying a little food so that multitudes are fed. Jesus performs these miracles by the spoken word/command and by touch. He heals those who are in his presence and those who are distant. The Synoptic Evangelists (Mark, Matthew, and Luke) tend to emphasize that Jesus' miracles are acts of power (e.g. Lk. 6.20; 24.19) and authority. In contrast, the Evangelist, John, emphasizes that Jesus' miracles are signs; that is, they are miracles with a message.

The fourth Evangelist reports that Jesus performed many signs on the principle of inclusio, i.e. from first to last (Jn 2.23; 20.30). Of the many signs which Jesus performed, John chose to write about just seven of these. Collectively, these seven signs illustrate that, 'Jesus is the Christ, the Son of God' (20.31). Of the seven signs that John has chosen, only two overlap with those many miracles which the synoptic writers report. These are the complementary Passover signs: 1) Jesus feeds the multitude and 2) Jesus walks on water (6.1-15; 16.22). Unique to John's gospel are the following: Jesus turns water into wine (2.1-11); Jesus heals the nobleman's son; Jesus heals a lame man (5.1-9); Jesus heals a blind man (9.1-7); and, most dramatic of all, Jesus raises Lazarus from the dead (11.1-44). Though these signs have a collective message – showing that Jesus is the Son of God (20.31) – each sign also has its own distinctive, singular message. This message can be perceived by the process of interrogating the report, asking three questions of it: 1) what is the general truth of this sign? 2) what is the specific truth of this sign? And 3) what does John report about the belief/unbelief of the participants in the event?

The first sign which John reports is that one time Jesus turned water into wine (Jn 2.1-11). When John's readers ask, 'what is the general truth of this sign?', they can infer that the sign illustrates the (sometimes embarrassing) reality of human inadequacy (the supply of wine runs out) which is dramatically contrasted by Jesus' abundant all-sufficiency. When they ask the second question, 'what is the specific truth which this sign conveys?' The answer is related to the transformation of Jewish purification (2.6) into the new wine of the new age (compare Lk. 5.37). What is the result of this unexpected, totally surprising miracle upon the disciples? John, who is not only

the Evangelist, but is one of Jesus' companions at the wedding, answers, 'his disciples believed in Him' (2.11). Because many interpreters are committed to interpreting John's gospel according to
their own non-biblical theology, they delay the belief/salvation to
either the outpouring of the Spirit upon the disciples on resurrection day (20.22) or on the Day of Pentecost (Acts 2.1-4). But John
is definitive, the disciples 'believe' and therefore are children of
God (1.12) and have eternal life (20.31). No amount of verbal gymnastics can overturn this interpretation (compare 6.68, 69).

Several of the seven signs have parallel, complementary general
truth, specific truth, and believing themes. This is most evident in
John's reports about Jesus' healing activity. As reported by the
Evangelist, Jesus heals the nobleman's son, a lame man, and also a
blind man (Jn 4.46-54; 5.1-9; 9.1-7). In each episode, the general
truth is to be found in the contrast between helplessness in the face
of disease (fever, paralysis, or blindness) and Jesus' power to heal.
The specific truth of the first two signs of healing is that Jesus is
the source of life (4.53; 5.21, 39). The specific truth of the third
healing sign is that Jesus is the light of the world (9.5). Those persons who experience their healing believe (4.53; 9.38); others are
uncertain or unbelievers (4.48; 5.38).

One sign, Jesus raises Lazarus from the dead (Jn 11.1-44; 12.18),
is a special kind of healing sign. Thus, Lazarus is sick unto death
and, in fact, actually dies and is buried. The general truth is that,
ultimately, man is helpless in the face of death, but Jesus has power
over death. The specific truth is that Jesus is the resurrection and
the life (11.25a). The believing theme is evident in Jesus' challenge
to faith: 'he who believes in Me shall live even if he dies' (11.25b),
and in the response – many believed, but others plan to kill him
(11.45, 53).

The two signs at a certain Passover season are complementary.
These are the sign that Jesus feeds the crowd of five thousand and
following this Jesus walks on water (Jn 6.1-15; 16-22). The general
truth of the first of these signs illustrates the inadequacy of human
resources (five loaves of bread and two fish) and Jesus' all sufficient
supply (twelve baskets full left over, 6.9, 13). The general truth of
the walking on water is humanity's helplessness in the face of natural forces and the contrast in Jesus' control of nature. The 'miracle

of the loaves and fish' is that Jesus is the bread of life (6.35) and the believing theme (6.29) is that God's 'work' is that disciples believe in Jesus whom God has sent (6.35; compare also 6.40, 47, 48, 68, 69). John reports neither a specific truth nor a believing theme for the sign of walking on water. But the complementary truths of both signs is that Jesus is not only the 'Prophet' (like Moses, Deut. 18.15), but that he is Israel's LORD, the 'I am' who has come to save 'walking on the paths in the mighty waters' (6.20; compare Ps. 77.19, 21; 78.21-33).

There is much more to the message of the seven signs than the above analysis gives. But the basic message of the seven signs is self-evident. Thus, the Evangelist illustrates that Jesus is abundantly capable of meeting every need (beyond the inadequate human resources). Further, Jesus has power to heal all kinds of diseases and afflictions (fever, paralysis, and blindness) and even to 'heal' from death itself. Finally, Jesus controls the dangerous forces of nature itself, such as deadly storms on the Sea of Galilee. In all of these miracles, the message is that Jesus can do what no other person can do; he can do what only a prophet like Moses can do. Indeed, as the Son of God, he can do what only God can do. These seven signs then contribute to John's assessment about the identity of Jesus. In the final analysis, Jesus is the Son who *explains* the Father (Jn 1.18), the Son who has been *sent* into the world by the Father (17.18, 21, 25), the Son of God who can do what no one else on earth can do, and ultimately, the Son who is 'in the Father, and the Father is in Him' (14.10). Those who see the Son in these seven signs also see the Father (14.9).

7.3.3. Jesus embodies and yet supersedes the Jewish feasts

In very important, meaningful ways the heart of Jesus' ministry before the Passion Week and its aftermath (John 13–21) is about the 'I am' statements and the signs which he performed (2–12). But when examined from another perspective, Jesus' public ministry before Passion Week is about the fact that Jesus not only embodies the significance of the Feasts, but that he also supersedes the Feasts. The Feasts at issue include Purification, Sabbath, Passover, and Dedication. In every episode which involves these feasts, Jesus shows himself to be superior in word and deed to the historical and spiritual significance of the Feasts. The following discussion about Jesus and the Feasts will focus on Sabbath (5.1-47), Passover (6.1-71), and Tabernacles (7.1–8.59). These three feasts form the primary subject of John's narrative, and are bracketed by Purification (2.1-11) and Dedication (10.22-39).

7.3.4. Jesus supersedes the Sabbath feast of the Jews (John 5.1-47)

On one occasion, after Jesus has healed the nobleman's son (Jn 4.46-54), Jesus travels from Galilee up to Jerusalem. Here, on a certain Sabbath day, Jesus heals a man who has been lame for 38 years (5.1-9). This is the same kind of thing that Jesus has also done earlier in Galilee. For example, there in one of the synagogues in Galilee, Jesus healed a man with a paralyzed hand (Mk 3.1-6). The result of that healing was that some Pharisees begin to plot with the Herodians about how they might destroy Jesus (3.6). Now, what happens here in Jerusalem provokes similar murderous responses to this violation of the Sabbath work laws, is that 'the Jews were persecuting Jesus, because he was doing these things on the Sabbath' (Jn 5.16). Jesus defends himself claiming, 'My Father is working until now, and I Myself am working' (5.17). Jesus' reply does not pacify the Jews; rather, it adds further provocation for '[these] Jews were seeking all the more to kill Him, because he was not only breaking the Sabbath, but was also calling God his own Father, making himself equal with God' (5.18). These Jews certainly understood Jesus accurately. By calling God his Father, Jesus actively asserts his deity, and emphasizes that as God's Son (compare 1.1, 18; 3.16, *et al.*), he only does what he has learned to do from his Father (5.19-29). The Father works on the Sabbath doing the basic issues of life and death, of birth and burial. Jesus' defense is twofold: 1) his own works, such as healing a lame man on the Sabbath, witness to the fact that the Father has sent Him, and 2) though his enemies because of their unbelief have not heard God's voice, the Father himself has borne witness about him (Jn 5.37).

The primary issue in this episode of Jesus' work and identity is about authority: biblical authority versus the authority of tradition (5.39-47). As Jesus observes, his opponents 'search the Scriptures' (5.39), but, in reality do not believe them (i.e. Moses' writings, 5.46, 47).

Therefore, since Moses wrote about Jesus, how will they receive the teaching from the One about whom Moses wrote. For example, in relation to the Sabbath, Moses wrote, 1) God blessed the Sabbath day and sanctified it (Gen. 2.3), and 2) the covenant which bears his name (Moses') reinforces the complementary themes about the Sabbath day, namely, rest and holiness (Exod. 20.8-11; Deut. 5.12-15). However, by Jesus' day, the Tradition of the Elders had developed a catalogue of prohibited 'works' such as, 'sowing, plowing, reaping, binding sheaves, … grinding [grain], sifting, kneading, baking, … tying [a knot], loosening [a knot], sewing two stitches, tearing in order to sew two stitches, etc. (*mShabbath* 7.2). More germane to the healing of the lame man is the prohibition that on the Sabbath, 'they may [not even] straighten a deformed child's limb (*mShabbath* 22.6). As the so-called 'Sermon on the Mount' (Matthew 5–7), as well as Jesus' defense reminds us, Jesus honors the Scriptures (Moses), but regularly repudiates, that is, set aside and/or violates the Tradition of the Elders. These traditions are so revered that those who lived by them consider that they are equal to, or even more binding than the Law of Moses.

Therefore, in summary, the episode of Jesus healing the lame man on the Sabbath illustrates that the God who first sanctified the Sabbath day (Gen. 2.3), and who later encoded this sanctity or holiness in his covenant with Moses (Exod. 20.8-11) with his Son, Jesus, alone determines whether healing on the Sabbath is a permitted or a prohibited work.

Simply put, by the sanction of Scripture and the authority of his own Sonship, Jesus is Lord of the Sabbath. In other words, Jesus supersedes the Sabbath, and before his life is over, he will also supersede the Feasts both Passover (John 6) and Tabernacles (John 7, 8).

7.3.5. Jesus supersedes the Passover (John 6.1-71)

John the Evangelist not only reports that Jesus supersedes the Sabbath (Jn 5.1-47), but he also reports that Jesus supersedes the Passover, the Feasts of the Jews (6.1-71). The setting for his narrative about Jesus and the Sabbath is Jerusalem. In contrast, the setting for his narrative about Jesus and the Passover is the Galilean countryside (wilderness?). John's Passover narrative includes the fourth sign – Jesus multiplies food (6.1-15), and the fifth sign – Jesus walks on water (6.16-21). It also includes Jesus' self-identification both the absolute 'I am' saying, 'It is I' (6.20), and the first of the 'I am' sentences, namely, 'I am the bread of life' (6.35).

Historically, Passover is the first feast in Israel's national history for it celebrates the exodus of Israel from Egypt (Exod. 12.1-51). Annually, it is also the first of three pilgrimage feasts, Passover, Pentecost, Tabernacles; it is celebrated on the 14th day of the first month, while Pentecost is celebrated 50 days later, and Tabernacles is celebrated on the 15th day of the seventh month. The Passover season unfolds in three stages. The first stage includes the sacrifice of a lamb and the sprinkling of its blood on the door posts and lintel of the Israelite houses. The second stage is the pathway of escape from the pursuing Egyptian army at the Red Sea (14.1-31), and the third stage is the gift of manna – bread for heaven – in the wilderness (16.1-36). While the Passover itself happens in a day, this cluster of three events identifies the Passover season, the setting for Jesus' miracle of multiplying food (John 6.4).

John reports events in Jesus' ministry spread over three Passover festivals: John 2.23; 6.4, and 12.1; 13.1. Jesus is in Jerusalem to celebrate the first and third Passovers, but is still in Galilee when he *recapitulates* the events of the exodus Passover. John's narrative identifies Jesus' initiating the fulfillment of the three stages of the original Passover. Stage one identifies the setting: 'Now the Passover, the feast of the Jews, was at hand' (6.4). The second stage is Jesus walking on water (6.16-21), a deliberate echo of Ps. 77.19 ('Thy paths in the mighty waters/And Thy footsteps may not be known'), and 78.13 ('he divided the sea, and caused them to pass through') (compare Isa. 51.10-12). The third stage is Jesus' identification as the bread of life (6.35). In spite of the sign – Jesus multiplies food – which he has just performed, some in the crowd challenge Jesus asking, 'What then do You do for a sign, that we may see and believe you?' (6.30). They contrast Jesus' sign (6.14) with the snide implication that, after all, Moses could do better, for (quoting Ps. 78.24), 'he gave them (Israel) bread out of heaven to eat'. This taunt leads to a lengthy discourse, in which Jesus identifies himself and exposes the unbelief of those who taunt Him.

Jesus has strong things to say to those who have unfavorably compared him to Moses. He accuses them, '... you have seen Me and yet do not believe' (Jn 6.37). Like Israel in the time of Moses, these unbelievers are grumblers: they grumble about Jesus' claim that he is 'the bread that came down out of heaven' (6.41) and in turn are rebuked by Jesus for their grumbling (6.43). They have no life because they reject the (spiritual) food which Jesus offers, namely, his (shed) blood and his body (6.52-58). As a result of these 'hard sayings', many of his disciples grumble, complaining 'this is a difficult statement, who can listen to it?' (6.60), and many of these grumblers 'withdrew and were not walking with him anymore' (6.66).

Jesus not only rebukes the unbelieving grumblers in the crowd, but he also reveals new dimensions of his self-identity. Thus, Jesus asserts, 'I am the bread of life; he who comes to Me shall not hunger, and he who believes in Me shall never thirst' (Jn 6.35). He claims, 'I have come down from heaven' (6.38). In contrast to every other person, he is 'the One who is from God, [and] he has seen the Father' (6.46). In plain, unambiguous language Jesus further claims, 'I am the bread of life' (6.48). Summing up his language of self-identity, he affirms, 'I am the living bread that came down; if anyone eats this bread, he shall live forever' (6.51) In contrast to those disciples who saw, but could not believe (6.37), Peter speaks for those who believe: 'You have words of eternal life. And we have believed and have come to know that You are the Holy One of God' (6.68, 69).

At this Passover season, Jesus initiates a variety of works and words which loosely recapitulate the three stages of the exodus of Israel out of Egypt. Jesus feeds the five thousand, recapitulating, and indeed, surpassing the gift of manna in the wilderness. Jesus walks on water, echoing the poetic accounts of God's steps upon the water. In many ways, Jesus is like Moses, but a greater prophet than Moses. He is like manna, but the life he gives is spiritual, eternal. Eating his [spiritual] flesh and drinking his [spiritual] blood recapitulates the unleavened bread and the cups of wine at the Passover meal. Much more can be said about the Jesus of John's Passover narrative but enough has been said to illustrate that Jesus not only fulfills the meaning of the Passover, but that he supersedes it. May we add our voice to Peter's, saying, We (I) have believed and have come to know that You (Jesus) are the Holy One of God.

7.3.6. Jesus supersedes the Feast of Tabernacles (John 7.1–8.60)

Following the Feasts of Passover and Pentecost, the Feast of Tabernacles is the third of the great pilgrimage Feasts. Like Passover and Pentecost, it has its origin in the exodus of Israel out of Egypt. It commemorates the nomadic life of Israel in the wilderness, hence its name 'tabernacles/tents' or 'booths' (Exod. 23.16; Lev. 23.34). It is a seven-day festival concluding on the eighth day, the 'great day' of the feast. To participate in Tabernacles, the Israelites moved into temporary booths made from willow branches. By Jesus' day, the feast had acquired several distinctive features which Jesus not only fulfills, but which he also supersedes (Jn 7.1–8.60).

As it was celebrated in second Temple Judaism (a.k.a. New Testament times) the Feast of Tabernacles had three distinctive liturgical practices which Jesus supersedes. These are: 1) the rite of the willow branch, 2) the water libation ceremony, and 3) the candlestick or torch ceremony. The rite of the willow branch involved a daily procession around the Temple altar, which was temporarily covered in willow branches. As part of the procession, the people chanted the refrain, 'Save now we beseech Thee, O LORD' (Ps. 118.25) and '*Ani waho*! Save us we pray!' (*Suk.* 4.5e) *Ani waho* literally means 'I and he', but without the conjunction (*wa*), the phrase *Ani ho* is often represented in the Septuagint as 'I am' (Greek *ego eimi*, see Deut. 32.39; Isa. 41.4; 46.4). Alert Bible readers will immediately recognize that *ego eimi* (Greek) is the name by which God identified himself to Moses in the wilderness (Exod. 3.14-16). Therefore, in Israel's prayer, *ani waho* appears to be an allusion to the divine name 'Yahweh'.[3] With this knowledge, the Bible interpreter recognizes that it is more than a coincidence that John's report about Jesus at the Feast of Tabernacles contains the highest concentration of absolute 'I am' sayings in the gospel (Jn 8.18, 24, 28, 58). Jesus supersedes the willow branch as the 'I am' who first appeared to Moses in the wilderness. Two of Jesus' 'I am' sayings have special 'saving' significance: 1) he asserts, 'you will die in your sins, unless you be-

---

[3] Cf. Andrew C. Brunson, *Psalm 118 in the Gospel of John: An Intertextual Study on the New Exodus Pattern in the Theology of John* (Tübingen: Mohr Siebeck, 2003), pp. 308-12.

lieve that I am' (8.24), and 2) he also affirms, 'Before Abraham was born, I am' (8.58). Jesus' audience clearly understands that Jesus is claiming to be their Redeemer God, and rejecting this claim (as blasphemous), the Jewish leaders pick up stones to throw at Him, i.e. kill him (8.59).

In addition to fulfilling and superseding the rite of the willow branch, in a dramatic scene on the Temple Mount, Jesus also supersedes the water libation ceremony. In the Jewish sacrificial system, a water libation is an offering of water which is poured out on the altar.

During the Feast of Tabernacles, a container of water is daily carried from the pool of Siloam up to the Temple courtyard. The officiating priest pours this water into a silver bowl which then funnels the water onto the altar. Apparently, at this very moment, Jesus interrupts the ceremony. He cries out, 'If any man is thirsty, let him come to Me and drink ...' (Jn 7.37). By doing this, Jesus turns the attention of the worshippers away from the altar and onto himself. Catching the attention of the crowd, Jesus offers the one who drinks 'from your innermost being shall flow rivers of living water' (7.38). The Evangelist explains for his readership what Jesus is doing, writing, 'But this he spoke of the Spirit, whom those who believed in him were to receive, for the Spirit was not yet given, because Jesus was not yet glorified' (7.39; compare 20.21). But the Temple crowd would not have understood this meaning. John reports three responses among the crowd: 1) some conclude that Jesus is the prophet (like Moses [Deut. 18.15]), 2) others that Jesus is the Messiah = Christ, and 3) others that he cannot be the Messiah, because he comes from Galilee and not from Judea (7.40, 41). The unbelievers in the crowd, 'wanted to seize him (i.e. kill Him), but John observes, 'no one laid hands on Him' (7.45).

Jesus also supersedes the final event of Tabernacles, namely, the candlestick or torch ceremony. On the Temple Mount, tall pillars were located at the four corners of the court of women. A large bowl surmounted each pillar. On the evening of the last day of the feast, the bowls were filled with olive oil to which was added a linen wick. When the candlesticks were lit, the Temple became 'the light of Jerusalem'. Probably, at the very moment when the candlesticks are being lit, Jesus cries out, 'I am the light of the world' (Jn 8.12a).

He also adds the promise, 'he who follows Me shall not walk in darkness, but shall have the light of life' (8.12b). He also performs a sign to validate his self-identity, and this is that he heals a blind man (9.5-7) who affirms that he believes that Jesus is the Son of Man (9.35-41).

In these narratives about Jesus and the Jewish Feasts, John illustrates from first (Jn 2.11) to last (10.22-39) that Jesus, by word and by deed, reveals that he is the Son of God who fulfills, but also supersedes the Jewish Feasts. There is no mistaking this, for his enemies in the crowds which gather around him repeatedly recognize his claims. For example, when Jesus states, 'My Father is working until now and I, Myself, am working' (5.17), John reports, 'the Jews were seeking all the more to kill him [because he was] making himself equal with God' (5.18). The aftermath to the sign of feeding the five thousand (6.1-15) is that many in the multitude grumble about him because this carpenter's son claims to have come down from heaven (6.42). Tabernacles is a particularly dangerous time for Jesus. Twice John reports that some Jews wanted to kill him (7.44; 8.59). Finally, at the Feast of Dedication (10.22-39), some of the Jews seek to kill him by stoning, because 'You [Jesus] being a man, make yourself to be equal with God' (10.33). Repeatedly, many people in the crowds at these festivals see his deeds and hear his words and believe; many others, however, see the same signs and hear the same words and do not believe. And some of those who do not believe repeatedly try to kill Him. But whether Jesus is believed or not, he supersedes the religion of his contemporaries because, truly, he is the great I AM.

7.3.7. Responses to Jesus' self-revelation: to believe or not

Jesus' words and works of self-revelation typically provoke strong responses of either trust or repudiation. Few people remain neutral or indifferent. So, the questions which Jesus' self-identity ask include the following. What kind of a person is he who identifies himself by works such as turning water into wine, healing various kinds of diseases and afflictions, multiplying a little bread into much bread, walking on water, and raising the dead back to life? What kind of a person is he who identifies himself to be the bread of life, the light of the world, the door of the sheepfold, the good shepherd, the resurrection and the life, the [only] way to God, and the true vine? What kind of a person is he who appropriates the sacred name of Israel's redeemer God: the I AM? What kind of a person is he who is Lord of the Sabbath, and the embodiment and supersession of the Passover and the Feast of Tabernacles? According to John the Evangelist, he is from the beginning the eternal Word of God (Jn 1.1) and therefore is the Christ, the Son of God (20.31). On the one hand, so credible is Jesus' self-revelation that many believe in Him. On the other hand, so difficult are his claims about himself that many reject Him. This is a matter of believing or disbelieving.

Second only to John's theme of Jesus' self-revelation is the theme of the varied responses to Jesus' self-revelation. This complementary theme is about the opposite responses of either 'believing' or 'disbelieving'. So important is this theme that one commentator of an earlier generation named his commentary on John's gospel, *The Gospel of Belief.*[4] In his narrative, John uses the verb 'to believe' in is variant forms over 80 times. Interestingly, he does not use the noun form 'belief/faith' at all. Thus, as found in John's gospel, believing is not an objective *substance*, but it is an *action* of heart and mind. The 'believe' theme has several secondary emphases.

One secondary emphasis of the believe theme is that believing is the basis for eternal life. John reports this emphasis from first to last in his gospel narrative. For example, as the gospel opens he reports, 'as many as received Him, to them he gave the right to become the children of God, even to those who believe in his name' (Jn 1.12). The most oft-quoted verse in all of the gospels promises, 'whoever believes in him will not perish but have everlasting life' (3.16). In the same context, this promise is reinforced by the affirmation, 'whoever believes in the Son has eternal life' (3.36). Later, Jesus challenges a crowd in Jerusalem: 'he who believes in him [God] who sent Me [Jesus], has eternal life' (5.24). After feeding the five thousand, Jesus announces that the Father's will is that 'everyone who believes in the Son has eternal life' (6.40). Much later in his ministry, as he is about to raise Lazarus from the dead, Jesus affirms, 'I am the resurrection and the life, whoever believes in Me,

---

[4] Merrill Tenney, *John: The Gospel of Belief* (Grand Rapids: Eerdmans, 1997), p. 195.

though he dies, yet shall he live' (11.25). Finally, John explains that to believe that Jesus is the Christ, the Son of God (because of his seven signs) results in life in his name (20.31).

Two, the signs are the basis for believing just as believing is the basis for eternal life. John reports that Jesus reported 'many' signs. This is true, whether John is reporting about Jesus' ministry in Galilee or in Jerusalem (Jn 2.1-11; 2.23). As John reports them, these miracles are more than simply acts of power; they are miracles with a message about Jesus. It is because of their 'sign' language about Jesus that the miracles become the basis for believing.

For example, after Jesus turned about 120 gallons of water into 120 gallons of wine, then his disciples 'believed in Him' (2.11). Similarly, after he had healed the nobleman's son, he and his household believed (in him [4.50, 53]), but many in the crowd do not believe (4.48). Later, Jesus performs a healing in Jerusalem (5.1-9) just as he had first performed a healing in Galilee. Here, the unbelief of many is much stronger than it may have been in Galilee (5.38). Nevertheless, as he had done in Galilee, Jesus challenges the crowd to believe (5.46, 47). At the Passover season, after Jesus feeds the five thousand, many of those who have been fed conclude that Jesus is the long-promised prophet like Moses (Deut. 18.15) and try to make him their King (6.14, 15). But, rather than acceding to their attempt, Jesus makes it clear to that crowd that God's will is that they accept him as the One who gives eternal life (6.29, 40). This is a hard saying and many begin to reject him (6.64); but the disciples, excepting Judas, are steadfast in their belief (6.68, 69). Jesus heals a blind man in Jerusalem, as an acted parable, demonstrating that his claim to be the 'light of the world' is true (8.12; 9.5); many of the Jews oppose Jesus, but the man, formerly blind, declares, 'Lord, I believe' (9.38). And finally, after Jesus has raised Lazarus from the dead, many believed (11.45). Some of the Jews were so adamant in their unbelief that some of the chief priests and Pharisees plotted to kill not only him (11.47-53) but Lazarus as well (12.11).

Three, the message of the signs is that Jesus is the Messiah/Christ. For example, after Jesus speaks to the 'woman at the well' in Samaria (Jn 4.1-38), many of the Samaritans believed in Him, believed because of his Word, indeed, believed that he is 'the Savior of the world' (4.39-42). Further, during the subsequent Passover season, the disciples believe that Jesus is 'the Holy One of God' (6.69). The man born blind, whom Jesus healed, believes that Jesus is 'the Lord' (9.38). Finally, Martha believes that Jesus is the 'Christ, the Son of God' (11.27).

Furthermore, after a resurrection appearance to Thomas, he believes that Jesus is his 'Lord and God' (20.28, 29). In spite of the evidence that Jesus is Savior, the Holy One of Israel, Lord, Christ, Son of God, and God, some do not believe. These include the multitude at the feeding of the five thousand (6.24, 36), the disciples, Judas (6.64), Jesus' own brothers (7.5), the rulers of the Pharisees (7.48, 49), other Jewish leaders (9.18; 10.25), and the world itself (16.9). Clearly, miracles as signs do not necessarily make believers out of unbelievers.

The overall lesson of the 'believe' theme is that eternal life, both in the here and now, and in the ages to come, cannot be experienced apart from believing in Jesus Christ, the Son of God (Jn 20.31).

8

CYCLE SIX, CONTINUED: THE GROWTH AND SPREAD OF CHRISTIANITY

In 68 CE long-simmering Jewish resentment against their Roman overlords breaks out in open revolt. By 70 CE, however, the Roman army has crushed the revolt. Palestine has been overrun; the once sacred city of Jerusalem has been recaptured; the Second Temple has been destroyed; and much of the population has been slaughtered and/or enslaved. This is the brutal ending to the fifth cycle of turning points in biblical history and theology. As was discussed in chapter five, this cycle of turning points had begun with so much promise for good in the time of Cyrus King of Persia and the leadership of Joshua and Zerubbabel. But as Israel's history advances from this era of restoration and rebuilding to the era of Second Temple Judaism, the good aspects have been squandered; and revolutionary Jews have brought this judgment upon the nation.

The sixth turning point, however, began about 75 years before the Jewish Revolt – resulting in an overlap of about two generations between the new start of the sixth cycle and the judgment of the fifth cycle. Historically, the actual turning point is the births of two males, John the son of Zacharias and Elizabeth and Joshua/Jesus the son of Mary. These two cousins, John and Jesus, are God's primary agents for the new start of the sixth cycle of turning points. The new start begins once John and Jesus reach their mature adult years, about age thirty. The previous two chapters have surveyed select themes of the new start, as they are to be found in the four gospels, namely, Mark, Matthew, Luke (chapter 6), and John the

Evangelist (chapter 7): four witnesses, one message. After the *turning point* – the births of John and Jesus – and the *new start,* itself – the fourfold witness to Jesus, the cycle advances to include Luke's witness to the *growth and spread* of the Jesus Movement, a.k.a. Christianity.

8.1. Secondary Agents of the New Start

As we have already discussed, Jesus is the primary agent of the sixth start/new start. Ultimately, as the Son of God, he is God in the flesh; and in this way, God becomes his own agent of the new start. But in a variety of ways and contexts, Jesus will call, commission, and empower many secondary agents. The Bible reader is indebted to Luke for writing a second volume to his witness about Jesus, namely, the Gospel according to Luke. This second volume, the Acts of the Apostles, reports about the roles of these secondary agents in the numerical growth and geographical spread of Christianity. Unfortunately, the English translation of the Bible obscures the close relationship between the Gospel and Acts in two ways. One, it gives the volumes distinctly different titles: The Gospel According to Luke, and The Acts of the Apostles. This creates the impression that these are two independent books. Two, it tears the two volumes apart by placing John's gospel between them. The result is that many Bible readers think of them as two separate books and tend to interpret them separately. But they are two parts of one book, Luke–Acts, and should be interpreted as such. In order to rehabilitate Luke's writings, the first five books of the New Testament could be positioned as follows: John, Mark, Matthew, and Luke–Acts. Luke–Acts could then be titled something like 'The History of Jesus', and 'The History of the Church', or 'The Beginning of Christianity', and 'The Growth and Spread of Christianity'. Bible readers will certainly interpret Luke–Acts better if Luke's two books were to be treated this way.

Luke is the only one of the four Evangelists to write a sequel to his witness about Jesus. Interpreted as a literary document, the Acts of the Apostles belongs attached to his gospel. But when read as historical narrative, Acts is in fact the historical sequel to all four gospels and not just to Luke's gospel. Therefore, just as the gospels can be described by the phrase: 'four gospels; one message', so there are also 'four gospels; one common history'. In this regard, Acts will be interpreted differently if it is understood to be the historical sequel to each of the four, as Mark–Acts, Matthew–Acts, Luke–Acts, and finally, as John–Acts.

All four Gospels witness to a combination of events which are associated with the call and commissioning of the disciples as secondary agents of Jesus' own ministry. These first witnesses are a group of disciples, from among whom Jesus will call twelve to be apostles. Numbering twelve, the apostles represent the twelve tribes of Israel (Mt. 19.28). They are to be with him throughout his ministry, as earlier the sons of the prophets were associated with Elijah and Elisha, or with him as disciples were followers of their Rabbi. Having apprenticed them to himself, Jesus periodically sends them out to multiply and extend his own ministry (e.g. Lk. 9.1-6; 10.1-24). After his death and resurrection Jesus will recommission his disciples, and of equal importance, will empower them. Mark is the only Evangelist who does not report about this post-resurrection re-commissioning.

John the Evangelist's report about Jesus' recommissioning the Twelve which takes place on resurrection-day evening. This evening Jesus comes to his disciples, and says, 'Peace be with you; as the Father has sent Me I also send you … receive the Holy Spirit' (Jn 20.21, 22). This report is often interpreted to be about the 'conversion-initiation' of the disciples,[5] but its meaning when taken on its own terms, is not about the disciples coming to salvation, but rather, it is about the disciples being *sent*. In this regard it parallels Jesus' own experience of being sent (compare Jn 17.18 *et al.*). It is also about receiving the sanctifying/consecrating work of the Spirit – being set apart for service – just as at the beginning of his ministry, the Father 'anointed' Jesus for ministry (1.29-34). It is also about witnessing about Jesus as the One who forgives those who repent and believe (20.23; compare 20.30, 31). And so, on this resurrection-day evening, Jesus transfers his own mission (being sent), em-

---

[5] James Dunn, *Baptism in the Holy Spirit: A Re-examination of the New Testament on the Gift of the Spirit* (Louisville, KY: Westminster John Knox Press, 1984).

powering of the Holy Spirit, and message of forgiveness from himself to his apostles.

Matthew and Luke (but not Mark) also report recommissioning episodes. For example, Matthew reports an episode when Jesus meets his disciples in Galilee. He affirms his right to recommission them saying, 'All authority has been given to Me in heaven and earth' (Mt. 28.18). On this basis he commands: 1) 'Go, therefore, and make disciples of all nations', 2) 'baptizing them ...', and 3) 'teaching them' (28.19, 20a). For this mission, Jesus assures the disciples, 'lo, I am with you always, even to the end of the age' (28.20b). Finally, Luke also reports that Jesus commissioned his disciples saying, 'You are witnesses of these things' (Lk. 24.48). 'These things' about which they are to witness include the following: 1) Jesus' charismatic ministry (miracles, wonders, and signs), 2) his death, and 3) his resurrection (Acts 2.22-25). For their role as witnesses Jesus assures his disciples, 'I am sending forth the promise of My Father upon you ... until you are clothed with power from on high' (24.49). As a later verse illustrates, Jesus' promise of 'power from on high' is an implicit promise of the Holy Spirit (Acts 1.8; compare Lk. 4.14). This, in their commissioning, the disciples will experience the Trinitarian God (Father, Son, and Holy Spirit) in their lives.

8.2. First Things First

In his narrative history about the acts of Jesus and his followers, namely, Luke–Acts, Luke reports extensively about how the Trinitarian God is collectively, interdependently involved in the spread of the Jesus Movement (a.k.a. Christianity). There are two examples of this early in Luke's narrative about Jesus. The first is his report about the virgin birth, which involves the Father's purpose, the Spirit's enabling power, and the Son of the Most High who will be born to Mary (Lk. 1.32-35). The second example is his report about the public inauguration of Jesus' ministry, at which time Jesus has been baptized by John the Baptist, the Father speaks from Heaven, and the Holy Spirit descends upon Him, anointing him to preach the gospel to the poor (3.21, 22; 4.18). What was true in Jesus' own inauguration for ministry is similarly true for Jesus' followers. Their experience of ministry preparation has various significant elements. These include, but are not limited to the facts that: 1) in answer to their prayer, the Father will *give* the Holy Spirit to the disciples (Lk. 11.13), 2) Jesus will *baptize* disciples in the Holy Spirit to inaugurate their ministry (Acts 1.4, 5), and 3) the Holy Spirit *speaks* (prophetic) utterances through their words (Acts 2.4).

These Trinitarian contributions to the inauguration of the disciples for ministry are sometimes misunderstood and, therefore, deserve a fuller explanation. In a comment on the (Lord's) model prayer (Lk. 11.1-13), Jesus taught that the Father in Heaven will *give* the Holy Spirit to those who ask Him, that is to those who pray. In this discussion with his disciples, Jesus makes several pertinent points. Disciples are to pray to the Father, 'Thy Kingdom come' (11.2b). Thus, on the one hand, the Father's gift of the Holy Spirit to the disciples is an aspect of the Father's will in their lives. Jesus also assured his disciples that when they pray to the Father to receive the Holy Spirit, on the other hand, they know the gift of the Holy Spirit is a good thing (compare Mt. 7.11), and not a harmful thing (11.11, 12). Finally, Jesus observed that (sometimes) the prayer for the Father's gift of the Holy Spirit may involve continuous asking, seeking, and knocking, but the answer is sure (11.9-10). Clearly, the disciples' prayers to receive the Holy Spirit are not about the imperceptible reception of the Holy Spirit in the conversion-initiation experience, but are about a tangible, subsequent gift of the Spirit. This is confirmed in the actual experience of the disciples' reception of Spirit-baptism on the day of Pentecost (Acts 1.4, 5; 2.1-21), which happens in the context of prayer (1.14; compare 8.15).

Not only will the Father give the Holy Spirit to his disciples in answer to their prayers (Lk. 11.13); but in a complementary act, Jesus will specifically, but not conclusively, *baptize* his disciples in the Holy Spirit. According to Luke, this is exactly what Jesus promised to do for the commissioning of the disciples. He reports that prior to his ascension (Acts 1.9-11), Jesus

commanded them not to leave Jerusalem, but to wait for what the Father had promised, 'Which', he said, 'you heard from Me; for John baptized with water, but you shall be baptized with the Holy Spirit not many days from now' (Acts 1.4, 5).

The nature of being baptized in the Holy Spirit is a deeply conflicted subject. It is beyond dispute that Jesus is applying John the Baptist's prophecy to the disciples' reception of the Holy Spirit on the
Day of Pentecost (2.1-21). The Father's promise, as earlier prophesied by John the Baptist is that his successor will baptize, 'in the
Holy Spirit and fire' (Lk. 3.16). John the Baptist, himself, explains
the meaning of Spirit baptism (3.17). Being baptized in the Spirit, in
the covenantal language is a 'blessing', like a grain harvest; being
baptized in fire is a 'cursing', like the burning up of the chaff. As
explained by John the Baptist, and as reported by Luke, when Jesus
baptized his disciples with the Holy Spirit on the Day of Pentecost,
he blessed them with the 'empowering' and 'filling' gifts of the Holy Spirit. There is nothing in Luke's narrative about Jesus as Spirit-
baptizer which points to the 'conversion-initiation' work of the Holy Spirit (1 Cor. 12.13). This is confirmed by the observation that
the inaugural reception of the Spirit by the disciples is functionally
equivalent to Jesus' own earlier inaugural reception of the Spirit.

Jesus' Inaugural Reception of the Spirit	Disciples' Inaugural Reception of the Spirit
The Father anoints Jesus with the Spirit (Lk. 4.18/Isa. 61.1)	Jesus baptizes the disciples with the Spirit (Acts 1.5/Lk. 3.16)
Result: Jesus is full of the Spirit (Lk. 4.1a)	Result: disciples are filled with the Spirit (Acts 2.4)
Result: Jesus is led by the Spirit (Lk. 4.1b)	Result: disciples are led by the Spirit (Acts 8.29)
Result: Jesus is empowered by the Spirit (Lk. 4.14)	Result: disciples are empowered with the Spirit (Acts 1.8)
Visual sign: Spirit descends in bodily form (Lk. 3.21)	Visual sign: tongues of fire (Acts 2.3)
Audible sign: voice from Heaven (Lk. 3.22)	Audible sign: Sound of wind (Acts 2.2); spoke with other tongues (Acts 2.4)

To deny that the Spirit-baptism of the disciples is functionally
equivalent to Jesus' own earlier Spirit-anointing is to put ecclesiasti-
cal tradition above the plain meaning of Scripture – surely an unjus-
tifiable hermeneutical principle.

The above discussion about Jesus baptizing his disciples in the Holy Spirit clearly demonstrates that their inaugural experience of the Spirit is functionally equivalent to his own earlier inaugural anointing by the Spirit. This can be further illustrated by a trajectory of inaugural vocational gifts of the Spirit which began in the time of Moses and advanced through Saul/David and Elijah/Elisha. In these and other examples the gift of the Spirit to the second party both consecrates and equips these newly commissioned leaders for charismatic, Spirit-empowered ministry. The following table illustrates the pattern for transfer of the Spirit from an incumbent leader to a second party.

Pattern	Transfer of Spirit to Israel's Elders	Transfer of Spirit to Disciples
Covenant Context	The Sinai Covenant	The New Covenant
Location	The Tabernacle	The Temple
Task	Elders given new leadership responsibilities	Disciples are given new leadership responsibilities
Transfer	The Holy Spirit is transferred from Moses to the Elders	The Holy Spirit is transferred from Jesus to his disciples
Number	From one to a group (70)	From one to a group (120)
Sign	The Elders prophesied	The disciples spoke in tongues = prophesied

The unmistakable parallels between the two episodes illustrates that in the generation when the covenant is given at Mt. Sinai, the 70 elders became the prophets of that covenant; so now, on the Day of Pentecost, the community of the 120 disciples become prophets of the new covenant.

Luke narrates a larger picture than just the Pentecost narrative he so dramatically reports. Luke–Acts reports that everyone who receives the Holy Spirit has already, earlier first experienced the essential spiritual prerequisite – they were in right relation to God. The following table summarizes all of the relevant data in Luke–Acts about the antecedent spiritual state of those whom Luke reports to have subsequently received the Holy Spirit.

Person(s)	Antecedent Spiritual State	Subsequent Experiences of the Spirit
Elizabeth	Lk. 1.6 righteous, walked blamelessly	Lk. 1.41 filled with Holy Spirit and prophesied
Zacharias	Lk. 1.6 righteous, walked blamelessly	Lk. 1.67 filled with Holy Spirit and prophesied
Simeon	Lk. 2.25 righteous and devout	Lk. 2.25 led by the Holy Spirit and prophesied
120 brethren	Lk. 6.13 disciples	Acts 1.5 **baptized in the Holy Spirit**
	Acts 11.17 believers	Acts 2.4, 17 filled with the Holy Spirit; spoke in tongues = prophesied
5000 Disciples	Acts 4.4 believers	Acts 4.31 filled with the Holy Spirit and gave inspired bold witness
Samaritans	Acts 8.12 believers	Acts 8.15–17 received the Holy Spirit
Paul	Acts 9.15 Chosen instrument to witness about Jesus before the Gentiles, Kings and Israelites	Acts 9.17 filled with the Holy Spirit (to witness)
Cornelius' house church	Acts 10.2–4 God-fearers, righteous Acts 11.17 believers	Acts 11.16 **baptized in the Holy Spirit** Acts 10.46 spoke in tongues = prophesied
Ephesian Twelve	Acts 19.1 disciples Acts 19.2 believers	Acts 19.6 (implied) **baptized in the Holy Spirit**; spoke in tongues and prophesied

The above data compels Bible readers to recognize that in Luke–Acts, receiving the Spirit is about Christian vocation or charismatic experience rather than about salvation. No amount of verbal gymnastics, linguistic slight-of-hand, or presuppositionally based Scripture twisting can overturn the evidence. To conclude, just as God anointed Jesus with the Holy Spirit to originate the gospel, so in the same way Jesus baptized his disciples in the Holy Spirit so that they might spread this good news throughout the Roman Empire and to different people groups.

To this point, the discussion of 'first things' has shown: 1) that God the Father gives the Spirit to his disciples in answer to their prayers, and 2) that Jesus baptizes his disciples in the Holy Spirit to anoint, that is, consecrate them for their Spirit-empowered, Spirit-filled, and Spirit-led ministry. In the Trinitarian gift of the Spirit, the Holy Spirit gives inspired 'utterance' and other gifts to the disciples. Luke reports this happening on the post-Easter Day of Pentecost writing, 'And they were all filled with the Holy Spirit and began to speak with other tongues as the Spirit was giving them utterance' (Acts 2.4). The Bible reader will make several observations. One, Luke emphasizes, 'all were filled and spoke' (1.15), and not just the twelve apostles (1.26). Two, Luke explains that these other tongues are the mother tongues or various dialects of the multi-tongued character of the crowd of Pentecost pilgrims (2.5-11). Three, speaking the various languages of the Temple crowd, the disciples are praising God (literally, 'speaking the magnificent things of God'), perhaps like Mary's hymn of praise to her 'magnificent' God (Lk. 1.46-55). Four, interpreting their experience of the Spirit to be a fulfillment of Joel's prophecy about a future outpouring of the Spirit, Peter identifies Spirit-inspired speech (2.4) to be a kind of prophesying (2.16-18).

Luke uses the term, 'filled with the Holy Spirit' more widely than any other term to describe people's experiences of the Spirit. He distributes the term as follows: three times in the infancy narrative (Lk. 1.15, 41, 67), three times in the life of the Spirit-baptized community in Jerusalem (Acts 2.4; 4.8, 31), and three times in Paul's experience (9.17; 13.9, 52). As Luke uses the term, it does not describe some general state of 'spirituality' (i.e. the Spirit-filled 'life'). Rather, it describes either prophethood (e.g. 1.15), or the Spirit's prophetic 'utterances' (e.g. Lk. 1.67; Acts 2.4; 4.8). Therefore, in all cases, the term, 'filled with the Holy Spirit' is restricted to prophetic speech or to the call to prophethood. Thus the term describes an important aspect of the kind of vocation or ministry which God's workers will follow.

This section about 'First Things' has briefly illustrated the works of God – as Father, he gives the Spirit, as Son, he baptizes his disciples in the Spirit, and as Holy Spirit, he inspires 'utterances' in the witness of his followers. In other words, God (Father, Son, and Spirit) is fully and directly involved in the success of the sixth New Start. All in all, at no turning point in Old Testament times did the one and only creator and redeemer God involve himself in human affairs as the triune God. What task is so important that the triune God involves himself in this way? The answer is to be found in the magnitude of the message which is involved in the sixth start/new start: 'For God so loved the world, that he gave his only begotten Son, that whoever believes in him should not perish, but have eternal life' (Jn 3.16). The answer is also to be found in the complementary mission of the disciples, who beginning on the post-Easter Day of Pentecost become a community of Spirit-baptized, Spirit-empowered, Spirit-filled, and Spirit-led workers in order to witness about Jesus locally (Jerusalem), regionally (Judea and Samaria), and ultimately, globally (to the ends of the earth [Acts 1.18]).

8.3. The Growth and Spread of the Community of Jesus' Followers

Early in the history of humankind, the Noah cycle of Turning Points ends in the judgment which was associated with the Tower of Babel episode (Gen. 11.1-9). Out of the international confusion of languages, which is the nature of God's judgment, God calls a man from Ur of the Chaldees to be his agent for the third new start. This is a certain Abram, to whom God promises to bless his family, the new nation which will grow up from his family, and also all of the nations of the world (Gen. 12.1-2). Time advances, and in the fourth and fifth New Starts, God prepares Israel for the forthcoming sixth New Start. This happens when, as Paul writes, 'the fullness of time came [and] God sent forth his Son, born of a woman, born under the Law, in order that he might redeem those who were under the Law' (Gal. 4.4, 5). The fourfold Gospel as reported about Jesus as God's primary agent for the sixth turning point, and now Luke's narrative, the Acts of the Apostles, reports about the local, regional, and international growth and spread of the Good News about Jesus.

In general terms, the gospels report that Jesus regularly teaches using parables (Mt. 13.3). Two of Jesus' many parables are about the growth and spread of the Kingdom of God. Luke reports Jesus teaching,

> The kingdom of God is like a mustard seen, which a man took and threw into his own garden; and it grew and became a tree, and the birds of the air nest in its branches ... it is like leaven, which a woman took and hid in three pecks of meal, until it was all leavened (Lk. 13.18-21).

Not all Bible interpreters agree about the meaning of these two parables. Nevertheless, all can agree that they are about the same basic subject, the Kingdom of God. Bible readers will observe that this is the general subject which bookends the opening and closing of Acts (Acts 1.8; 28.31). The parable of the mustard seed emphasizes the *growth* of seed from a very small beginning to a very large ending. Whatever nuances this parable may have, it is clearly about the growth of the kingdom among God's people in Jerusalem, such as Luke reports in Acts 1.4–7.60. Similarly, the parable of the leaven complements the parable of the mustard seen, with the difference that it is about the *spread* of the kingdom, such as Luke reports in Acts 8.1–28.31.

8.3.1. The growth of the community of disciples

In his Acts narrative, Luke reports about the growth in the number of Jesus' followers in Jerusalem (Acts 1.1–7.60). First, he identifies the Eleven (apostles) as God's secondary agents of this new Turning Point (1.2; the Twelve [1.26]). When devout Jews begin to gather in Jerusalem to celebrate the Feast of Pentecost, some of Jesus' followers from Galilee swell the number of disciples to 120 (1.15). From the Day of Pentecost onward, the city of Jerusalem is rocked by a series of unexpected wonders and signs, of which, three happen on this festival day. These signs include: 1) the sound of a gale-force wind, but no wind blows (2.2), 2) a fireball in the sky which bursts and rains down tongues of fire upon the 120 (2.3), and this group finds itself to be doing the most unexpected thing, namely, praising God in languages which they have never learned (2.4). Shortly thereafter, Peter and John heal a well-known crippled beggar, one example of the many wonders and signs which are being done at the hands of the apostles (2.43; 2.1-9). Later, the deacon Stephen will perform extraordinary wonders and signs (6.8). These miracles, which the narrative suggests are commonplace, call for an explanation, and Peter conducts city-wide evangelistic crusades on the Temple Mount preaching that Jesus is Lord and Christ, and that he is God's Servant and the Prophet like Moses (2.36; 3.13, 22). For these and other reasons, the number of Jesus' followers explodes. This apparently unstoppable growth stirs the leaders of Judaism to act against the disciples. First, they command Peter and John to stop preaching that Jesus rose from the dead (4.18); next, the Twelve are flogged because they continued to preach about the resurrection (5.40), and finally, they put Stephen to death for witnessing about Jesus (6.10; 7.60). This escalating opposition drove many disciples, such as Philip the Evangelist, to flee Jerusalem, the city that kills the prophets (8.5; Lk. 13.34). But, ironically, this opposition does not quench the gospel, it simply results in the spread of the gospel.

Clearly, the many miracles as signs and wonders and the Spirit-filled preaching bring many devout Jews to accept Jesus as their Messiah/Christ. For example, on the Day of Pentecost, about three thousand Jews, both residents of Jerusalem and visiting pilgrims, are added to the small number of original disciples. And it does not stop there, 'for', as Luke reports, 'the Lord was adding to their number day by day those who were being saved' (Acts 2.47). By the time that Peter and John have healed the lame beggar at the Temple gate the number has grown to about five thousand believers (4.4). Soon, 'constant addition' has raised the number to the size of a multitude (4.32), and finally to 'the multitudes' (5.14). This rapid multiplication of Jesus' followers helps Luke's readership to understand his refusal to identify the believing community as the 'church' until the time of the Ananias and Sapphira episode (5.1-11). The Greek word for church is *ecclesia*. This word is often used by the Greek translators of the Hebrew Bible to identify the *nation* of Israel. Therefore, Luke delays using the term, *ecclesia*, until the number of the believing community grows to the size of a small nation (i.e. a nation within the nation). And it is only when the church in Jerusalem has grown to this size that God permits it to be scattered by the events which are associated with the death of Stephen (8.1-4).

The death of Stephen is a turning point in Luke's narrative. Prior to Stephen's death, Luke emphasizes the growth of the number of disciples in Jerusalem. After Stephen's death, Luke emphasizes the spread of Christianity to other lands and nations (Acts 8.1–28.31). But even with the shift in emphasis, Luke periodically reminds his readership of the ongoing, phenomenal growth in the number of Jesus' followers. For example, as a result of Philip's preaching in Samaria about Jesus the 'multitude' who gave attention to his preaching believed and are baptized (8.5-13). Further, in Lydda, all who saw (the lame man now healed) turned to the Lord (9.35). Similarly, in Joppa many who learned that Dorcas/Tabitha had been raised from the dead 'believed in the Lord' (9.42). Finally, Luke concludes his narrative about the spread of the gospel to Samaria and Judea (8.5–12.23) by reporting, 'but the word of the Lord continued to grow and to be multiplied' (12.24). Years later, James, the de facto leader of the church in Jerusalem can report to Paul that there are 'many ten thousands (literally, myriads) among the Jews of those who have believed, and they are all zealous for the Law' (21.20).

Two clichés describe the basis for the phenomenal growth in the number of believers in Jerusalem. These are: 1) 'bloom where you are planted', and 2) 'redeem the time'. In other words, the growth arises out of the providential circumstances in which the disciples find themselves. For example, the earliest post-Easter community of disciples was planted in Jerusalem and it was there that circumstances yielded opportunities to witness about Jesus. In this sense, in Jerusalem there is the empowering of the Spirit but no leading of the Spirit. Circumstances such as the three wonders and signs on the day of Pentecost (Acts 2.2–4.19) and later the healing of the lame beggar at the Temple gate (3.1-9) produces the occasions for effective evangelism. But once the Christian community in Jerusalem is dispersed after the Stephen episode (6.8–7.60), specific opportunities to witness about Jesus are orchestrated by the Spirit (e.g. 8.29; 10.19; 13.2-4, *et al.*).

8.3.2. The geographic spread of the gospel

In his prologue to the book of Acts, Luke reports about Jesus' strategy for the Spirit-baptized and Spirit-empowered witness of the disciples, locally, regionally, and internationally (Acts 1.1-8). Indeed, Luke's narrative, itself, loosely follows this structure, as Jesus' followers witness about Jesus, first in Jerusalem (Acts 1–7), then in Samaria and Judea (chapters 8–12), and, finally to the ends of the earth, that is, Rome (13–28). But the spread of the gospel actually begins immediately after the Day of Pentecost when devout Jewish pilgrims who have come to believe that Jesus is 'Lord and Christ' (2.36) take back with them the good news about Jesus to the lands of the Jewish Diaspora (2.9-11). This is 'centripetal' missions – when people are drawn to the center (e.g. Jerusalem) to be evangelized. The 'centrifugal' spread of the gospel – witnesses being sent out from the center (from Jerusalem to Judea [8–12], and then from Jerusalem to the ends of the earth) is the second phase in the spread of the gospel.

8.3.3. The spread of the gospel

Before his ascension, Jesus recommissions his disciples to witness about him locally, regionally, and internationally (Acts 1.8). From this standpoint, Luke narrates the story of this witness according to the strategy of: 1) witness in Jerusalem (1.12–8.4), 2) witness in Samaria and Judea (8.5–12.24), and 3) the witness to the 'ends of the earth', i.e. Rome (12.25–28.31). But the spread of the gospel actually begins immediately after the Day of Pentecost when devout Diaspora Jewish pilgrims who have come to believe that Jesus is Lord and Christ (2.36) carry the gospel with them back to their native lands and ancestral homes (2.9-11). This witness is first centripetal – God's people come up to Jerusalem and are saved (2.39) – and centrifugal – those who are saved take their newfound faith back to their families and to their communities. Later, after the death of Stephen in Jerusalem, the centrifugal movement of the gospel out from Jerusalem is highlighted, first, by the witness of Philip in the province of Samaria, and, second, the witness of Peter in the province of Judea. Luke's reports about Philip and Peter prepare the way for the subsequent witness by Paul from Jerusalem, to Antioch, and round about the northern Mediterranean world to the city of Rome itself.

8.3.4. The gospel spreads from Jerusalem to Samaria and Judea

The witness of Stephen in Jerusalem is a significant point in Luke's narrative strategy. On the one hand, Luke closes his Jerusalem narrative reporting the martyrdom of Stephen (Acts 6.8–7.60) and the persecution of Jesus' followers (8.1-4). At this point, Luke shifts the focus of his narrative from Jerusalem to Samaria (8.5-25). On the other hand, Luke's focus on the community of God's people, including the apostles, ends with the choosing of the seven deacons (6.1-7). From this point in his narrative (6.1-7), Luke will focus his narrative on the acts of six charismatic leaders – God's secondary agents for the spread of the gospel. These six secondary agents are Stephen, Philip, Barnabas, Agabus, Peter, and Paul. Luke reports about them in pairs, namely two deacons (Stephen and Philip), two prophets (Barnabas and Agabus), and two apostles (Peter and Paul). Each leader is, in his own right, a Spirit-baptized, Spirit-empowered, Spirit-filled, and Spirit-led secondary agent in the spread of the Gospel.

As a result of murderous persecution instigated by a certain Saul of Tarsus, Philip flees the city of Jerusalem and takes the gospel to Samaria (8.5-25). Historically, this is the third time that Jesus and/or his agents have taken the gospel to Samaria. The first time, Jesus witnesses about himself to 'the woman at the well' (Jn 4.1-42). She, in turn, witnesses to her own townspeople, and they come and hear Jesus for themselves. As a result, they come to believe that he is 'the Savior of the world' (4.39-42). Later, as Jesus departs from Galilee for his final journey to Jerusalem (Lk. 9.51), he will for the second time approach, 'a village of the Samaritans, but they did not receive Him' (9.52). Now, after Philip finds refuge in a city of Samaria, he not only preaches the Word, but he also casts out demons and heals the sick (8.6-8). As a result, there was much rejoicing in the city (8.8). They rejoiced not only because of the wonders and signs but also because, 'they believed … the good news about the Kingdom of God and the name of Jesus Christ' (8.12).

When Philip's preaching (i.e. evangelism) is finished, an angel (or a messenger) instructs Philip to leave Samaria and go to the Gaza road which descends south of Jerusalem (8.26). Once Philip has obeyed, the Spirit of the Lord directs him to a chariot which is passing by, and which is carrying an Ethiopian Court official (8.29). This man is reading from the scroll of the prophet Isaiah, but he doesn't fully understand the message. Therefore, 'beginning from this Scripture, he preached Jesus to him' (8.36). He believes Philip's witness, and Philip baptizes him. The court official then goes on his way back to Ethiopia 'rejoicing' (8.38) – taking the 'good news' about Jesus to the royal court. Many interpreters for theological reasons discredit Philip's evangelistic ministry in Samaria, but the parallels between the two narratives – Philip's preaching, belief, rejoicing, and baptism – confirms the effectiveness of his witness to both the Samaritans and the Ethiopian, and that of his reputation as 'the Evangelist' (21.8). Ending this encounter, 'the Spirit of the Lord snatched Philip away' (8.39), and he continues to preach the gospel in other cities, finally coming to Caesarea Maritima where he apparently settles.

Having reported how the gospel came to Samaria (Acts 8.5-25), and, eventually, to Ethiopia (8.26-40), Luke reports a series of episodes which result in the ongoing spread of the gospel. These include, but are not limited to, the commissioning and early preaching of a certain Saul of Tarsus (9.1-30). In the context of the spread of the gospel, the conversion of Saul is significant in two ways: 1) Jesus commissions him to be his 'chosen instrument ... to bear [Jesus'] name before the Gentiles and Kings and the sons of Israel' (9.15). For this great task Saul (who is later called 'Paul') will be filled with the Holy Spirit (9.17), and 2) his later recommissioning and Spirit-filled experiences qualify him to be a prophet and teacher (13.1), set apart and sent out by the Spirit (13.2-4).[6]

Paul's mentor and senior partner in this Spirit-led ministry is a certain Barnabas, who is a Levite of Cyprian birth (Acts 4.36). He has earned a reputation in the church in Jerusalem as an encourager (4.36-37). Being a Spiritful encourager, teacher, and prophet (4.36-37; 11.22-24; 13.1), the church in Jerusalem will send him to the fledgling church in Antioch in Syria to encourage these recent converts to Christianity, as it had earlier sent Peter and John to Samaria to encourage the believers there (8.14-17). Eventually, Barnabas adds Paul to the leadership team of the church in Antioch, and within the year, the Holy Spirit will send them out, bearing the name of Jesus before diasporan Jews, Roman officials, and Gentiles (13.1-14.28). But, before the team of Barnabas and Paul begin to spread the Gospel in Gentile lands, Peter will witness about Jesus in

---

[6] Hereafter, Saul of Tarsus will be referred to as 'Paul', which is the preferred name in the Acts narrative after chapter 13.

Judea, and here, in Caesarea, he will begin the church's mission to the Gentiles (15.7-11).

8.4. Peter's and Paul's Prophetic Missions to the Gentiles

At the heart of Luke's second book – the continuing narrative about all that Jesus began to do and teach – lies the fact of the Gentile mission (Acts 9.1–22.21). Prior to this the disciples had witnessed about Jesus to Jews (2.1-8.4) and Samaritans (8.4-40). This witness had been spectacularly successful, and in the short time between the Day of Pentecost episode and Stephen's martyrdom (2.1–7.60) the number of Jews who had become followers of Jesus had grown from a gathering of 120 persons to more than 5,000 believers and then to multitudes large enough to be called a nation or church (1.15; 4.4; 5.11). This rapid growth threatened the leadership of the coalition of leading Sadducean and Pharisaic families, and soon followers of Jesus experienced a series of persecutions of escalating severity (Acts 4.1–7.60). One result of this persecution was that, fleeing Jerusalem, Philip took the evangel to Samaria (8.5-42) with an effectiveness proportional to the earlier witness in Jerusalem. All of these events prepare the way for the 'problematic' prophetic mission to the Gentiles.

8.4.1. Narrative pattern: four prophetic tours to the Gentiles (9.1–22.21)

Two cities, Jerusalem and Rome, each great in her own way, bookend Luke's narrative about the spread of the gospel (Acts 1.12–7.60; 28.11-31). But the heart of Luke's narrative consists of reports about four peripatetic (walk about) tours of the two foremost prophets, Peter and Paul (9.1–22.21). Luke's reports about the travels of these two prophets span about 12 to 15 years and circle the lands surrounding the northeastern Mediterranean. These reports yield a massive amount of detailed, potentially confusing information. But by inventing a common narrative pattern for reporting these four prophetic tours of Peter and Paul to the Gentiles Luke not only makes this information easily understandable, but he also reinforces fundamental theological themes.

Luke reports the prophetic witness of Peter to Jews (Acts 1.12–5.42), Samaritans (8.14-25), and Gentiles (10.1–11.18). His report about Peter's witness to Gentiles, namely, the household of the Roman Centurion, Cornelius, establishes the pattern for his subsequent reports about Paul's so-called first, second, and third missionary journeys. These are best identified as itinerant or prophetic tours. As Luke works out his narrative strategy for describing Peter's travels through western Judea the pattern includes three elements: 1) one or more short introductory reports (9.32-43), 2) a major report about ministry in one city (10.1-48), and 3) a concluding aftermath in Jerusalem (11.1-18). With two variations Luke adapts this pattern to his report about Paul's three journeys around the rim of the Mediterranean (13.1–22.21). The two variations are: 1) Luke explicitly identifies the activity of the Holy Spirit in the introductory reports to each tour, and 2) he also inserts a series of summary reports between each major report and its aftermath. The following chart illustrates Luke's narrative pattern.

Prophetic Tour	Introductory Episodes	Major Report	Series of Summary Reports
Peter's First	Implicit emphasis is on the **power** of the Holy Spirit	Focus is on Caesarea Acts 10.1-48	**Aftermath** in Jerusalem
Paul's First	Explicit emphasis is on the **initiative** of the Holy Spirit	Focus is on Antioch Acts 13.13-52	Journey resumes and concludes in Antioch with an **aftermath** in Jerusalem Acts 4.1-15.30
Paul's Second	Emphasis is on the **leading** of the Holy Spirit	Focus is on Philippi Acts 16.11-40	Journey resumes and concludes in Antioch with an appendix about Apollos Acts 17.1-18.28
Paul's Third	Emphasis is on the **gift** of the Holy Spirit	Focus is on Ephesus Acts 19.8-41	Journey with **aftermath** concludes in Jerusalem Acts 20.1-22.21

These narratives yield their fullest meaning when each one is interpreted as part of a larger pattern.[7]

---

[7] Typical of a truncated interpretation of Paul's Gentile mission is the chapter by Philip H. Towner, 'Mission Practice and Theology', in I. Howard Marshall and David Peterson (eds.), *Witness to the Gospel: The Theology of Acts* (Grand Rapids: Eerdmans, 1998), pp. 417-36. Towner's focus is primarily limited to Luke's 'Cor-

8.4.2. Peter's first prophetic tour and its aftermath in Jerusalem (Acts 9.32–11.18)

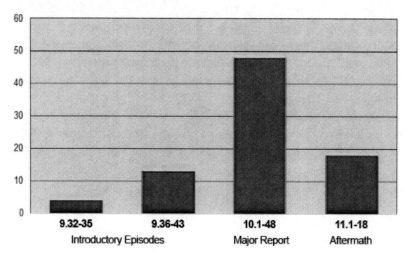

Luke structures his report of Peter's prophetic tour according to this pattern:

1. Series of introductory reports (9.32-35; 9.36-43). These two reports describe the implicit power of the Holy Spirit in Peter's ministry (healing the lame man and raising the dead).

2. A major report of Peter's ministry in one city, namely Caesarea (10.1-48).

3. The aftermath, where in Jerusalem Peter defends his visit to the Gentile house church in Caesarea (11.1-18).

For Luke, Peter is the prototypical prophet. According to Luke's narrative he is baptized in the Spirit, empowered by the Spirit, and filled with the Holy Spirit (Acts 1.5, 8; 2.4, 17-21). Like Jesus earlier, he is a prophet powerful in works, such as healings (3.1-9; 5.12-16) and words (3.10-26; 4.8-12). Along with other disciples, Peter is commissioned to witness about Jesus in Jerusalem, Judea, and Sa-

---

inth' and 'Ephesus' narratives (Acts 18–19), thereby, cutting himself off from: 1) the significance of Peter's first prophetic tour, 2) Luke's programmatic short introductory narratives, 3) the explicit prophetic make-up of the teams, and 4) the ominous opposition to the Gentile mission from believing Jews in Jerusalem.

maria, and to the ends of the earth (1.8). By the time that Luke reports about Peter's first prophetic tour, Peter (with John) has already given effective prophetic ministry in Jerusalem (3.1–5.42) and Samaria (8.14-25). Now Peter is about to give prophetic ministry in western Judea, but to his surprise, he will not only minister to Jews, but he will, albeit reluctantly, be the first to minister to Gentiles (9.32–11.18). In western Judea he will experience both triumph and certain levels of tragedy.

Luke briefly reports Peter's ministry in two communities, Lydda and Joppa; each of which contains communities of 'saints' and 'disciples' (9.32, 36). In Lydda he heals a certain saint named Aeneas, and in Joppa he raises a certain disciple named Tabitha from the dead (9.33, 37, 40-42). These wonders and signs, which echo similar earlier miracles of Jesus, result in many turning to the Lord (9.36) and many believing in the Lord (9.42). These miracles represent the triumph of implied charismatic prophetic ministry and prophetic evangelism. In Luke's narrative strategy these episodes introduce Luke's major report about Peter's ministry to the Roman centurion who is based at Caesarea in Joppa.

As earlier at Lydda and Joppa, where Peter ministered to Jews who were saints and disciples, so, next when Peter comes to Caesarea he will minister to a man who is 'righteous' and a 'believer' (10.22; 11.17). The difference is that this man, named Cornelius, is not a Jewish believer like Aeneas and Tabitha, but he is a Gentile believer. This presents Peter with a cultural problem disguised as a spiritual problem, for Jews did not fellowship with Gentiles. In fact, it required both a vision and a command from the Holy Spirit (10.9-23) to compel this reluctant prophet to visit the household of this Gentile 'without misgivings' (10.20; 11.4-12). But God not only initiated this visit of Peter to this household of 'righteous' Gentile believers,[8] but he also demonstrated his acceptance of these believers by baptizing them in the Holy Spirit (10.44-48) as he had earlier on the Day of Pentecost baptized the disciples in the Holy Spirit

---

[8] See John Calvin, *Commentary on the Acts of the Apostles* (trans. Henry Beveridge; Grand Rapids, Baker, n.d.). Calvin writes that Cornelius, 'a true worshipper' has 'this commendation that [he] had a church in his house', p. 407.

(11.15-17; compare 1.4, 5). This was a triumph of obedience over prejudice, of inclusivism over exclusiveness.

Luke's Cornelius narrative is foreshadowed earlier in Luke–Acts. For example, in his 'Infancy Narrative' (Luke 1.5–2.42), Luke reports that the Spirit who inspires prophecy is given to Elizabeth, Zacharias, and Simeon, each of whom are first reported to be 'righteous and devout' (Lk. 1.5, 2.25). Luke reports that Cornelius has the same spiritual qualifications as these earlier men and women of the Spirit (Acts 10.2, 22). With the same qualifications, might Cornelius also be a candidate to have the Spirit of prophecy poured out on him? In addition, Luke reports an episode in Galilee which involves a centurion who is a man of faith (Lk. 7.1-10). Might Cornelius the centurion, also a man of faith, be acceptable to God – on the basis of his faith and apart from the necessity of Law-keeping? Finally, Jesus baptizes his disciples in the Holy Spirit on the first post-Easter Day of Pentecost, commissioning and empowering them for prophetic vocation (1.5, 8; 2.1-21). Might Cornelius, though he is a Gentile believer, also be baptized in the Holy Spirit, similarly commissioning and empowering him for prophetic service (10.44-48; 11.15-17)? Luke's major report about Cornelius demands that a 'yes' answer be given to all three questions. Righteousness, faith, and prophetic commissioning trumps law-keeping and racial exclusiveness.

In spite of the Cornelius episode being a triumph of divine inclusiveness over Jewish Christian exclusiveness, Peter's visit to this Gentile household casts a shadow over the Gentile mission. When Peter returns to Jerusalem from Caesarea he is sharply criticized by good, law-keeping Jewish believers. It is significant that he is challenged, not because the Gentiles had received the Word of God (11.1; compare 8.14), but because Peter 'went to uncircumcised men and ate with them' (11.3). This is the issue, not of the salvation of the Gentiles but of table fellowship between Jewish Christians and Gentile Christians. After Peter had explained God's role in the episode of his visit to Cornelius, the Jewish Christians in Jerusalem were mollified, and so, 'they quieted down' (11.18). In this way a potential tragedy was apparently averted. But in reality it was only postponed until the results of Paul's first prophetic tour became known. Paul's prophetic tour had the potential to divide the church irrevocably into two factions – law-keeping Jewish believers and non-law-keeping Gentile believers. Peter's experience with Cornelius proved to be one of the decisive factors in preventing this division.

8.4.3. Paul's three prophetic tours (Acts 13.1–22.21)

At an indeterminate time after Peter's prototypical prophetic tour in western Judea and its conflicted aftermath in Jerusalem (9.32–11.18), Paul will finally begin his own mission to the Gentiles. This will be the dominant passion of his life for the next 12 to 15 years. Just as Peter's mission began among the Jews in Judea and then transitioned to a resident Gentile household, so Paul's mission begins among Jews of the Diaspora and then also transitions to Gentiles. When Luke comes to reporting about Paul's ministry to Jews and Gentiles he adapts his narrative, with modifications, to his earlier narrative about Peter in Western Judea.

8.4.3.1. Paul's first prophetic tour and its aftermath in Jerusalem (Acts 13.1-15.35)

The following bar graph illustrates how Luke proportions and divides his narrative episode by episode.

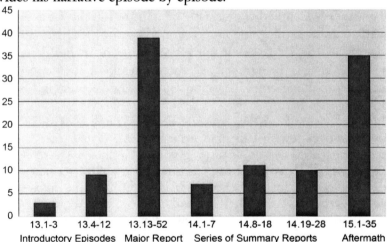

Paul's so-called 'first missionary journey' (hereafter, 'first prophetic tour') begins about ten or more years after his prophetic commissioning in Damascus (9.1-19).[9] This tour is about the team

---

[9] For a brief discussion of the chronology of Paul's missionary journeys see S.E. Porter, 'Chronology, New Testament', in Craig A. Evans and Stanley E. Porter (eds.), *Dictionary of New Testament Background* (Downers Grove, IL: InterVarsity Press, 2000), pp. 201-208.

of Barnabas and Saul and their helper, John Mark. It sets out from Antioch in Syria, moves across the water to Cyprus and finally advances onto the Anatolian highlands of Turkey where, Luke reports, churches were established in the Galatian cities of Pisidian Antioch, Iconium, Lystra, and Derbe. With modifications, Luke reports about the progress of this tour according to the narrative pattern which he developed when he earlier narrated the events of Peter's ministry in Judea.

For the purposes of this chapter I will focus my discussion on several select features of Luke's narrative, rather than giving a complete exposition of the narrative. First, Luke explicitly identifies Barnabas and Saul to be 'prophets and teachers' (Acts 13.1). This identification makes explicit for Barnabas the significance of his earlier experiences of the Spirit (11.24) and for Saul when he was filled with the Spirit (9.17). Knowing that Barnabas and Saul are prophets helps Luke's readership better understand: 1) Paul's conflict with the Jewish false prophet, Bar-Jesus (13.6-17), 2) the boldness of their witness (13.42, compare 4.31), 3) their role as 'a light for the Gentiles' (13.47, compare Isa. 49.6), and 4) the many 'signs and wonders' which they performed (14.3). It is at this point that Luke first identifies this team of prophets as apostles. In other words, Barnabas and Saul are prophets who are 'sent out' to bring the light of salvation to the Gentiles (14.4).

A second feature is the difference between the summary introductory reports which Luke gives for Peter's prophetic tour (Acts 9.32-43) and which he gives for Paul's prophetic tour (13.1-11). Having already written extensive reports about Peter's Spirit-baptized, Spirit-empowered, and Spirit-filled ministry in Jerusalem, Luke is content to imply the same reality for Peter's ministry in western Judea. This work of the Spirit is implied in Peter's role as the agent for the healing of Aeneas and the raising of Tabitha from the dead. But for the recommissioning of Barnabas and Saul, Luke makes the work of the Spirit explicit. He writes that the Holy Spirit said, 'Set apart for Me Barnabas and Saul for the work to which I have called then' (13.2). This recommissioning means for Luke that Barnabas and Saul have been, 'sent out by the Holy Spirit' (13.4). These two references to the Spirit are programmatic for the rest of the narrative. In other words, from the beginning to the (implied) end of the narrative Barnabas and Saul minister as Spirit-filled prophets (13.9, 52).

A third feature is the transition for Barnabas and Saul between ministering to Jews and ministering to Gentiles. As part of his commissioning in Damascus (Acts 9.15-17) to witness about Jesus to Gentiles, Paul is also called to witness about Jesus to Jews. In other words, just as Peter ministered to both Jews and Gentiles on his first prophetic tour, so Paul will also minister to both Jews and Gentiles on his first and subsequent tours. Paul's strategy is to minister to Jews *first* and then to the Gentiles (13.46). This, in fact, is what the Lord commanded (13.47). Since their ministry to the Gentiles fulfills the prophecy of Isaiah, it is a secondary fulfillment, of which Jesus is the first (Lk. 2.29-32).

The ministry of Barnabas and Saul (a.k.a. Paul [Acts 13.9]) to the Jews appears to have ready success for Luke simply reports in Salamis, 'they *began* to proclaim the Word of God in the synagogues of the Jews' (13.5). Journeying across the island to Paphos their witness triumphs in two opposite ways: 1) Paul, filled with the Spirit, curses a Jewish false prophet who is opposing their witness, and 2) the Roman proconsul 'believed ... being amazed at the teaching of the Lord' (13.6-12). Opposition and belief also typify the responses to their witness in Pisidian Antioch. On the one hand, many Gentiles believed and, on the other hand, Paul and Barnabas enacted Christ's curse (they shook off the dust of their feel [13.51, compare Lk. 9.5; 10.11, 12]). In spite of the opposition which these prophets experience in city after city their tour triumphs in the midst of this persecution.

On this first prophetic tour of theirs, Barnabas and Paul experience what it means to be rejected prophets – first by some Diasporan Jews and second by some disciples in Jerusalem. Luke has earlier foreshadowed this 'rejection' motif, initially for Jesus (Lk. 4.24-30) and most recently for Peter (Acts 11.1-3). Jesus identified this rejected prophet motif by the maxim, 'no prophet is welcome in his home town' (4.24). Now Paul and Barnabas will experience similar opposition to their prophetic mission to the Gentiles. Returning to Antioch in Syria from Pisidian Antioch, Iconium, Lystra, and Derbe (13.15–14.28) they reported that God, 'had opened a door of faith for the Gentiles' (14.27). However, after a long time some men came from Judea and began teaching the brethren, 'unless you are circumcised according to the custom of Moses, you cannot be saved' (15.1). Whether or not these teachers were some of the same ones who had earlier agitated against Peter (11.1-3) they had a similar mindset. But they have escalated the issue of witnessing to Gentiles from the level of table fellowship to the level of salvation itself.

The teaching of these agitators from Jerusalem jeopardized the very nature of Paul's calling to witness about Jesus to the Gentiles (9.15-17). It discounted Paul's teaching about being saved on the basis of faith and replaced it by the principle of law-keeping. The issue is whether Gentiles can be saved by faith alone or must they also become proselytes to Judaism (i.e. undergo circumcision, baptism, and mandatory sacrifice)[10] in order to be saved. Not surprisingly, Luke reports that Paul and Barnabas 'had great dissension with them' (15.2). On one level at stake was the legitimacy of Paul's calling, but at a more foundational level at stake is whether Christianity must remain as one sect among others within Judaism, or might it break away as an independent faith. The so-called Jerusalem Council will decide (15.1-35).

Though the Jerusalem Council will publicly rule on the issue, they actually would not decide it. It is God's decision. This decision is already, before they meet, decided by God. At the Council meeting Peter testifies, 'God made a choice among you, that by My mouth the Gentiles should hear the word of the gospel and believe' (15.7). Barnabas and Paul then report 'what signs and wonders God had done through them among the Gentiles' (15.12). Finally, James adds that even the Prophets wrote about the salvation of the Gentiles (15.14-21). And so, for the second time the Gentile mission is vindicated. Will these two decisions which are made in Jerusalem in support of the Gentile mission remain unchallenged? Will the decision stand? Will the very nature of Christianity as Paul proclaimed it prevail? Paul's second and third prophetic tours will decisively determine the issue.

---

[10] S. McKnight, 'Proselytism and Godfearers', in Craig A. Evans and Stanley Porter (eds.), *Dictionary of New Testament Background* (Downers Grove, IL: InterVarsity Press, 2000), pp. 844-45.

8.4.3.2. Paul's Second Prophetic Tour (Acts 15.36–18.23)

Once again, the following bar graph illustrates how Luke proportions and divides his narrative episode by episode.

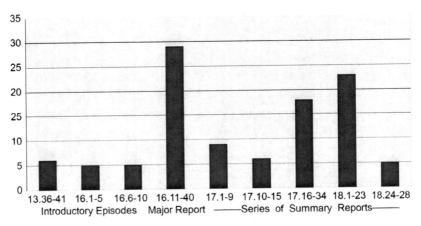

Luke established his narrative pattern for reporting about the prophetic tours to the Gentiles first with Peter (Acts 9.32–11.18), and he then adjusted it when he reported about Paul's first prophetic tour (13.1–15.35). When he next reports about a second prophetic tour he continues to use the same narrative strategy: 1) a series of introductory episodes (15.36–16.10), 2) a major report of Paul's ministry at Philippi (16.1-40), and a series of summary reports following Paul from Philippi to Thessalonica, Berea, Athens, and Corinth. However, in contrast to his earlier reports about Peter's and Paul's first prophetic tours, in his report about this tour there is no Aftermath in Jerusalem.

There are personnel changes for the team which now accompanies Paul. Because of an irreconcilable dispute with Paul, Barnabas, accompanied by his nephew, John Mark, returns to Cyprus after the Jerusalem Council (Acts 15.36-41). Therefore, as a result, Silas replaces Barnabas, Timothy replaces John Mark, and at Troas the author of Luke–Acts joins the team. These changes signify two important changes: 1) from this time forward Luke will be a sometime companion of Paul, which means that Luke becomes a firsthand participant in some of the history which he reports, and 2) Silas is, like Barnabas and Paul, also a prophet, which means that the team on the second tour is fully a team of prophets as was the team on the first tour (15.32). Not only is Paul's new team a team of prophets, it is also a team of Roman citizens (16.37).[11] This will have a bearing on Paul's relationship with Roman law and Roman officials extending through to the end of Paul's life.

Luke's narrative strategy has been to include at least one programmatic report about the Holy Spirit in the short reports which introduce the narrative. For Peter's first prophetic tour the activity of the Spirit is implied in the miracles of healing and raising the dead (Acts 9.32-43); for Paul's first prophetic tour the Holy Spirit initiates the timing of the tour (13.2). Now, in his narrative about Paul's second tour, he continues to emphasize the work of the Spirit (16.6-10). This is about the leading of the Spirit. At the first, the leading is negative. Apparently, Paul has purposed to travel to Asia (whose leading city is Ephesus). The Holy Spirit forbids him to do this (16.7). Paul, therefore, turns toward Bithynia. Once again the Spirit forbids this (16.7). At this point God's leading becomes positive and, at Troas, Paul is called through a prophetic vision to go to Macedonia (16.8-10). This leading by Spirit and by vision echoes Peter's earlier leading to Caesarea by vision and by Spirit (10.9-22). These programmatic references to the Spirit are Luke's way of telling his readership that the story which he is about to tell is the story of God at work by Spirit-empowered, Spirit-called, and Spirit-led prophets.

On his second prophetic tour Paul continues to follow the strategy which he (and Peter earlier) had already used. This strategy continues to be to witness about Jesus to Jews first, and then, as circumstances unfold, to witness about Jesus to Gentiles. For example, in Philippi, a Roman colony, there is no synagogue so on the Sabbath Paul seeks out a 'place of prayer' outside the city where worshippers would gather. In contrast to Philippi in the cities of Thessalonica, Berea, Athens, and Corinth Paul first witnessed to synagogue congregations (17.1-18.17).

On his inaugural prophetic tour Paul, a true prophet had been forced to confront a Jewish false prophet who was attempting to

---

[11] Brief articles on Roman citizenship and colonization can be found in *The Oxford Classical Dictionary* (ed. N.G.L. Hammond and H.H. Scullard; Oxford: Oxford University Press, 2nd edn, 1970), pp. 243-44; 265-66.

thwart his witness (13.6-12). This confrontation between a true and
a false prophet had echoed Peter's confrontation with Simon the
magician in Samaria (8.18-25). Now for the third time Luke reports
a similar confrontation between two prophets. In Philippi there is a
slave girl, who is apparently a devotee or imitator of the Delphic
oracle (16.16). Day by day she disrupted Paul's witness, much in the
same way that at the beginning of Jesus' ministry a demon-
possessed man interfered with Jesus' teaching (Mk 1.22-27). An-
noyed by this slave girl's activity Paul silenced her by casting out the
Delphic pythonic spirit.[12] Just as Paul's victory in the confrontation
with the Jewish false prophet resulted in the Roman governor at
Paphos coming to faith (13.12), so also the silencing of the slave
girl in Philippi through a variety of dramatic circumstances results
in the salvation of the Philippian jailer and his household (16.19-
34).

In different ways in each city in what modern readers call Europe, i.e. from Philippi south to Corinth, Paul and his companions
establish faith communities. Thus: 1) at Philippi both Lydia's
household and the jailer's household are saved (16.14, 15; 29-34); 2)
in Thessalonica some Jews and many Greeks were persuaded that
Jesus was the Christ (17.4); 3) in Berea many Jews and a number of
prominent Greeks believed (17.12); 4) at Athens some men and
women believed (17.34); and 5) many of the Corinthians were believing and being baptized (18.8). Three of the churches which Paul
established in these cities, namely Philippi, Thessalonica, and Corinth, will later receive letters from Paul. But Luke's reports about
Paul's successful witness are matched by intense, often brutal opposition. For example, at Philippi Paul and Silas were beaten and im-
prisoned (16.19-23); in Thessalonica and later in Berea they were
forced to flee from mob violence (17.1-16); and in Corinth Divine
protection alone kept Paul from being physically assaulted (18.9-17).

Also to be observed is that at Corinth Paul is opposed by a
group of Jews, who not only resist his witness but who also actively
blaspheme Jesus (Acts 18.6). In response to this blasphemy Paul: 1)
enacts a curse (he shook out his garments), 2) pronounces prophetic judgment upon them (your blood *be* upon your own heads [com-

---

[12] John R. Levison, *Filled with the Spirit* (Grand Rapids, MI: Eerdmans, 2009).
Levison interprets Luke's report about Paul and the slave girl at Philippi in a radi-
cally different way. For example, he writes, 'this slave-girl was *not* a threat, that her
divining because she had a pythonic spirit did *not* lie in opposition to his (Paul's)
mission; that her inspiration was *not* illicit' (pp. 320-21).

pare Ezek. 18.13]), and 3) announces that in Corinth from this point on he will go to the Gentiles (18.6). This episode of Jews at the local level rejecting Jesus as their Messiah, with the result that Paul turns to the Gentiles, echoes Paul's earlier experience in Pisidian Antioch (13.46-48). But, in spite of local opposition throughout this prophetic tour, there is no hostile aftermath in Jerusalem as had occurred earlier (13.1-3; 15.1-5). Luke simply reports, 'he set sail from Ephesus. And when he had landed at Caesarea, he went up and greeted the church, and went down to Antioch' (18.22). Luke's readers are left to speculate why at this point in his narrative he does not even identify Jerusalem by name. Perhaps the answer lies in the future, when he reports the tragic aftermath in Jerusalem at the conclusion of Paul's third prophetic tour (21.15–22.21).

8.4.3.3. Paul's Third Prophetic Tour and Its Aftermath (Acts 19.1–22.21)

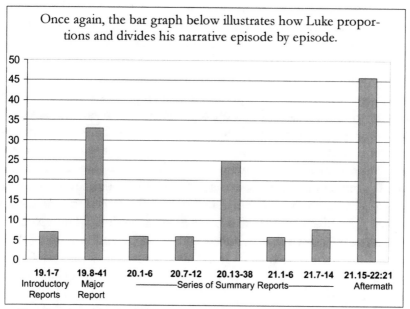

By the time that Luke's readership has advanced to this point in the history of the prophetic missions to the Gentiles, the alert reader knows what to expect. And (s)he will be right. For example, Luke for the fourth time begins his narrative with a short introductory report which identifies an activity of the Holy Spirit (Acts 19.1-7). (S)he will recall that earlier introductory reports have, in turn, emphasized: 1) the (implied) *empowering* of the Holy Spirit (9.32-43), 2)

the *initiative* of the Spirit (13.1-4), and 3) the *leading* of the Spirit (16.6-8). Now, Luke's fourth and final introductory report emphasizes that Paul is the agent for the Ephesian Twelve to be baptized in the Holy Spirit.

The alert reader will also have anticipated that Luke will follow up his introductory report (Acts 19.1-7) with a major report about Paul's prophetic witness in one city: Ephesus (19.8-41). Earlier in his narratives Luke had reported about Paul's desire to visit Asia (=Ephesus, 16.6-8). More recently, Paul had spent three months visiting this city while he was enroute from Corinth to Jerusalem and Antioch, promising, 'I will return to you again if the Lord wills' (18.18-21). As Luke reports Paul does return to Ephesus, which will prove to be the final city where he will be free to give a bold,[13] prophetic witness to Jews and Gentiles.

In Ephesus Paul's prophetic ministry to Jews and Gentiles includes extraordinary miracles, an episode involving Jewish exorcists (=false prophets), and mob violence against Paul (Acts 19.11-41). But by now Luke's readership has observed that no opposition to Paul's prophetic witness, no matter how vigorous, no matter whether it comes from false prophets, unbelieving Jews or Gentiles; no matter whether it is mob action or official, can thwart the advance of the gospel. Paul's experience in Ephesus confirms this. For example, within two years, not only does everyone in the city hear his prophetic witness, but 'all who lived in Asia hear the word of the Lord, both Jews and Greeks' (19.10). Further, the seven sons of Sceva's failed attempt at exorcism (19.13-17) resulted in fear within the city and the name of the Lord being magnified. The result of Paul's prophetic witness by word and by signs and wonders (19.8-12) is that many believed (19.18). This is so much so that the Christian faith seriously undermined the dominant cult of Diana = Artemis (19.21-41).[14]

---

[13] Note, Luke's report about 'bold witness' always presupposes 'being filled with the Holy Spirit' (e.g. Acts 2.4, 29; 4.31; 9.17, 27, etc.).

[14] For a discussion of Ephesus and its Temple see Harold W. Hoehner, *Ephesians: An Exegetical Commentary* (Grand Rapids, MI: Baker Academic, 2002), pp. 78-89.

The series of summary reports which follow Luke's Ephesus narrative show Paul in his role as pastor rather than evangelist; that is, he exhorts disciples rather than evangelizes nonbelievers. He spends three months doing this in Macedonia and Greece (20.1-3). Enroute to Jerusalem, but while he is at Troas, he raises a young man, Eutychus, from the dead (20.7-17), a miracle which is uniquely associated with charismatic prophets such as Elijah, Elisha, Jesus, and Peter (1 Kings, 2 Kings, Luke, Acts). At Miletus he affirms: 1) he has been led by the Holy Spirit (20.22, 23); and 2) he has been obedient and faithful (20.26). Finally, at Tyre and Caesarea he is also the subject of prophecies about what awaits him when he comes to Jerusalem, namely, his fate as a rejected and persecuted prophet (21.1-14). These prophecies cast a dark shadow over his visit to Jerusalem – perhaps darker than on any previous visit to this center of Judaism. Both Paul and his companions and also Luke's readership know beyond any doubting that Paul faces a tragic reception in this city that kills the prophets (Lk. 11.45-52; 13.31-35).

Luke reports the aftermath to Paul's third prophetic tour, writing, 'when we came to Jerusalem, the brethren received us gladly' (21.17). Moreover, the following day Paul met with James and the Elders, testifying about 'the things which God had done among the Gentiles through his ministry' (21.19). Hearing Paul's report, these leaders of the church in Jerusalem 'began glorifying God' (21.20a). This initial reception of Paul appeared to give the lie to the ominous prophecies which had so recently been given. But the situation begins to change almost immediately. As a counter to Paul's report about what God had done among the Gentiles, James reports about the Jewish believers in Jerusalem: 'You see, brother, how many thousands there are among the Jews of those who have believed' (21.20b). This is good news, indeed! But then James adds the ominous words that these believers 'are all zealous for the law' (21.20c). James next informs Paul that he is reputed to have taught Diasporan Jews 'to forsake Moses, telling them not to circumcise their children nor to walk according to the customs' (21.21). Suddenly, Luke's readership understands that the compromise decision made at the Aftermath to Paul's first prophetic tour was, at best, a temporary solution. James' words inform Paul that something must be done to rehabilitate Paul's reputation. James instructs Paul to undergo, at his own expense, a public purification rite to demonstrate that he still lives according to the Law (21.22-25). Hearing this, what may have flashed through Paul's mind? No one, not even Luke ever learned. Paul simply followed James' instructions (22.26). And so, the tragedy unfolds with the result that Paul is soon victim of angry mob violence, arrest, imprisonment, a plot to kill him, two years' imprisonment at Caesarea, followed by another two years of house arrest in Rome. The tragedy in this aftermath is not found in the 'bonds and afflictions' which Paul experiences in Jerusalem, Caesarea, and Rome. The Holy Spirit, by revelation and prophecy had prepared Paul for this (20.22-24; 21.1-14). No, the real tragedy is that James, who led the Jerusalem Council with courage, wisdom, and spiritual insight now, however inadvertently, not only sends Paul into danger and death, but also, by default, allowed a permanent wedge to be driven between believing Jews and believing Gentiles. From this point forward, believing Judaism is sentenced to becoming a marginalized, declining sect within Christendom.

8.5. Conclusion

This chapter has briefly surveyed some aspects of Luke's 'Gentile Mission' narrative. This narrative, which is central to Acts, tells the story of the prophetic witness of the two leading prophets in Acts, namely, Peter, and Paul. Several conclusions follow from this analysis of Acts 9.1–22.21.

1) Historically and in the present, the Church is enamored by the term 'apostle'. But Luke is not. Though he does use the term apostle, he regularly portrays Peter and Paul functioning in their role as prophets. For Peter this function begins as early as the post-Easter Day of Pentecost when the Spirit was poured out on Jesus' disciples (Acts 2.1-21). Like Jesus earlier (Lk. 24.19), Peter will function as a prophet who is powerful in works and words (Acts 1–12). Similarly, at the beginning of Paul's first two peripatetic tours, Luke identifies the members of the teams to be prophets, thus: 1) Barnabas and Paul (Acts 13.1), and 2) Paul and Silas (13.1; 15.32). Like Peter, Barnabas, Paul, and Silas are all prophets who are powerful in works and words.

2) It is somewhat commonplace for interpreters to impose the Gentile Mission motif upon Luke's narrative as early as his report about the outpouring of the Spirit on the Day of Pentecost. Luke's perspective differs. Of course, like every reader of the Greek Old Testament (the Septuagint), Luke's Bible, Luke knows about the prophecies which foretell a mission to the Gentiles (e.g. Isa. 42.6; 49.6). However, Luke does not introduce an actual, historical witness about Jesus to the Gentiles until he tells the story of Paul's commissioning as the prophetic witness to the Gentiles (Acts 9.15-17). Even so, it is Peter and not Paul, who by vision and by the Spirit is led to witness first to the Gentiles. It is a decade or more after his Damascus Road call and commissioning before the Spirit actually initiates Paul's witness (13.1-3).

3) Before the Gentile Mission begins, Peter, a true prophet, had clashed with a certain Simon the magician (Acts 8.18-24). Similarly, early in his first tour, Paul, a true prophet (13.1) clashes with the Jewish false prophet Bar Jesus (13.6-11). Later, when he is in the Roman colony of Philippi, Paul also clashes with a Gentile fortune teller (16.16-18). In addition to these iconic one-on-one true prophet against false prophet confrontations, there are also more widespread clashes, such as in Ephesus between Paul and the entire religious community which is devoted to the worship of Artemis/Diana (19.23-41).

4) The prophetic witness about Jesus by Peter and by Paul among the Gentiles is inevitably successful or triumphant. It had been triumphant earlier first in Jerusalem (Acts 1–7) and then in Samaria (8.4-40). It is likewise triumphant in Judea, Galatia, and the Aegean world. Its success is best demonstrated by the opposition which it evokes, namely, jealousy, fear, mockery, mob violence, and rioting. The episodes of prophetic witness which Luke reports are not about the slow, steady, progressive, and peaceful advance of the gospel. Rather, more often than not, these episodes are about confrontation and physical violence. But despite this, Spirit-filled prophets, both individuals and teams, continue to heal the sick, raise the dead, cast out demons, witness boldly, and establish faith communities. And so, looking back on years of faithful, Spirit-empowered, Spirit-led prophetic witness, Paul can observe that

from Jerusalem round about the Illyricum the gospel has been fully preached.

5) There is, however, a dark side to this prophetic witness. The triumphant progress of Peter's and Paul's prophetic witness is regularly accompanied by tragedy. It is that tragedy that everywhere their witness about Jesus is accepted by some it is also rejected by many others. Peter and Paul witnessed to the Jews first, but many of them reject Jesus as their Messiah, sometimes with blasphemy. On the other hand, Peter and Paul also witness to the Gentiles, but many of them reject the good news – often under the influence of non-believing Jews. But the greatest tragedy of all is that many believing Jews oppose the message that Gentiles can be saved on the basis of faith. In the end, because of their persistent zeal for the Law, believing Jews forfeit their *leadership* among believing Gentiles.

9

CYCLE SIX, CONTINUED:
PAUL – APOSTLE AND PROPHET-TEACHER TO
GOD'S NEW PEOPLE

This chapter continues to explicate the sixth cycle of turning points in biblical history and theology. As I have been discussing this cycle, the exposition began with a discussion in Chapter 6 about the primary agents of the turning point, namely John the Baptist and Jesus of Nazareth, and their role in the new start according to the Synoptic Gospels (Mark, Matthew, and Luke). Chapter 7 described the new start according to the Gospel According to John, and Chapter 8 advanced the discussion by examining the theme of the numerical growth and geographic spread of God's people. The present chapter (9) focuses on a different kind of growth – the theological growth of God's people. This discussion will be limited to Paul's writings – specifically emphasizing Paul's teaching about the complementary themes of anthropology, that is, his doctrine of humanity, and soteriology, his doctrine of salvation. Chapter 10, which will be about terrestrial and cosmic judgment, will conclude the pattern of this sixth turning point in biblical history and theology.

9.1. Growing the New People of God

The newly-planted churches, which were to be found in the cities along the shores of the northern Mediterranean seaboard, typically suffered various combinations of leadership crises, doctrinal confu-

sion, and moral and religious ambivalence. Paul's two canonical letters to the church in Corinth illustrate many of these issues, including divisions about leadership, cult prostitution, meat offered to
idols, and the doctrines of the charismata (gifts of the Holy Spirit),
and of the resurrection. These problem issues illustrate that numerical growth needed to be followed by spiritual growth – growth in
the grace and in the knowledge of the Lord Jesus Christ (2 Pet.
3.18). So, Paul writes to the church at Corinth to rebuke them for
inappropriate attitudes and conduct, and also to teach them sound
doctrine. Thus, as Paul explains, God used him to sow the seed, and
God used Apollos to water the young plant, but God gives the
growth (1 Cor. 3.6).

9.1.1. Paul: apostle and prophet-teacher to God's people

Whether he is writing to individuals, such as Timothy, or to the
churches, Paul invariably identifies himself as either an apostle of
Jesus (e.g. Rom. 1.1; 1 Cor. 1.1; or Gal. 1.1) or as a servant of Jesus
(1 Thess. 1.1; Tit. 1.1). The result is that in many modern churches,
the name 'Paul' almost always connotes the title 'apostle'. This is
unfortunate, not because to attach the title to his name – Paul the
apostle – is wrong, but it is a far too limited or too narrow description of his ministry. When Paul identifies himself as an apostle, he
is identifying his ambassadorial or delegate status. But though his
status is that of an ambassador (2 Cor. 5.20; Eph. 6.20), his letters
are written as prophetic letters, and he functions as prophetic-
teacher.

To help us understand the fact that Paul has the status of an
ambassador, yet he writes as a prophetic-teacher, the modern Bible
reader needs to remind him/herself that there are a variety of separate, but often overlapping ministry functions in the church of the
first century (and also today). Writing to the church at Ephesus,
Paul identifies some, but not all, of these functions. He observes,
'And He', that is Christ, 'gave some as apostles, and some as prophets, and some as evangelists, and some as pastors and teachers' (that
is, 'pastor-teachers' [Eph. 4.11]). These functions are 'graces' given
by Christ, who, himself, is the **measure** of these gifts (4.10). In
other words, as the primary agent of the sixth start/new start, Jesus
is the 'proto-apostle', 'the proto-prophet', 'the proto-evangelist', 'the
proto-pastor' (shepherd, Jn 10.10), and the 'proto-teacher' (of Israel

[Jn 3.2]). Christ is the fullness of these giftings, but Paul, the servant of Christ, in a limited way, measured up to Christ's standard, as did the other secondary agents who also ministered to the churches of his generation. The following table illustrates these gifts among Christ, the primary agent of the new start, and Paul and the other secondary agents.

Jesus: Primary Agent	Paul: Secondary Agent	Other Secondary Agents
Proto-apostle – sent (*apostellō*) from God	Paul the Apostle (apostolos, 1 Cor. 9.1)	Andronicus and Junias (Rom. 16.7)
Spirit-anointed Prophet (Lk. 3.22; 4.18)	Paul the Prophet (Acts 13.1)	Agabus, Barnabas, Silas (Acts 11, 13, 15)
The Evangelist preaching good news (*evangelion*) (Lk. 4.18)	Paul the Evangelist (preaching good news about Christ, Acts 9.20)	Philip the Evangelist
The Good Pastor (shepherd, Jn 10.10)	Paul the Pastor	Elders: shepherd the flock among you (1 Pet. 5.2)
The Teacher (of Israel Jn 3.2)	Paul the Teacher (Acts 9.26)	Aquila and Priscilla, Apollos (Acts 18.25)

Observation: the above table illustrates that Jesus (anointed by the Holy Spirit), and Paul (filled with the Holy Spirit) manifest the same range of grace gifts. Also, other secondary agents in the church individually manifest one or more of these grace gifts. Indeed, the church itself, called to do the work of the ministry will manifest these and many more grace gifts. But of course, Paul and other secondary agents are all inferior to Jesus, for the Son of God is superior to these redeemed sons of Adam. And Jesus is not only superior, but He, himself, is the one who gives these, and other, grace gifts to his secondary agents in ministry (Eph. 4.11).

The above round-about discussion about Paul's own grace gifts has one purpose. This is to illustrate that though he has the *status* of an apostle, when he writes letters to individuals or churches, he *functions* as a 'prophetic-teacher'. The observation that Paul functions as a prophetic-teacher reminds the modern Bible reader that by-and-large, his letters are circumstantial. This means that their function is to instruct those whom he addresses about specific issues of doctrine and/or practice. Complementing this instruction, he typically exhorts the recipients of his teaching to live by both right thinking and right actions.

Biblical scholars and other informed and thoughtful Bible readers traditionally identify eight major doctrinal subjects. These classic doctrines include the doctrine of revelation, the doctrine of theology proper, of humanity, of sin, of Christ, of salvation, of the church, and, last, but not least, the doctrine of last things. These eight doctrines are usually given Greek or Latin names, for the earliest theologians of the church spoke Greek or Latin. The following table identifies the traditional names which are given to the doctrines.

	Biblical Subject	Formal Theological Name
1	Doctrine of Revelation	Revelation
2	Doctrine of God	Theology Proper
3	Doctrine of Man	Anthropology
4	Doctrine of Sin	Hamartology
5	Doctrine of Christ	Christology
6	Doctrine of Salvation	Soteriology
7	Doctrine of the Church	Ecclesiology
8	Doctrine of Last Things	Eschatology

Each of these doctrines has its own combination of primary, secondary, and tertiary sub-themes. Collectively, the themes follow a natural, logical progression. Paul's letter to the Romans is his most sustained, systematic doctrinal discussion of the full range of Christian doctrine. This chapter (9) will not discuss the full range of doctrine. Rather, it will focus on three interdependent themes, namely, Paul's doctrine of humankind (anthropology), his doctrine of human sinfulness (hamartology), and his doctrine of salvation (soteriology). Other doctrines, such as God as Creator and redeemer have been discussed in earlier 'turning points'. Others, such as 'last things' will be discussed later. This discussion of the theological 'growth' of God's people, which complements the previous discussion of the numerical growth and theological spread of God's people (Chapter 8), will limit itself to Paul's doctrine of humankind, humans as sinners, and God's saving activity.

9.2. Paul Teaches about Humankind and its Sinful Nature

Paul's teaching about humanity is rooted in the Scriptures, specifically in the Genesis narratives about the creation and the fall of humanity (Genesis 1–3). Thus, his doctrine of humankind and human sinfulness begins with Adam. Drawing on the revelation within these narratives, he observes, 'through one man sin entered the world, and death through sin, and so death spread to all men, because all sinned' (Rom. 5.12). He adds that death, and therefore, 'sin [descended] from Adam until Moses' (5.14). But, Paul adds there are two proto-typical persons and not just one – the Adam of creation. These are Adam, who is a type (*tupos*) and also 'the one Man, Jesus Christ' (5.15). In this way, Paul's discussion about Adam and of the origin and pervasiveness of sin Adam's ante-type, Jesus Christ.

9.2.1. Paul teaches about the first and Last Adam

Paul's teaching about humanity depends on a 'first Adam/last Adam' typology (Rom. 5.12-21). But these two proto-typical humans are not equals. Paul explains: Adam is the person of *transgression*; the last Adam (a.k.a. Jesus) is the person of *righteousness*. The first person brought *condemnation*; the last brought the free gift of *grace*. Adam brought *disobedience*; the last Adam gave *obedience*. As a result, Adam brought *death*; Jesus brought *eternal life*. Therefore, Paul concludes, God forbid that his people of the new humanity, which is characterized by righteousness, grace, obedience and eternal life, should not continue in sin (6.1).

Within months of writing to the saints at Rome about the first and last proto-typical men, Adam and Jesus, Paul writes to the church at Corinth about these two shapers of humanity and destiny (1 Cor. 15.45-49). His context in this discussion is the contrast between the natural body and the spiritual body (15.44). The contrast includes the following differences:

The First Man (Adam)	The Last Man (Jesus)
Adam was a living soul.	Jesus becomes a life-giving Spirit.
Adam was from the earth, earthly.	Jesus is from heaven, heavenly.
Humanity bears the image of the earthly.	Jesus' followers bear the image of the heavenly.
Flesh and blood cannot inherit the Kingdom of God.	The dead in Christ shall be changed.
The perishable do not inherit the imperishable.	The dead (in Christ) will be raised imperishable.

The monumental contrast between what the first Adam brought to humankind and what Jesus, the last Adam, effects by gift and by grace elicits the following response: 'Therefore ... be steadfast, immovable, always abounding in the work of the Lord, knowing that your toil is not in vain in the Lord' (15.58).

9.2.2. Paul teaches about the sinful nature

By the time that Paul first begins to write his pastoral letters of instruction and exhortation, he is already an experienced teacher (Acts 11.32). From reading these letters, it is evident that he is already well-versed in the lively art of metaphor. For example, when he teaches about the church, he uses metaphors such as, 'the body', 'the Temple', and 'a marriage' (1 Cor. 12.14-28; Eph. 2.26-28; 5.22-32). Similarly, when he teaches about the legacy of the first Adam upon contemporary humankind, he also uses a variety of metaphors.

9.2.2.1. Two metaphors of the sinful nature

Paul describes the sinful human nature as both 'the flesh' and 'the old man'. He employs the metaphor of 'the flesh' in Gal. 5.1-25 and Rom. 8.1-11. Paul writes about 'the flesh' in the context of his teaching about Christian liberty observing, 'it was for freedom that Christ set us free' (Gal. 5.1). As he begins his discussion, the term 'the flesh' refers to the Jewish rite of circumcision (5.2). This is a boundary marker or sign of membership within Judaism. At this point, 'the flesh' is morally neutral. Paul goes off on a word and the term 'the flesh' becomes a negative metaphor. And so, he writes, 'do not turn your freedom into an opportunity for the flesh' (5.13).

The metaphor is no longer describing a bodily substance. It now describes the domain of sin; a collection of sinful attributes and works. These sinful works are evident, that is, they are tangible and observable (5.19). Examples of the works of the flesh include: '[sexual] immorality, impurity, sensuality, drunkenness, carousing, and things like these' (5.19-21). Paul has previously warned the Galatian believers about these works of the flesh, and this present teaching represents a second warning (5.21b). But the antidote to living by the flesh is not simple abstinence – as an act of the will, as important as this is. No. The works of the flesh need the transforming work of the Spirit. The fruit of this transformation is 'love, joy, peace, patience, kindness, goodness, faithfulness, gentleness, and self-control' (5.22, 23). Paul observes, 'those who belong to Christ Jesus have crucified the flesh with its passions and desires' (5.24). Those who belong to Christ, therefore, need to 'walk by the Spirit' (5.25).

In Rom. 8.1-11, Paul's teaching about 'the flesh' echoes his earlier teaching about 'the flesh' which he gave to the churches in Galatia. His teaching is about those 'who do not walk according to the flesh, but according to the Spirit' (Rom. 8.4). Paul's teaching about 'flesh' and 'Spirit' advances by a series of contrasts, as the following table illustrates.

	Walking According to the Flesh	**Walking According to the Spirit**
8.4	Some walk according to the flesh.	Others walk according to the Spirit.
8.5	These set their minds on the things of the flesh.	These set their minds on the things of the Spirit.
8.6	The mind set on the flesh [leads to] death.	The mind set on the Spirit is life and peace.
8.7 8.8	The mind set on the flesh: Is hostile toward God Does not submit to God Cannot please God.	Believers are not in the flesh: Spirit of God dwells in them Christ is in them.

When Paul wrote about 'flesh' and 'Spirit' to the Galatians, his teaching is an explicit warning to crucify the flesh with its deeds/works and its passions (Gal. 5.21b). When he writes to the church at Rome, the warning is implicit in the contrast between the 'flesh/death' and 'Spirit/life' contrast (8.6). However, later in his

letter to the Roman believers he exhorts, 'let us behave properly ...
Put on the Lord Jesus Christ, and make no provision for the flesh in
regard to its lusts' (13.13, 14).

For Paul, 'the flesh' is an important metaphor to describe the
sinful nature which humans inherit from Adam. Another such metaphor is the 'bath/old man-new man' metaphor which Paul highlights in his letters to the saints in Ephesus and Colossae. In both
the Greco-Roman and Jewish worlds of Paul's day, public baths
were an important aspect of daily life. These baths served various
functions: 1) bodily cleansing, 2) ritual purity, and 3) religious initiation rites. For the Jews, their religious baths included proselyte baptism into the Jewish faith. As Paul teaches about it, the 'bath' metaphor seems to echo the actual experience of proselyte baptism.
Thus, the candidate approaches the bath, puts off his old garments,
goes down into the waters and is baptized, and then exits the bath
and, transformed, puts on new clothes. As a metaphor of the new
life in Christ, the old clothes which the baptismal candidate wears to
his/her baptism symbolizes the 'old man' of his previous sinful nature; the waters of life signify the transformation and initiation into
the new faith community, and the new garments which are put on
signify the new person.

In the hortatory section of his letter to the saints at Ephesus
(Eph. 4.1–6.20), Paul utilizes the 'bath/old man-new man' metaphor. He writes:

> ... that in reference to your former manner of life, you lay aside
> the old self [Lit., 'old man'], which is being corrupted in accord-
> ance with the lusts of deceit, and that you be renewed in the
> Spirit of your mind, and put on the new self [Lit., 'new man'],
> which in the likeness of God has been created in righteousness
> and holiness of the truth (4.22-24).

In this pastoral letter, Paul exhorts, 'Therefore, laying aside falsehood, speak the truth, etc.' (4.25). Here, Paul identifies the 'old man'
to be falsehood, and, in addition, to be thieving, unwholesome
words, grieving the Spirit, bitterness, anger, wrath, clamour, slander,
and malice (4.25-31). Paul's pastoral exhortation, however, is two-
sided. Not only are the saints to lay aside the 'old man' garments,
but they are to put on the 'new man' garments; that is, truth, good
labor, edifying words, grace, kindness, tender-heartedness, and for-

giveness (4.25-32). The old person, 'gives the devil opportunity' (4.27); the new person will act, 'just as God in Christ' also acts (4.32).

Similarly, Paul exhorts the saints at Colossae:

since you have laid aside the old self ['man'], and have put on the new self ['man'] ... put on a heart of compassion ... bearing with one another, forgiving each other ... and beyond all these things put on love, which is the perfect bond of unity (3.9-14).

Paul concludes his old person/new person contrast exhorting, 'Let the peace of Christ rule in your hearts ... [and] let the word of Christ richly dwell within you' (3.15, 16).

Whether Paul utilizes the 'flesh/Spirit' metaphor or the old person/new person metaphor, these metaphors clearly teach that the Christian must wage war against his old, sinful nature. Being in Christ effects the victory of the Spirit over the flesh (Gal. 5.13-26). In this way, 'saints' – born bearing the image of Adam (Rom. 5.12) are in the process of being transformed into the new image of Christ (Rom. 8.28).

9.2.2.2. Human sinfulness: a whole body experience

As an evangelist who worked in both the Greco-Roman and the Jewish cultures, Paul observes that the Gentile world, though it had the witness about God in creation, was guilty of sin (Rom. 1.18-32). Many of his contemporary Jews would have fully agreed with Paul about this. But as a follower of Christ Jesus, Paul came to understand that the Jewish world, in spite of its gift of the Law, was also guilty before God (Rom. 2.1–3.8). Many of Paul's Jewish contemporaries would have vehemently repudiated this insight. Nevertheless, Paul concludes, 'all have sinned and fall short of the glory of God' (3.23). But Paul's indictment of the Gentile and Jewish worlds gets worse. He observes that not only are all of Adam's descendants sinners, but that every part of 'sinful man' is tainted by sin.

Paul reminds his readership in Rome, 'we have already charged that both Jews and Greeks are all under sin' (Rom. 3.9). He then validates this fact by quotations from various Psalms (and also from Isa. 59.7), which teach that from head to toe, humans give themselves to sinfulness. Thus, not only are all humans sinners (3.10-12), but their throats, tongues, lips, mouths, feet, and eyes are instruments for the manifestation of sin (3.13-18). Obviously, Paul does not identify how every part of the human body can be used to effect sinfulness, but his examples demonstrate the inclusiveness of the sinful nature – from head to foot and every part (e.g. heart, hands, etc.) in between. This data from the Scriptures, however, is more than illustrative, though it is that. It is proof so 'that ever mouth may be closed, and all the world may become accountable to God' (3.19). This means that by the works of the Law, no flesh will be justified in his sight (3.20). For those who have eyes to see and ears to hear, Paul has not only proven that sinfulness is pandemic, but that it is absolute – all have sinned. Properly understood, this divine assessment robs humanity of any and all hope, and evokes the plaintive cry, 'Wretched man that I am! Who will set me free from the body of this death?' (7.24).

9.3. Paul Teaches about Salvation

Paul's teaching about humankind indicts humanity before God to be sinful by nature and a sinner by action. This indictment, in and of itself, robs humanity of HOPE. But is Paul's doctrine of sin merely a negative exaggeration of a zealot? Actually, it was Jesus who a generation earlier established the absolute inability of humanity to solve the problem of the sinful nature. Once, when Jesus was travelling on the road going up to Jerusalem to celebrate the Jewish Passover, he observed to his disciples that a rich person, because of his wealth, has no advantage over a poor person for entering into the Kingdom of God. This amazed Jesus' disciples who by their reaction obviously had presumed that wealth was a spiritual asset (Mk 10.17-27). Astonished, they ask, '[if wealth gives no advantage before God], then who can be saved?' (10.26). Jesus teaches, 'with men it is *impossible*' (italics added, 10.27). But Jesus does not leave humanity with no hope of salvation. He, therefore, replies, '[impossible], but not with God; for all things are possible with God' (10.27). So, there is hope for the hopeless. God can do what no person can do. This is good news, indeed! Anointed by the Spirit of the Lord, Jesus preached this good news even to the poor (Lk. 4.18).

Not only can God do what no person on earth can do, but, from the beginning, he has announced that he will deal with the problem: '[the seed of the woman] shall bruise you [the serpent] on the head, and you shall bruise him on the heel' (Gen. 3.15). But this is an enigmatic promise, whose meaning only becomes clear as the turning points in history and theology advance God's saving purposes to their historical fulfillment. Paul, himself, was astutely aware of this historical process. He taught, 'when the fullness of time came, God sent forth his Son, born of a woman, born under the Law, that he might redeem those who are under the Law, that we might receive the adoption as sons' (Gal. 4.4, 5). Thus, God was involved in human history from Adam to Jesus to effect redemption 'at the right time' (Gen. 3.15; Gal. 4.4, 5). Paul emphasizes this point when he writes to Titus about, 'the hope of eternal life, which God, who cannot lie, promised long ages ago, but at the proper time manifested' (Tit. 1.2, 3a). Here, Paul identifies the God of the gospel proclamation to be 'our Savior' (1.3b).

And so, God will do what no one else on earth can do – effect the salvation of the sinner. In addition, God can do what the Law, itself, cannot do for the Jewish sinner. Paul teaches:

> Christ Jesus has set you free from the law of sin and death. For what the Law could not do, weak as it was through the flesh, God did: sending his own Son in the likeness of sinful flesh and as an offering for sin, he condemned sin in the flesh (Rom. 8.2, 3).

Earlier in his letter to the churches at Rome, Paul reminded the saints there about what God had actually done 'in the fullness of time', 'at the proper time'. He writes about:

> Being justified as a gift by his grace through the redemption which is in Christ Jesus; whom God displayed publicly as a propitiation in his blood through faith. This was to demonstrate his righteousness (Rom. 3.24, 25).

Paul brings the threads of his teaching about God the Savior together in Romans 8. Arguably, this is the most profound and comforting single discussion of the doctrine of salvation in all of the New Testament. He begins his teaching about salvation with the triumphant truth that, in spite of the spiritual frustrations which he identified in the previous paragraph (Rom. 7.14-25), 'there is therefore now no condemnation for those who are in Christ Jesus' (8.1). He then moves his discussion forward, recapitulating aspects of his earlier doctrinal teaching (1.16–7.25), and re-emphasizing many of the primary, secondary, and tertiary themes of salvation. This teaching about salvation is robustly Trinitarian, but it seems to fall under two headings: 1) Life in the Spirit (8.1-27), and 2) God is the One who justifies (8.28-39). He concludes his discussion on a higher note of triumph affirming, 'I am convinced that [nothing terrestrial or celestial] shall be able to separate us from the love of God which is in Christ Jesus our Lord' (8.39). And he is so overwhelmed at the mystery and the magnificence of God's mercy that he exclaims: 'Oh, the depth of the riches both of the wisdom and knowledge of God!' (11.33). In these ways, Paul carries his readership to the highlights of his teaching about God's salvation.

9.3.1. Life in the Spirit (Romans 8.1-27)

In earlier chapters of his letter to the saints at Rome, Paul has taught about the works of God in Christ. But in that discussion, he wrote very little about the works of the Holy Spirit. Now, in Romans 8, while not ignoring the saving activity of Christ, he emphasizes the place of the Holy Spirit in the Christian life. For example, following upon his opening statement about the believer's freedom from condemnation, he contrasts 'the law of the Spirit of life in Christ', from 'the law of sin and death' (8.2). Further, those who have this freedom 'do not walk according to the flesh, but [live] according to the Spirit' (8.4). They are the ones who set their mind, not on the flesh, '[but] on the things of the Spirit' (8.5). Therefore, 'the mind [which is] set on the Spirit is life and peace' (8.6). In addition, at Rome, and indeed, throughout the world, Christians do not live according to the flesh, 'but live in the Spirit since, indeed, the Spirit of God dwells in you' (i.e. believers, 8.9). The obvious corollary is, 'if anyone does not have the Spirit of Christ, he does not belong to Him' (8.9b). Paul's cluster of observations about the Spirit extends beyond this life to the resurrection, for 'he who raised Christ Jesus from the dead will also give life to your mortal bodies through his Spirit who indwells you' (8.11).

Having just taught his readership about the imperceptible experiences of the Spirit, namely, the believer 'lives' in the Spirit and paradoxically, the Spirit 'dwells' in the believer (8.1-11), Paul begins to teach about the more tangible, active works of this Spirit (8.12-17). These works include active, rather than positional, sanctification, being led by the Spirit, adoption as sons, etc. First, Paul reminds his readers about active sanctification. He writes that believers are obligated, 'by the Spirit to put to death the deeds of the body' (8.12, 13). Second, Paul writes about their family relationship with God, observing, 'all those being led by the Spirit of God, these are sons of God' (8.14). At this point, Paul may recall some of his own recent experiences of being led by the Spirit (Acts 16.6-8). Third, Paul assures his readership that the Spirit, who leads God's children, is not a Spirit of slavery, but he is the Spirit of adoption (8.15). This adoption is about the son's 'coming of age', 'about being given adult privileges and responsibilities'. It is about family intimacy – entitlement to address God as 'Abba! Father', as Jesus, himself did. And, it is also about praying the prayer of the Son's submission (Mk 14.36). The cry of sonship (Abba! Father) also assures God's people that they are children of God (8.16). Fourth, of course this status, which the Spirit bestows, also means that God's children are 'heirs', heirs of God and fellow heirs with Christ' (8.17). This guarantees that 'present suffering' (such as Paul, himself, experienced, 2 Cor. 11.21-33) will, of a certainty, be followed by 'future glorification' (8.17). From present sanctification to 'present suffering' (8.12-17), the Spirit leads God's children, brings them to adult maturity, and privileges them in ways that are parallel to Jesus' own relationship to the Spirit. This is 'good news', indeed!

In God's plan of salvation, the work of the Spirit is much larger than the salvation of the individual, or of people from every tribe and tongue and people and nation (Gen. 12.2; Rev. 5.10). It extends beyond humanity to include creation itself. This is because when Adam disobeyed, the very earth – as well as humanity – became tainted by sin (Gen. 3.17, 18; 4.10, *et al.*). Therefore, the plan of salvation must extend to what God had created and then had cursed. Paul does this in Rom. 8.18-27.

By way of transition about his discussion about the Spirit and salvation, in v. 18, Paul repeats the 'present suffering/future glorification' principle which he had identified in 8.17. As only someone who has suffered greatly can do, Paul minimizes present suffering in comparison to future glorification. He writes, '*I consider* (italics added) that the sufferings of the present time are not worthy to be compared with the glory that is to be revealed to us' (8.18). This bold statement is Paul's springboard to discussing the 'redemption' of creation. Earlier in this chapter, we observed that Paul's doctrine of 'man' began with the creation account (Genesis 1, 2). Similarly, Paul's doctrine of the curse upon creation begins with the judgment narrative (Genesis 3). Personifying creation, Paul writes, 'for the anxious longing of the creation waits eagerly for the revealing of the sons of God' (Rom. 8.19). In other words, the redemption of creation is directly dependent upon the salvation of humanity. This relationship between 'curse' and 'salvation' is not permanent: 'creation was subjected to futility … in hope' (8.20). As Paul explains, 'creation itself will be set free from its slavery to corruption into the freedom of the glory of the children of God' (8.21). In fact, 'the whole creation (still personified) groans and suffers the pains of childbirth together until now' (8.22). Paul adds a personal perspective: 'we know' [this] (8.22a) – perhaps signifying the droughts, storms, earthquakes, etc., of which he had direct experience (2 Corinthians 11; Acts 11, 16, 27).

Christian experience is similar to creation's experience, with some significant differences. One difference is that we (Paul and all other believers) have 'the firstfruits of the Spirit' including but not limited to our sonship with God. These firstfruits of the Spirit evoke eagerness for the fullness of our adoption as sons. This fullness of firstfruits is, in fact, the resurrection of the body. In other words, in spite of our present experiences of the Spirit, our salvation experience remains incomplete until the redemption (resurrection) of the body. Therefore, in this life, salvation always has an aspect of hope (8.24), and it is this hope which gives sons a sense of eagerness for the resurrection (8.25).

In this life, the believers' experiences of the Spirit remain 'firstfruits'. They always remain incomplete. This is true of our communication with God. It remains 'firstfruits/incomplete'. This is expressed by the word 'groaning' (*sustenazō*). Therefore, the **groaning** of creation (Rom. 8.22) and the **groaning** of the believer (8.23) are matched by the **groaning** of the Spirit (8.26). In each case, the 'groanings' identify 'inarticulate speech' which transcends the limitations of articulate speech. For the believer, this inarticulate speech is the highest form of speaking to God, BECAUSE it is one of the languages by which the Spirit speaks to his Father (8.26, 27; compare 8.15). Many Bible readers interpret this text to describe 'speaking in tongues' (1 Cor. 12.10; 13.1; 14.1) and/or 'praying in the Spirit' (Eph. 6.18; compare Jude 20).

9.3.2. God is the One who justifies (Rom. 8.28-39)

At some length, Paul has just written about some of the aspects of what it means to live in the Spirit (Rom. 8.1-27). He concluded his discussion with some observations about groaning (praying) in the Spirit (8.26, 27). This is the highest form of communication which humans can have with God, for it is the primordial language by which the Spirit speaks within the Trinity. Now, abruptly, Paul begins to write about the fact that God is the one who justifies (8.28-39). He returns to his teaching about justification written earlier in his letter (3.21–5.10).

9.3.3. God works all things together for good (Rom. 8.28)

Paul resumes his earlier teaching about justification, affirming (what modern readers might identify as) his thesis statement. He writes: 'And we know that God causes all things to work together for good to those who love God, to those who are called according to his purpose' (Rom. 8.28). This work of God is a shared theological/experiential principle, for it is something that 'we know'. Therefore, Paul is not introducing a new principle for a new insight. Though he has neither planted the church in Rome, nor even visited it, Paul knows that he has this 'knowledge' in common with his readers.

This theological/experiential knowledge is, 'that God causes all things to work together for good' (8.28). In the context of what he has just written, this knowledge would include the 'present sufferings' which are the prelude to 'future glorification' (8.17, 18). On a personal level, Paul may be thinking about his beating in Philippi at the hands of the magistrates there, and the 'good' salvation which came to the household of the jailer as a result (Acts 16.31). On the larger canvas of history, the great judgments which God imposed on humankind also work together for good, because at appropriate times, they wipe the slate clean, and, thereby, prepare the way for a new start. Of course, all Christians recognize that the greatest act of human sinfulness in the world, namely the crucifixion of Jesus, unleashed the greatest possible good – the blessing of potential justification. This is from God's side a generous, gracious, merciful, and loving thesis.

To interpret this theme out of context will invariably lead to various distortions. Paul is not proposing that every catastrophe of nature, or the oppression of totalitarian governments, or the brutal suffering of war, *et al.* is good. Yet some Christians take this as a theological truism, twisting Scripture and shaming the very character of God. In context, Paul's meaning is unambiguous. Paul is affirming the redemptive goodness of God from the sin of Adam to the justification which God effects.

9.3.4. The fivefold chain of justification (8.29-30)

Immediately after advancing his thesis – that God can do redemptively what no one else on earth can do – Paul writes about the broad, sweeping, extra-terrestrial scope of salvation. As Paul understands it, redemptive history begins in eternity (God foreknew) and, ultimately, will also end in eternity (God glorified) (Rom. 8.29, 30). As he writes about God's plan of salvation, which begins and ends in eternity, he identifies five links in a chain of redemptive history. Thus, God's foreknowing works together with God's predestining, which together work with God's calling, justifying, and glorifying activity. This five-link chain of salvation is not fully comprehensive; it is representative and illustrative. The Bible reader recognizes that Paul could have identified alternative and/or additional links in the chain. For example, he could have constructed his chain from links such as God wills, he redeems and/or reconciles, and raises the dead. One point of this observation is to caution the Bible reader/interpreter about attributing absolutist status to these terms. They make salvation much too narrow. Often, Paul writes about the eternal purposes of God using different language which *adds equally important* nuances to the doctrine of salvation.

The following table identifies the Greek words which lie behind the English translations with which Bible readers are so familiar. The table illustrates that Paul expresses his theological understanding of the broad sweep of terminology in the common everyday Greek language of the common people. He does not use some technical, esoteric, or sacred language which only the 'initiated' might understand. For example, the first two links in the chain of salvation, 'he foreknew (*proegnō*), and he foreordained (*proōrisen)*', describe the beginning process of salvation in eternity. But no reader of Paul's letter has any frame of reference for understanding words about eternity. This is particularly true for the term, '*proōrisen*', which is traditionally translated by the English language word, 'predestined', but this is misleading and is not justified by the context in which Paul writes. In this contextual frame of reference, predestination is about being 'conformed to the image of Christ' (8.29), and elsewhere it is about the elect being 'adopted as sons' (Eph. 1.5). *These two contexts mean that God determined beforehand to treat those whom he would justify as adult sons.* In these contexts, predestination has nothing to do with the God of the Calvinists predestining some sinners to heaven and others to hell.

English Translation	Greek Word	Basic Meaning
God foreknew	*proegnō*	Know before about a matter
he foreordained	*proōrisen*	Determine beforehand
he called	*ekalesen*	Express something aloud; summon
he justified	*edikaiōsen*	Justify, set right (in connection with forgiveness of sins predicated through Jesus)
he glorified	*edozasen*	Grant of higher status

The next two links in the chain of salvation, he called and he justified, happen in time. Assuming that the above observations about the meaning of the term, 'he foreordained', are correct, God's 'calling' is about the service to God which all of his people are commissioned to perform. This interpretation is supported by Paul's salutation at the beginning of the letter. There, he identifies himself as, 'Paul, a *bond-servant* of Christ, *called* as an apostle' (italics added, Rom. 1.1; compare Acts 9.15). Clearly, the calling is about servanthood and apostleship. It is not about 'election' to salvation. And so, it is for the term, 'he justified', which will be discussed in the following verses of Romans (8.31-34). The fifth and final link in the chain, 'he glorified' is a transitional term, shifting the perspective from initial glorification on earth in the present to complete/final glorification in eternity. In another letter, Paul observes, 'But we all, with unveiled face, beholding as in a mirror the glory of the Lord, are being transformed into the same image from glory to glory, just as from the Lord, the Spirit' (2 Cor. 3.18). Clearly, being glorified is a process (like metamorphosis), and ultimately guarantees that those who are foreordained will be conformed to the image of Christ. In other words, those created in the image of God (Gen. 1.27), but tainted by indwelling sinfulness (3.1-27), in God's saving process, will ultimately experience a greater glory, namely, the eternal glory of the Lord.

9.3.5. God is the One who justifies (Rom. 8.31-39)

Earlier in his letter to the Romans, Paul has affirmed that believers in Christ who have fallen short of the glory of the Lord (Rom. 7.14-21) are, nevertheless, free from condemnation because they are 'in Christ' (8.1). Their freedom from condemnation has a judicial or legal nuance or aspect, which Paul illustrates by having his readership image a court scene with him (8.31-34).

Persons	Function
God sits as judge	God is the one who justifies
The Devil (implied) is the prosecutor	The Devil lays a charge against God's elect
The Prisoner	God's elect (tainted by a sinful nature [7.14-21])
The Counsel for the defense	Jesus intercedes for the elect
God's verdict	(implied) Guilty as charged
God's sentence	Guilty, but ACQUITED!
Basis for the sentence of acquittal	Jesus has died, paying the penalty for the believer's sins

The above table illustrates that first and foremost 'God is for us' (8.31). In context, Paul has demonstrated this by identifying the five links in the chain; namely, God foreknew, foreordained, called, justified, and glorified his people (8.29, 30). Since God has brought the process full circle – from eternity to eternity – and since God has paid the penalty for all human sinfulness (including the believer's) – he did not spare his own Son – and even though the Prosecutor's charges are true – the God who has done everything for us that is necessary DOES NOT CONDEMN; HE JUSTIFIES.

This is the gospel. It is the good news that God does not condemn the believer. Neither does he ignore or condone sin. He condemned sin vicariously by giving his Son to die a substitutionary death. Therefore, having himself paid the penalty for sin, he justifies the believer when he falls short of the glory of God. Paul is not ashamed to declare this gospel, for it is the power of God unto salvation (Rom. 1.15, 16). Since God justifies the sinner, exercising his authority and prerogative as Judge, God's people 'overwhelmingly conquer through him who loves us' (8.37). It is true! God can do (for his people) what no one else on earth or in the heavens can undo. Nothing 'shall be able to separate us from the love of God, which is in Christ Jesus our Lord' (8.39). With Paul, all of God's people can exclaim:

> Oh! The depth of the riches both of the wisdom and knowledge of God! How unsearchable are his judgments and unfathomable his ways! FOR WHO HAS KNOWN THE MIND OF THE Lord, OR WHO BECAME HIS COUNSELLOR? OR WHO HAS FIRST GIVEN TO HIM THAT IT MIGHT BE PAID BACK TO HIM AGAIN? For from him and through him and to him are all things. To him be the glory forever, Amen (Rom. 11.33-36).

Not surprisingly, the letter to the saints at Rome ends with a doxology: 'to the only wise God, through Jesus Christ, be the glory forever, Amen' (16.27).

10

Cycle Six, Continued:
Judgment – The Climax of History

There is a well-known cliché which aptly describes some people. It is that you cannot see the forest for the trees. In other words, the person is so focused on the individual tree – the small, detailed picture – that they are unable to see the forest – the big picture. When discussing the sixth cycle of turning points in biblical history and theology, the cliché needs to be reversed: 'you cannot see the trees for the forest'. In this case, because the literature of the turning point is, with minor exceptions, the entire New Testament, the individual tree, such as the 'judgment' theme may be lost sight of. This chapter focuses on God's judgment upon the terrestrial and celestial enemies of God and his people. This will bring our discussion of the sixth cycle to an end.

The judgments of God upon a sinful world have never been a 'darling' doctrine. And that is how it should be, for in the words of one writer, 'all discipline (one aspect of judgment) for the moment seems not to be joyful, but sorrowful' (Heb. 12.11). And so it is for God's judgments, however necessary they are. God is always a reluctant judge, and therefore, his judgments are always tempered by patience, longsuffering, love, mercy, and grace. Though each cycle of turning points ends in judgments, no judgment is capricious or inappropriate. Paul's doctrine of humanity and sin makes explicit what is everywhere implicit in the Bible, namely, 'all (that is both the Jewish and the Gentile worlds) have sinned and fallen short of the glory of God' (Rom. 3.23). The sixth cycle ends with God's kindness and goodness still rejected by 'the many' and as a result, God's just judgments upon an unrepentant world order will bring that world order to a well-deserved and necessary end.

10.1. Judgments: Global and Cosmic

Many Christians throughout history have projected their individual and/or group sentiments onto God. In this way Christians have, ironically, tended to make God after their own image. A propos to our subject, many Christians have turned God into a pacifist. Their God as 'human pacifist' does not believe in capital punishment or warfare. However, in spite of these fine sentiments, such as, 'make love, not war', 'love conquers all', *et al.*, God is not a pacifist. And, of course, neither is he a bully. Rather, he is a holy and righteous judge and when it is appropriate, he is a warrior. This is why history as we know it will end in one final great battle between God and his enemies. English language Bible readers identify this last battle as, 'The battle of Armageddon'.

When they think about it, Bible readers identify God's two fundamental works to be Creation and Redemption. In a manner of speaking this is correct, but it can be refined as follows: 1) God is the One who creates, and 2) God is the One who justifies. Point two needs to be refined further so that, as the One who justifies, his verdict is that some put their trust in Him, are found guilty, but are acquitted on the basis of Jesus' atoning Redemption. However, as the One who justifies, the rest of humanity is found guilty, and because they do not put their trust in Him, are condemned – and sentenced to their just punishment. The book of Revelation is primarily about the just judgment/punishment which befalls those who refuse to submit to Him.

10.1.1. John's vision about God (Rev. 4.1-11)
Who is this God who presumes to condemn and punish sinful humanity? Who is this One who acts as it the whole world is accountable to himself? The answer is the God who is the creator. He is also the God of new beginnings – such as the new starts which punctuate human history. John's prophetic vision of the creator God is reported in Rev. 4.1-11. In context, this vision follows his earlier vision of the Son of Man (1.9-20), who will systematically

assess the spiritual condition of the 'seven churches of Asia' (2.1–
3.22). After this two-part context, John has a vision about, 'One
who is sitting on the throne' (4.2). This is an actual vision, for he is,
'in the Spirit' (compare 1.10). In reporting his vision, he must describe the indescribable One. The One who made humans in his
own image cannot be described by the image of humans. Therefore, John does not see one like Adam; he sees some One greater.
This One can best be pictured in terms of light, color, and radiance:
the colors of the rainbow and semi-precious stones such as jasper,
sardius, and emerald (4.4). This One is enthroned in the center of a
community of living beings. This community includes 24 elders,
who apparently represent the twelve sons of Jacob (i.e. Israel) and
the twelve apostles (i.e. the Church). It also includes four living
creatures – apparently the cherubim of Ezekiel's visions (4.8; Ezek.
1.10).

The 24 elders and the four living creatures function as two
'praise and worship' teams. The four living creatures sing the ancient song of the seraphim, saying, 'Holy, Holy, Holy is the Lord
God, the Almighty, who was and who is and who is to come' (Rev.
4.8; compare to Isa. 6.2) This worship by creatures of creation (lion,
calf, human, and eagle) echoes the LORD God's command, both to
Israel and to the Church: 'You shall be holy, for I am holy' (Lev.
11.44; 19.2; 1 Pet. 1.16). Complementing the adoration of the Holy
One, the 24 elders worship Him, saying 'Worthy art thou, our Lord
and our God, to receive glory and honor and power; for thou didst
create all things, and because of Thy will they existed, and were created' (Rev. 4.11). This worship is unceasing. It also compensates for
the inadequate worship which is given to God on earth by the
twelve sons of Jacob and of the twelve apostles, that is, of all of
God's people of both testaments. In heaven, these representatives
of creation give in full measure, 'glory and honor and thanks to him
who sits on the throne' (4.9).

This, then, is the God of all creation. He is pure and radiant
light. He is the royal, sovereign God sitting on his throne (in authority and power). He is the eternal One (who was, is, and is to
come). He is the thrice Holy One (Father, Son, and Holy Spirit).
And he is the creator of everything that exists. But not all of his
creation heeds the command to pursue holy living. Not all of his

creation submits to his sovereign authority and gives to him that perfect obedience which he deserves. Their stories of unholy attitudes and conduct and willful disobedience are written in a book which has been sealed with seven seals (5.1). The breaking of these seven seals will, therefore, unleash God's judgments upon the earth (6.1-8, *et al.*). These judgments include, but are not limited to, conquest, warfare, agricultural scarcity, and death. They are carried out by the Lion of the tribe of Judah, who is also known as the Lamb (5.5-6; 6.1).

10.1.2. John's two visions about Jesus (Rev. 1.12-18; 5.1-14)

In addition to and complementing his vision of the One who is sitting on his throne, John also reports two visions about Jesus Christ. The first is a vision about Jesus, revealed to be the Son of Man (1.12-18), and the second vision is about Jesus revealed to be the sacrificial Lamb (5.1-14). Both visions about Jesus lead to him as God's prophet or spokesman of judgments (2.1–3.22; 6.1-8, *et al.*).

Exiled to the island of Patmos, John is 'in the Spirit' on the Lord's day and has a vision of Jesus. The Jesus of his vision is much different than his earlier experience of Jesus, whom he had *seen* with his own eyes, and *handled* with his own hands – the Father's own Son, Jesus Christ (1 Jn 1.1-4). In contrast, the Jesus of his vision is transcendent; and in order to portray this transcendence adequately, he utilizes 'Son of Man' imagery taken from the prophet Daniel (Dan. 7.13). Jesus may be the Son of Man, but as John sees Him, 'his head and his hair were white like wool, like snow'; 'his eyes were like a flame of fire'; 'his feet were like glowing, burnished bronze'; 'his voice was like the sound of many waters'; and 'his face was like the sun shining in its strength' (Rev. 1.13-16). This Son of Man is different than all other 'sons of man', from the first one (Adam) onward (Gen. 2.7). Strengthening the picture, he is, 'the first and the last, the living One', who has defeated death – who has the key of death and Hades (Rev. 1.17-19). Later in Revelation Jesus will break the fourth seal and will unleash 'Death and Hades' upon sinful humanity (Rev. 6.8).

Following the vision, Jesus prophesies through John to the seven churches of Asia: Ephesus, Smyrna, Pergamum, Thyatira, Sardis, Philadelphia, and Laodicea (2.1–3.22). Numbering seven, these actual, individual churches represent the condition of the church at large, in John's day and throughout the generations. Each letter reveals what Jesus knows about the church: 'I know your deeds' (Rev. 2.11, 19, 3.1, 8, 15); 'I know your tribulation' (1.9); 'I know where you dwell' (2.13). Each letter concludes with the call to hear what the Spirit says to the churches (2.7, 11, *et al.*). These prophetic exhortations from Jesus, by the Spirit, through John address both the individual church and the church at-large. The main message (to be discussed in the following section) is that the churches are accountable to the all-knowing Son of Man, who will bless those who 'hear' (i.e. obey) and bring judgment to those who persist in disobedience.

In John's second vision of Jesus, he is portrayed, not as the 'Son of Man', but as the sacrificial, redeemer 'Lamb' (5.1-14). This vision is not an independent one, but is the second, complementary section of John's vision of the Holy, Creator God (4.1-11). The vision is about the tribe of Judah, the 'Root of David' (5.5, compare Gen. 49.9; Isa. 11.1). Thus, the vision shows that the sovereign Lord holds the book (of condemnation) in his right hand (5.1) and a royal descendant (Judah/David) will break the seals, unleashing God's judgments (6.1). But, in the typical fluidity of visionary images, when John looks, he does not see a lion, but, instead, he sees a Lamb (5.6). This Lamb has been sacrificed (and resurrected), for it is standing 'as if slain' (5.6). The image may be that of a Lamb, but it is unearthly for it has seven horns – i.e. it is all powerful (omnipotent) and it has seven eyes – i.e. it is all knowing (omniscient) (5.6c). The One worthy to loose God's judgments upon the earth, then is the royal prince, all powerful and all knowing, worthy because of his sacrifice.

The lion is the lamb, and if the sovereign God is worthy of all praise because he is the Creator (4.11), the Lamb is worthy because he is the Redeemer (5.8). The four living creatures and the 24 elders, who worship the Creator, also worship the Lamb because he is the sacrificial Redeemer Lamb. This Lamb 'didst purchase for God with Thy blood men from every tribe and tongue and people and nation' (5.9). Those who are redeemed, have been made to be 'a Kingdom and priests to out God; and they will reign upon the earth' (5.10; compare to Dan. 7.14, 25). In other words, what God earlier did for Israel in the time of Moses, redeeming them and making them to be a royal priesthood (Exod. 19.5, 6), the Lamb has now done on a larger, universal scale.

This vision of God as Creator and the Son of Man as Redeemer Lamb evokes the greatest, most absolute worship in the cosmos. Thus, myriads of the redeemed blend their voices with the four living beings and the 24 saying, 'worthy is the Lamb that was slain to receive power and riches and wisdom and might and glory and blessing' (Rev. 5.12). In addition, John reports:

> And every created thing which is in heaven and on earth and under the earth and in the sea and all things them (John) heard, saying, 'To him who sits on the throne and to the Lamb, be blessing and honor and glory and dominion forever and ever' (5.13).

Even the Hallelujah chorus, which comes later in the book of Revelation (19.1-10) does not get any better than what John here sees and hears.

10.1.3. John's revelation of judgment and vindication

As the Book of Revelation advances, John's vision of the transcendent Son of Man, who is also the Lamb of God (1.12-16; 5.1-14), and his vision of the One sitting on his throne (5.1-11) give way to scenes of Judgment. No alert Bible reader will be surprised by this shift. For example, **History prepares for it.** Previously, each of the cycles in biblical and historical theology have always ended in judgments. There is nothing in the sixth new start to indicate that this cycle will be different. Moreover, **God's character demands this transition** from the transcendent visions of glory to the grim gloom of Judgment, God is revealed in his attribute of Holiness (5.8), and this holiness spurned cannot go unpunished forever. Finally, **God's people pray for it.** When the Lamb breaks the fifth seal, the faithful martyrs cry out, 'How long, O Lord, holy and true wilt Thou refrain from judging and avenging our blood on those who dwell on the earth' (6.10). And, finally, **God is worshiped for having vindicated his people;** 'Hallelujah … his judgments are true and righteous … [and] he has avenged the blood of his bond-servants' (19.2). Justice (punishment and/or vindication) will not be delayed forever.

As it is revealed in the Book of Revelation, eschatological, apocalyptic, and global judgment has four dimensions. One, it reports about God's chastening judgments upon the sevenfold Church of Asia (Rev. 2.1–3.22). Two, it reports about God's punitive cycles of sevenfold judgments upon the nations of the world (6.1-16.21). Three, God's punitive judgments are upon the Beast, which is the dominant world power (17.1–18.24); and four, the final punitive judgment brings human history, as God's people know it, to an End (19.1-20.15). Cumulatively, these judgments advance history throughout the sixth cycle, from the first coming of Jesus – The Prince of Peace – through to the second coming of Jesus – the Warrior Prince.

10.1.3.1. Jesus announces chastening judgments upon the Church (Rev. 2.1–3.22)

In the book of Revelation Jesus first warns the Church, which is typified or represented by the 'seven Churches' about their actual and/or potential wrong attitudes and actions (2.1–3.22). Many readers may be surprised by this fact. One reason for this surprise is that many Christians expect that once their sins have been forgiven Jesus' exclusive interest for them is in their individual, family, and/or community comfort, security, and even prosperity. But Jesus has a different set of values and standards than these self-serving expectations. Jesus' standards are faithfulness, holiness, truthfulness, etc. These standards are as old as the beginnings of the nation of Israel and extend across the generations to his new Ecclesia, the Church. Peter identifies this principle of accountability in one of his letters to the churches. He writes, '*it is* time for judgment to begin with the household of God, and *if it* begins with us first, what *will be* the outcome for those who do not obey the gospel of God' (1 Pet. 4.17).

Jesus' prophetic warnings about disobedience, disloyalty, and sexual immorality are embedded in his seven letters to the seven churches of Asia, namely the churches in Ephesus, Smyrna, Pergamum, Thyatira, Sardis, Philadelphia, and Laodicea (Rev. 1.11). Jesus is the author of these letters, and John, who writes them, is his scribe. Cumulatively, the letters give a composite identity of the author. He is, 'the One who holds the seven stars in his right hand, the One who walks among the seven golden lampstands' (2.1); he is also 'the first and the last, who was dead and has come to life' (2.8). Also, he is 'the One who has the sharp two-edged sword' (2.12); in addition, he is 'the Son of God, who has eyes like a flame of fire, and his feet are like burnished bronze' (2.18). Further, he is the One, 'who has the seven spirits of God, and the seven stars' (3.1). Moreover, he is the One, 'who is holy, who is true, who has the keys of David, who opens and no one will shut, and who shuts and no one opens' (3.7); and finally he is, 'the Amen, the faithful and true Witness, the beginning of the creation of God' (2.14). These attributes re-capitulate the earlier vision of Jesus as the transcendent Son of Man (1.12-18). Surely, the two-fold emphasis by vision and by composite picture of Jesus' identity is sufficient motivation for God's people to obey, remain loyal, and pursue truth and holiness to such a One. Or is it?

The message and the ambience of each letter from Jesus are specific to the church to which it is sent. Paradoxically, while being church specific, each letter is only one part of Jesus' overall prophetic warning to the church. Therefore, collectively, the letters have a message for churches in every culture, generation, and locality. The individual warnings are as follows:

Church	Prophetic Warning	Prophetic Exhortation
Ephesus	They have left their first love	Remember ... repent, do deeds as at first
Smyrna		Do not fear the persecution
Pergamum	Some hold the teaching of Balaam, Balak, and Nicolaitans	Repent
Thyatira	They follow 'Jezebel' a false prophet	Jezebel has not repented; the rest are to hold fast
Sardis	Their deeds remain uncompleted	Wake up! Remember; repent
Philadelphia	Testing is about to come	Hold fast to what you have
Laodicea	Their deeds – neither hot, nor cold	Jesus comes; he stands at the door and knocks

Except for the church at Smyrna, every church has one or more issues that need to be addressed. These issues include: 1) leaving their first love (Ephesus), 2) idolatry and sexual immorality (Pergamum), 3) false prophets (Thyatira), 4) danger of not persevering (Sardis, Philadelphia), and 5) spiritual pride (Laodicea). The grace that is offered (the exhortations) cannot be ignored with impunity.

However, the churches which positively respond to grace will be rewarded. These letters and their messages are addressed to individual churches and to the Church as a whole. Implicit in this is the principle that what is true of churches is sometimes (often?) true of individual believers. Thus, these letters not only expose individual personal spiritual attributes and actions which displease the transcendent Son of Man, but warnings, which if they go unheeded, will provoke justified and appropriate judgment.

10.1.3.2. Punitive judgments upon the nations/humankind (Rev. 6.1–16.21)

As we have observed above, judgment begins first with God's people, but it falls more severely upon those people who persist in spurning God's offer of mercy and grace. This is the sober, even frightening message of Rev. 6.1–16.21, which reports the outpouring of the punitive judgment of the seven seals, the seven trumpets, and the seven bowls/vials. It was Jesus, by virtue of the fact that he is the Redeemer Lamb, who announced imminent judgment upon the seven churches. Similarly, on behalf of God the creator, it is Jesus who unleashes the three cycles of judgments upon the nations. Except for their magnitude, these judgments are not unprecedented. For example, they resemble the Ten Plagues – the diseases which God poured out on the nation of Egypt (Exod. 7.1–12.51). In addition, before his death as the Passover Lamb in Jerusalem, Jesus prophesies judgments such as wars, earthquakes, famine … and persecution (Lk. 21.1-36). The following table illustrates how the eschatological judgments of Revelation (6–16) echo Jesus' own eschatological prophesies.

Jesus (Luke 21)		The Seven Seals (Revelation 6-8)
1	Wars and tumults (21.9)	Conquest (6.2)
2	Nation vs nation (21.10)	Bloodshed (6.3-4)
3	Earthquakes (21.11)	Famine (6.5-6)
4	Famines (21.11)	Death (6.7-8)
5	Pestilences (21.11)	Persecution (6.9-11)
6	Signs in heaven (21.11)	Earthquake (6.12-17)
7	Persecution (21.12)	Silence in heaven (8.1)

In addition, the following table illustrates the interrelationship between the three cycles of the judgments which are prophesied in the Book of Revelation.

	Seven Seals	Seven Trumpets	Seven Bowls
1	Conquest (6.2)	Drought (8.7)	Disease (16.2)
2	Bloodshed (6.3-4)	Sea becomes blood (8.8)	Sea becomes blood (16.3)
3	Famine (6.5-6)	Water becomes bitter (8.10-11)	Water becomes blood (16.4)
4	Death (6.7-8)	Darkness (8.12)	Scorching sun (16.8-9)
5	Persecution (6.9-11)	Locust-like demons (9.1f)	Darkness/pain (16.10-11)
6	Earthquake (6.12-17)	Cavalry invasion (9.13f)	Invasion from east (16.12-16)
7	Silence in heaven (8.1)!	No more delay (10.6)!	It is done!

The above table invites the following observations. The seven-fold pattern of eschatological judgments describes in apocalyptic language the history of humankind from the first coming of the Son of Man (Jesus) to his second coming (Lk. 21.9, 27). Each cycle of seven judgments is grouped in the 4-2-1 pattern. Further, each cycle of judgments concludes with God's direct and decisive attention (note the language of theophany in 8.5; 11.15; 16.18), which leads up to the end of the age (8.1; 10.6; 15.1; 17.17). Not only do these cycles of judgment echo Jesus' 'eschatological discourse' (Luke 21), but the seven trumpets and the seven bowls, in particular, also reflect the exodus typology (i.e. the Ten Plagues). Also, in most cases, God effects judgments by natural calamity or disaster; in other cases, judgments result from human activity, primarily warfare. In addition, the cycles of judgment indicate an intensification of judgment as the end time approaches – compare the limited scope of the seven trumpets to the global scope of the seven bowls. In part, these judgments come in response to the prayers for vindication made by God's longsuffering people (6.10; 8.3-5). Finally, these judgments are intended to bring people to repentance (9.20; 16.11) though humankind as a whole remains impenitent.

Because God is the Creator (Rev. 4.11) he holds not only his redeemed people accountable (2.1–3.22), but he also holds all peoples accountable (6.1–16.21). As is self-evident in the overlapping cycles of judgment, God's instruments of judgment are often horrendous natural disasters; at other times wars are his agents of judgment. But sinfulness is so deeply embedded in human nature that even repeated cycles of chastening judgments are often unheeded, and humanity continues to march towards God's final solution.

10.1.3.3. Punitive judgments upon 'Babylon' (Rev. 17.1–18.24)

The prophecies about God's judgments inexorably advance toward God's final cosmic judgment. The focus of the Book of Revelation shifts from visions of chastening judgments against the Redeemed, and punitive judgments against the nations, to God's judgments against the dominant anti-God world power (17.1–18.24). John the revelator identifies the world power by the mystic name, BABYLON (17.5). Every alert reader of the Book of Revelation, from the first century to the present, will see in the name, Babylon an allusion to Babel (Gen. 11.1-11), which led the city-states of Shinar/Sumer in false worship – polytheistic and idolatrous. This connection – BABEL > BABYLON – will be extended by historical references to Nebuchadnezzar's Neo-Babylonian empire and its patron god, the dragon Marduk. In the historical context of the Book of Revelation, Babylon is the cryptic name for the Roman Empire, ruled by Domitian (81-96 CE) who styled himself to be, *Dominus et Deus* – 'Master and God'.

10.1.3.4. John identifies the contemporary dominant world power (Rev. 17.1-18)

Revelation 17.1-18 is about, 'the judgment of the great harlot who sits on many waters' (17.1). The 'many waters' represent the coalition of the kings of the earth and those who dwell on the earth (17.2). The great harlot sits on a scarlet beast. This beast is full of blasphemous names, including, but not limited to, Marduk, the patron god of Babylon, and Jupiter, the chief god of the Romans. It is a composite beast, having seven heads and ten horns. The woman is clothed in purple and scarlet, full of idolatrous blasphemies. John reveals the full name of this Prostitute-City-Empire:

'BABYLON THE GREAT'
THE MOTHER OF HARLOTS AND OF THE
ABOMINATIONS OF THE EARTH (17.3-5).

The Empire is not only judged for its false worship (i.e. Emperor Worship) but also for its murderous persecution of the saints (17.6). Though John is the agent for the vision, he wonders at the mystery of the prostitute and the beast (17.6b). An angel explains the apocalyptic imagery (17.7). The following table summarizes the angel's explanation of the vision.

The Vision	The Explanation
The beast's seven heads	The seven heads are the seven mountains of Rome
The seven mountains	These are seven kings
The beast itself	It is an eighth king, who is also a seventh king
The ten horns	These are also ten kings
The lamb	he is the greatest King (King of Kings – compare Rev 1.5) he is the greatest Lord (Lord of Lords)
The waters	The peoples, multitudes, nations, tongues

The angel's explanation of John's vision is about God's judgment on the current world power, namely, imperial Rome. In the vision there is a contrast between God's people as 'saints' (7.6) and Rome as a prostitute (17.5). There is an implied contrast between the Redeemed (5.8, from every tribe and tongue – and people and nation), and the rest of humanity (17.15, peoples and multitudes and nations and tongues). Further, there is an implicit contrast between Jesus – King of Kings and Lord of Lords – and every other king and Lord, whoever has or whoever will rule on the earth. Finally, there is the contrast between God, who bends the nations to his will as agents for judgment (17.1; 17b) and the kings who purpose to serve the beasts (17.17).

10.1.3.5. God's judgment upon Rome is prophetically fulfilled (Rev. 18.1-24)

The vision of judgment against Rome (Rev. 17.1-18) is prophetically triumphantly celebrated in the vision of Rev. 18.1-24. In 18.7-19 the vision portrays the glory, wealth, and power of Rome – but none of these prevail, 'for the Lord God who judges her is strong(er)' (18.8). The great angel, therefore announces, 'fallen, fallen is Babylon the great!' (18.2 *et al.*). This angel invites heaven and (redeemed) earth, 'Rejoice over her, O heaven, and your saints and apostles and prophets, because God has pronounced judgment for you against her' (18.20). Inevitably, God's judgment against Rome illustrates older truths and/or lessons, such as the following: One, 'the Most High is ruler over the realm of humankind and bestows it on whomever he wishes' (Dan. 4.17). In addition, in the time of Isaiah, the LORD reminded Sennacherib, king of Assyria, that he is Yahweh's servant: 'Have you not heard? Long ago I did it, from ancient times I planned it. Now I have brought it to pass, that you [Sennacherib] should turn fortified cities into ruinous heaps' (Isa. 37.26-29). Also, the Creator God declares, 'It is I who says to Cyrus (the Persian), he is My Shepherd! And he will perform all My desire' (Isa. 44.27-28). These Old Testament texts illustrate what Rome did not recognize, namely, that the God of Israel (and of the Church) is the One who controls empire builders, such as Sennacherib (Assyria), Nebuchadnezzar (Babylon), Cyrus (Persia), and Caesars and Emperors (Rome). What was true for ancient emperors and empires, such as Assyria, Babylon, Persia, and Rome is also true of other past and present world powers, for example, whether they be Russia, the United States of America, or any other world power. Finally, what was true about God's judgments against the seven churches of Asia (2.3), the Nations (6–16), and the World Power (i.e. Rome), is true for the ultimate coalition of powers, global and cosmic (chs. 19, 20).

10.1.3.6. God's punitive judgments against the coalition of global and cosmic powers (Rev. 19.1–20.15)

John has one final vision of God's judgments (19.1-20.15). A chorus of praise (19.1-7) is the transition from the vision of judgments against the dominant World Power (17.1–18.24) and this vision of God's judgments against an almighty Coalition which will gather against him (19.7–20.15). This transition is the original Hallelujah Chorus (and is not to be confused with Handel's Hallelujah Chorus). John's Hallelujah Chorus is made up of four songs of festive joy – rejoicing at God's defeat of Babylon/Rome. The following chart summarizes the themes of the songs of festive joy.

	Joy	Theme
1	Hallelujah	Salvation and glory and power belong to God. His judgments are true … he has judged the great Prostitute.
2	Hallelujah	Her defeat is eternal. The smoke of her ruins rises forever.
3	Hallelujah	The twenty-four elders and the four living creatures say, 'Amen'
4	Hallelujah	The great multitude affirms: the Lord God, the Almighty, reigns

These songs of praise are the prelude to two great festive banquets (19.7-18). The first of these Banquets is the festive joy of a Wedding banquet (19.7-10). This is identified as the marriage supper of the Lamb (19.9). It is a festive meal, in response to the invitation, 'Let us rejoice …' (19.7). This banquet is *glorious*. It is pure, bright and clean (19.8), which is a sharp contrast to the earlier image of the Great Prostitute (17.1-7). The bride is made up of the saints (from both before and after the cross). These saints are the redeemed from every tribe and tongue and people and nation (compare 5.9). But John's vision also reports about a second banquet.

The second of the two Banquets may be identified as the great supper of God (Rev. 19.11-18). The meal is provided by the King of Kings and the Lord of Lords (19.16). The (carrion) birds of the air are invited to attend (19.17). In contrast to the glorious feast of the marriage supper, the supper of God is *gory*. It consists of the slain and rotting carcasses of the defeated Coalition armies (19.18). Specifically, it consists of the flesh of Kings, commanders, the mighty, and all people (who are *slain* by the Lamb of God, 19.11-16). Therefore, the Lamb who was slain by sinful people at the end of the world will slay sinful people who have refused the opportunity to become saints.

The vision of the Hallelujah Chorus (19.1-7) and of the two great banquets (19.7-18) concludes with a vision of three great judgments (19.19-20.15). First, the beast and the false prophet are thrown alive into the lake of fire which burns with brimstone (19.19-21). Second, the dragon, who deceived the beast and the false prophet, was also thrown into the lake of fire and brimstone (20.1-10). And finally, God who sits on his great white throne makes his final judgment. Everyone will be judged according to their deeds. The dead, whose names were in the 'books', were thrown into the lake of fire. In contrast, the dead (in Christ), whose names were in the 'book of life' are (implied) confirmed to live forever (20.12-15). And so, judgment ended.

And so also the sixth cycle of turning points in biblical history and theology ends. As we have observed: 1) Jesus was the primary agent of the new start (the fourfold gospel); 2) the disciples in Acts empowered by the Spirit spread the gospel from Jerusalem round about to Rome; 3) Paul, the prophetic-teacher, *par excellence* taught the fledgling church theology and ethics; and 4) finally, John the revelator, prophesied judgments upon wayward churches, the nations, the dominant World Power (Babylon/Rome), and the 'unholy trinity' (i.e. the beast, the false prophet, and the dragon). But this ending is not the whole story. It merely introduces the next (seventh) cycle of turning points, which advances from time into eternity.

11

CYCLE SEVEN: FROM THE SECOND COMING OF JESUS TO EVERLASTING BLESSEDNESS

God's chastening judgments of the churches and his punitive judgments upon the peoples of the world, the current world power, and upon the unholy trinity (the Beast, the False Prophet, and the Dragon) bring human history as we know it to an end. But at one and the same time the end of the sixth cycle is the beginning of the new start of the seventh and final new start. However, with the seventh new start the cycle of turning points collapses. There will be no spread in the number and location of God's people. Therefore, God's earlier command to be 'fruitful and multiply' (Gen. 1.28 *et al.*) will never again be given. Also, Jesus' command to his disciples to engage in Spirit-empowered witness about him to the ends of the earth is null and void (Acts 1.8). At the end of the sixth cycle God's global and cosmic enemies have been defeated and punished. Therefore, there will be no more sinning and no new judgments. By this time everyone's destiny, in heaven and on earth, is fixed. Therefore, there will never again be another new start or eighth cycle. It is finished.

11.1. Agent of the New Start

As Bible readers know the name 'Jesus', both in the Hebrew and the Greek languages means 'God Saves'. Therefore, it seems to be more than a mere coincidence that the agents of the last four of the seven cycles of turning points all have the name Joshua/Jesus (Josh.

1.1; Ezra 2.2; Mt. 1.1; Rev. 22.20). Uniquely, the agent of both the sixth and seventh cycles of turning points is *one* person (historically in his first coming and prophetically in his second coming).

The sixth cycle of turning points in biblical theological history began with the first coming of Jesus (Matthew 1; Luke 1, 2). This cycle concludes with the prophetic announcement upon all those people who have spurned that salvation which he effected. John's vision of final Judgment is loaded with symbolic representation. For example, Jesus is the Lamb, newly married (Rev. 19.9-11). He is also the Field Marshall, or five-star General of God's army (19.11, 14). In addition, he is the Word of God (creative at the beginning of history [Gen. 1.3 *et al.*], but now destructive at the end of history [19.13]). Furthermore, he is the Vintner, who treads the wine press of God's wrath (19.5). Moreover, he is the all-conquering General (20.1-3); and finally, he is the Judge of cosmic and human destinies. He effects punishment – the second death – upon his enemies, and vindication – eternal life – for his followers (20.11-13). The reality which this symbolism evokes is the setting for the second coming of Jesus.

The future or second coming of Jesus was announced at the time of his Ascension into Heaven (Acts 1.9-11). Interestingly, Jesus' return to earth will simply reverse the ascension; he will return as he left, with the difference that his departure was private, but his return will be public. What is possibly an early church Christological hymn celebrates his first coming to earth as a slave, his second coming as a conquering hero (Phil. 2.5-11). Finally, John earlier reported that he will come again riding on the clouds (1.7; Compare Dan. 7.13). John's vision, however, is not so much about the actual coming of Jesus, but it is more about the people whom he comes to bless (Rev. 21.1-4).

11.2. The New Creation

Together, the Father, Son, and Spirit effect a new creation. This new creation is about: 1) a new heaven and new earth (21.1), 2) the New Jerusalem (21.9-27), and 3) the new Garden of God (22.1-5).

11.2.1. A new heaven and a new earth (Rev. 21.1)
Creation had a beginning. Genesis reports: 'In the beginning God created the heavens and the earth' (Gen. 1.1). From the materials of

creation God systematically, step-by-step created an environment hospitable to the as yet uncreated humankind: light, air, water and land, the sun and moon and stars, and swarms of living things in the waters, and birds in the air, and living creatures on the land (1.3-26). Once an environment hospitable for humankind has been fashioned, God created humankind in his own image to 'subdue' and to 'rule' over the earth (1.27-30). And so it is at the start of the seventh cycle of turning points in biblical history and theology. God will create a new heaven and a new earth to be a hospital environment for the redeemed humankind, conformed to the image of Christ.

John reports a vision of this 'new heaven and new earth' (Rev. 21.1). That's it! Unlike the creation narrative of Gen. 1.3-30 there is no report of God's step-by-step creative activity. His report simply reports that 'the first heaven and the first earth passed away' (21.1b). This advance from the first heaven and earth to the new heaven and earth of John's vision is similar to the description of the advance from the old covenant to the new covenant about which the author of the epistle to the Hebrews writes. Having quoted Jer. 31.31 he observes, 'When he said, "A new covenant", he has made the first obsolete. But whatever is becoming obsolete and growing old is ready to disappear' (Heb. 8.13). The new covenant, about which he writes, is better than the old covenant which it has replaced, because it has been enacted on better promises (8.6). In the same way, the new heaven and the new earth is better than the first sin-cursed earth (Gen. 3.20), which it will replace. That is all John reports to his readership; and, indeed, it is all that Bible readers need to know. A more important part of the vision relates to God's redeemed people, the bride, the wife of the Lamb (21.2, 9-10).

11.2.2. The new Jerusalem (Rev. 21.2-27)

In his sequence of the last three visions of the Revelation, John first saw 'a new heaven and a new earth' (21.1). Immediately after this he saw another vision, 'the holy city, new Jerusalem ... made ready as a bride adorned for her husband' (21.2). This is a vision of the new transformed people of God. The vision itself is dominated by two metaphors: 1) a bride (21.2, 9) and 2) a city (21.3-27). The metaphors are fluid and both describe the same reality – God's people of both covenants. Their transcendent reality is that they are re-created in the image of God (compare Gen. 1.27), 'having the glory of God' (21.11). John describes the New Jerusalem using a kaleidoscope of shapes and sizes, numbers, colors (gemstones), and metaphors. For example, it is a walled city, for protection and exclusion; it has twelve gates, three on each side; the gates are guarded by twelve angels, like the cherubim who guarded Eden (compare Gen. 3.24); the wall is 144 cubits thick (12x12); and each gate is named after one of the twelve tribes of Israel (21.12, 13).

The wall is built on twelve foundation stones: jasper, sapphire, chalcedony, emerald, sardonyx, sardius, chrysolyte, beryl, topaz, chrysoprase, jacinth, and amethyst (21.14-20). Just as the twelve gates bear the names of the twelve tribes of Israel, so the twelve foundation stones are named after the twelve apostles (21.14). This imagery echoes the ephod which was worn by Israel's high priest, to which was attached a gemstone, each of which represented one of the twelve tribes of Israel (Exod. 28.17-20). In addition, the New Jerusalem is laid out as a square, with the three dimensional shape of a cube (21.15). This shape, therefore, echoes the holy of holies in the tabernacle/temple of Yahweh. In John's vision its shape means that, 'the tabernacle of God is among men … his people' (21.3). Unlike David's Jerusalem, which was holy in name only, the New Jerusalem of John's vision will be the holy city in fact (21.2, 10). This holy city is an echo of the glory of God, first seen in John's vision of the thrice holy God (compare 4.2; 21.18-20). The glory of God's people, having the radiant splendor of gemstones echoes the eternal radiance of God's own personhood.

11.2.3. The new garden (Rev. 22.1-5)
When God created a suitable environment for humankind, he created the earth to be a garden – an early and earthly paradise (Gen. 1.27-31). Having created this environment, God commissioned humans to be his gardeners. Their purpose was to 'subdue' and 'rule' over everything that lived in the sea, in the air, and on the land (1.28). God's act of creating/commissioning was 'very good' (1.31). But this garden, pristine and good as it was, pales in comparison to the 'new garden' of God, which he has prepared for his people (22.1-5).

John's vision of the new earth/garden echoes the creation narrative and other biblical texts (Genesis 2). For example, in his penultimate vision of 'new things', John is shown, 'a river of the water of life' (Rev. 22.1). Alert Bible readers will be reminded of the first garden, where 'a river flowed out of Eden to water the garden' (Gen. 2.10). Ezekiel adapts this imagery when he prophecies about the (to be rebuilt) new Temple, observing, water was flowing from under the threshold of the house = restored Temple (Ezek. 47.1). Later, standing on the very Temple mount itself Jesus promises 'from his innermost being shall flow rivers of living water' (Jn 7.37). In John's final vision this water 'flows from the throne of God and the Lamb' (Rev. 22.1).

The river of life supplies water to 'the tree of life' (Rev. 22.4). The 'tree of life' language is part of the language of the first creation account (Gen. 2.9) and of Ezekiel's new Temple imagery (Ezekiel 47). In John's vision, 'the tree of life' (singular) is actually, 'the trees of life', for they produce twelve fruit (compare Ezek. 47.7) – one kind of fruit for each month. Both images – 'water' and 'fruit' here connote life in it fullest measure and delight. One of the factors which enhances the delight is that in the new garden of God, 'there shall no longer be a curse', such as sin brought to the garden of Eden (22.3; compare Gen. 3.14-19). The absence of curse is replaced by the *presence* of God and the Lamb. The vision ends with the triumphant affirmation, 'they shall see his face' (22.4, 5). This is an intimacy which had even been denied to Moses in this life (Exod. 33.20). What had been denied to Moses, John himself has earlier prophesied to be the future experience of the children of God: 'We know that, when he appears, we shall be like him, because we shall see him just as he is' (1 Jn 1.5).

EPILOGUE

THE SPIRIT SAYS, 'COME!'
THE BRIDE SAYS, 'COME!'
THE LISTENER SAYS, 'COME!'
THE THIRSTY ONE SAYS, 'COME!'

JESUS AFFIRMS, 'I AM COMING QUICKLY.'

THE BRIDE REPLIES, 'AMEN. COME, LORD JESUS.'

SELECTED BIBLIOGRAPHY

The following selected bibliography makes no effort to be comprehensive. Rather, it identifies a modest number of sources which illustrate the range of bibliographic which is available.

1.   Old Testament Theology

Achtemeier, Elizabeth. *The Old Testament and the Proclamation of the Gospel.* Philadelphia: Westminster, 1973.

Anderson, B.W. *From Creation to New Creation: Old Testament Perspectives.* Minneapolis: Fortress, 1994.

_____. *Contours of Old Testament Theology.* Minneapolis: Fortress Press, 1999.

Barth, Christoph. *God With Us: A Theological Introduction to the Old Testament.* Grand Rapids: Eerdmans, 1991.

Birch, Bruce, Walter Brueggemann, Terrence Fretheim, David Petersen. *A Theological Introduction to the Old Testament.* Nashville: Abingdon Press, 1999.

Brueggemann, Walter. *Old Testament Theology: Essays on Structure, Theme, and Text.* Ed. Patrick D. Miller; Minneapolis: Augsburg Fortress, 1992.

_____. *Theology of the Old Testament: Testimony, Dispute, Advocacy.* Minneapolis: Fortress Press, 1997.

Childs, Brevard S. *Biblical Theology in Crisis.* Philadelphia: Westminster, 1970.

_____. *Old Testament Theology in a Canonical Context.* Philadelphia: Fortress, 1985.

_____. *Introduction to the Old Testament as Scripture.* Philadelphia: Fortress, 1979.

_____. *Biblical Theology of the Old and New Testaments: Theological Reflection on the Christian Bible.* Minneapolis: Fortress, 1993.

Clements, R.E. *Old Testament Theology.* Edinburgh: John Knox, 1978.

_____. *Wisdom for a Changing World: Wisdom in Old Testament Theology.* Berkeley: BIBAL Press, 1990.

Dyrness, William. *Themes in Old Testament Theology.* Downers Grove: Inter-Varsity Press, 1979.

Eichrodt, Walther. *Theology of the Old Testament.* 2 vols. Philadelphia: Westminster, 1961, 1967.

Farris, T.V. *Mighty to Save: A Study in Old Testament Soteriology.* Nashville: Broadman Press, 1993.

Feldmeier, Reinhard and Herman Spiekermann. *God of the Living: A Biblical Theology.* Baylor, 2011.

Gileadi, Avraham. *Israel's Apostacy and Restoration.* Grand Rapids: Baker Book House, 1988.

Goldingay, John. *Theological Diversity and the Authority of the Old Testament.* Grand Rapids: Eerdmans, 1987.

Gowan, Donald E. *Theology of the Prophetic Books: The Death and Resurrection of Israel.* Louisville: Westminster John Knox Press, 1998.

Hasel, Gerhard. *Old Testament Theology: Basic Issues in the Current Debate.* 3rd ed.; Grand Rapids: Eerdmans, 1982.

Hayes, John and Frederick Prussner. *Old Testament Theology: Its History and Development.* Atlanta: John Knox, 1985.

Hubbard Jr., Robert L., Robert K. and Robert P. Johnston and Meye, eds. *Studies in Old Testament Theology: Historical and Contemporary Images of God and God`s People.* Dallas: Word Publishing, 1992.

Kaiser, Walter G. Jr. *Toward an Old Testament Theology.* Grand Rapids: Baker Book House, 1987.

Knierim, Rolf P. *The Task of Old Testament Theology: Substance, Method and Cases.* Grand Rapids: Eerdmans, 1995.

Longman III, Tremper, Daniel G. Reid. *God is a Warrior: Studies in Old Testament Biblical Theology.* Grand Rapids: Zondervan, 1995.

Martens, Elmer A. *God`s Design: A Focus on Old Testament Theology.* Grand Rapids: Baker Book House, 1981; 2nd ed. 1994.

McKim, Donald K. ed. *Historical Handbook of Major Biblical Interpreters.* Downers Grove: InterVarsity Press, 1998.

Nicholson, Ernest W. *God and His People: Covenant and Theology in the Old Theology in the Old Testament.* Oxford: Clarendon Press, 1986.

Ollenburger, Ben, Elmer Martens, Gerhard Hasel, eds. *The Flowering of Old Testament Theology: A Reader in Twentieth-Century Old Testament Theology, 1930-1990.* Winona Lake: Eisenbrauns, 1992.

Payne, J. Barton. *The Theology of the Older Testament.* Grand Rapids: Zondervan, 1962.

Preuss, Horst Dietrich. *Old Testament Theology.* Louisville: Westminster John Knox Press, 1995.

Rad, Gerhard von. *Old Testament Theology.* 2 vols.; New York: Harper & Row, 1962, 1965.

Rentdorff, Rolf. *Canon and Theology: Overtures to an Old Testament Theology.* Minneapolis: Fortress, 1993.

Reventlow, Henning Graf. *Problems of Old Testament Theology in the Twentieth Century.* Philadelphia: Fortress, 1985.

Routledge, Robin. *Old Testament Theology: A Thematic Approach.* Downers Grove: InterVarsity, 2008.

Sailhamer, John H. *Introduction to Old Testament Theology: A Canonical Approach.* Grand Rapids: Zondervan, 1995.

Scheiner, Thomas R. *The King in His Beauty: A Biblical Theology of Old and New Testaments.* Grand Rapids: MI, Baker Academic, 2013.

Seitz, Christopher R. *Word Without End: The Old Testament as Abiding Theological Witness.* Grand Rapids: Eerdmans, 1998.

Smith, Ralph L. *Old Testament Theology: Its History, Method, and Message.* Nashville: Broadman and Holman Pub., 1993.

Waltke, Bruce K. *An Old Testament Theology.* Grand Rapids: Zondervan, 2007.

Westermann, Claus. *Element of Old Testament Theology.* Trans. Douglas W. Scott; Atlanta: John Knox Press, 1982.

Zimmerli, Walther. *Old Testament Theology in Outline.* Trans. David E. Green; Edinburgh: John Knox Press, 1978.

Zuck, Roy B. ed. *A Biblical Theology of the Old Testament.* Chicago: Moody, 1991.

2.   New Testament Theology

Alexander, T. Desmond, et al. *New Dictionary of Biblical Theology.* Downers Grove: InterVarsity, 2000.

Barr, James. *The Concept of Biblical Theology.* Philadelphia: Fortress Press, 1999.

Bock, Darrell. *A Theology of Luke and Acts.* Zondervan, 2012.

Boers, Hendrikus. *What is New Testament Theology?* Philadelphia: Fortress Press, 1979.

Bruce, F.F. *The New Testament Development of Old Testament Themes.* Grand Rapids: Wm. B. Eerdmans, 1968.

Burge, Gary M. *The Anointed Community.* Grand Rapids: Wm. B. Eerdmans, 1987.

Burke, Trevor J. and Keith Warrington. *A Biblical Theology of the Holy Spirit.* Eugene, OR: Cascade Books, 2014.

Cook, W. Robert. *The Theology of John.* Chicago: Moody Press, 1979.

Ellis, E. Earle. *Pauline Theology.* Grand Rapids: Wm. B. Eerdmans, 1989.

Enns, Paul. *The Moody Handbook of Theology.* Chicago: Moody Press, 1979.

Fee, Gordon D. *God's Empowering Presence.* Peabody: Hendrickson, 1994.

_____. *Pauline Christology.* Peabody: Hendrickson, 2007.

Gloer, W. Hulitt (ed.). *Eschatology and the New Testament.* Peabody: Hendrickson, 1994.

Green, Joel B. *The Theology of the Gospel of Luke.* Cambridge. CUP, 1995.

Guthrie, Donald. *New Testament Theology.* Downers Grove, Illinois: InterVarsity Press.

Jeremias, J. *New Testament Theology: The Proclamation of Jesus.* London: SCM Press, 1971.

Jervell, Jacob. *The Theology of the Acts of the Apostles.* Cambridge. CUP, 1996.

Kim, Seyoon. *The Origins of Paul's Gospel.* Grand Rapids: Wm. B. Eerdmans, 1981.

Kostenberger, A. *A Theology of John's Gospel and Letters.* Zondervan, 2011.

Ladd, G.E. *The Pattern of New Testament Truth.* Grand Rapids, Mich.: Eerdmans, 1968.

_____. *A Theology of the New Testament.* Grand Rapids: Wm. B. Eerdmans, 1974.

Lincoln, Andrew. *Truth on Trial.* Peabody, MA.: Hendrickson, 2000.

Longenecker, R.N. *Paul, Apostle of Liberty.* Grand Rapids: Baker repr., 1964.

_____. *The Ministry and Message of Paul.* Grand Rapids: Zondervan, 1971.

Marshall, I.H. *Luke: Historian and Theologian.* Grand Rapids: Zondervan, 1970.

_____. *New Testament Theology.* Downers Grove: IVP, 2004.

Marshall and Peterson (eds.). *Witness to the Gospel.* Grand Rapids: Eerdmans, 1998.

Martin, R.P. *Mark: Evangelist and Theologian.* Grand Rapids: Zondervan, 1973.

Matera, Frank J. *New Testament Theology.* Louisville: Westminster John Knox, 2007.

Mead, James K. *Biblical Theology*. Louisville: Westminster John Knox, 2007.

Morris, L. *The Apostolic Preaching of the Cross*. Grand Rapids: Wm. B. Eerdmans, 1960.

_____. *The Atonement*. Leicester: InterVarsity, 1983.

_____. *New Testament Theology*. Grand Rapids: Zondervan, 1986.

_____. *Testaments of Love*. Grand Rapids: Wm. B. Eerdmans, 1981.

Parsons, Mikeal. *Luke: Storyteller, Interpreter, Evangelist*. Peabody: Hendrickson, 2007.

Rainbow, Paul A. *Johannine Theology*. Downer's Grove, IVP Academic, 2014.

Ridderbos, H. *Paul: An Outline of His Theology*. Grand Rapids: Wm. B. Eerdmans, 1975.

Shelton, James B. *Mighty in Word and Deed*. Peabody: Hendrickson, 1991.

Smalley, Stephen. *John: Evangelist and Interpreter*. Greenwood: Attic Press, 1978.

Stronstad, Roger. *The Charismatic Theology of St. Luke*. Grand Rapids, Baker, 2013.

_____. *The Prophethood of All Believers*. Cleveland: CPT, 2010.

Thomas, John Christopher. *The Devil, Disease and Deliverance*. Sheffield, 1998.

Vanhoozer, Kevin. *Dictionary for Theological Interpretation of the Bible*. Grand Rapids: Baker Academic, 2005.

Warrington, Keith. *Pentecostal Theology*. London: T&T Clark, 2008.

**Note relevant articles in the eight IVP "Black" dictionaries.

INDEX OF BIBLICAL (AND OTHER ANCIENT) REFERENCES

OLD TESTAMENT

Genesis

1	1, 201, 225	1.29	12, 16	3.14-24	13
1–2	3	1.31	10, 21, 227	3.15	14, 15, 198
1–3	192	2	201, 227	3.16	16
1–8	18	2.1	7, 9	3.17	14, 16, 20, 200
1.1–2.4	8, 14	2.3	144	3.18	200
1.1–8.22	7	2.4-25	11, 12	3.19	14
1.1	7, 8, 9	2.5	12	3.20	226
1.1–2.1	9	2.7	12, 13, 211	3.22-24	15
1.1–2.4	11	2.8	21	3.24	16, 227
1.2	9	2.9	12, 13	4	17
1.3	9, 225	2.10	228	4–5	15
1.3-5	9	2.10-14	12	4.1-2	16
1.3-30	226	2.14	23	4.1-8	16
1.4	10	2.15	21	4.1-24	17
1.6-8	10, 18	2.16	13	4.3	16
1.8	9, 13	2.17	13	4.4	16
1.9	10	2.18-20	13	4.5-8	16
1.9-10	18	2.21-22	13	4.9-11	16
1.9-30	9	2.22-23	12	4.10	24, 200
1.10	9, 10, 13, 16	2.24	13	4.12	16
1.11	10	3	201	4.14	17
1.12	10, 12	3–6	25	4.17	23
1.14-18	9	3.1–6.7	8	4.21	23
1.14-19	9	3.1	14, 15	4.22	23
1.18	10	3.1-7	16	4.23	20
1.20	10	3.1-8	36	4.24	20
1.20-22	10	3.1-24	13, 14, 15	5.1-32	15, 17, 20
1.22	10	3.2	14	5.28-32	20
1.25	10	3.3	14	6–8	17
1.26	12	3.4	14	6.3	15
1.26-30	7	3.5	14	6.5	17, 20
1.27	10, 12, 15, 16, 21, 25, 205, 227	3.6	14	6.6	17
		3.7	14	6.7	17
		3.8	14, 21	6.8	17, 20
		3.8-11	17	6.8–8.22	8
1.27-31	11, 227	3.12	16	6.9	20, 21
1.28	2, 21, 224, 227	3.13	14	6.11	24
		3.14	14, 15	6.13	17, 20, 22, 24
		3.14-19	228		

Gen. Cont'd

6.13-22	18, 21	11.6	25	15.18-21	33, 59, 71
6.17	17	11.7	25	15.19-21	33, 60
6.17-21	17	11.8	25	16.1-16	34, 35
7.11	18	11.9	25	17	75
7.21-23	18	11.10-32	29	17.1	34, 38
7.23	18	11.27-30	29	17.1-8	35
8.13-19	21, 22	11.30	34	17.1-22	35
8.20	22	12	28, 75, 113	17.1-27	33
8.20-22	21	12–50	48	17.1-6	30
8.20–9.17	21	12.1	30, 33, 59	17.2	2, 34
8.21	22	12.1-2	47, 53, 94	17.4	34
8.21-22	22	12.1-5	29	17.5	34
9.1	2, 21, 22	12.1-4	31, 34, 35, 60	17.6	34, 65, 74
9.1-7	22	12.2	30, 57, 74, 75,	17.8	34
9.1–11.9	18, 28		200	17.7	34
9.2	21, 22	12.3	30, 33	17.8	34
9.3	22	12.4	29	17.9-14	34
9.4	22	12.5	34, 60	17.15-21	34
9.5-7	22	12.7	30	17.16	34, 57
9.7	23	12.10-20	35	17.17	34, 35
9.8	22	12.10-14.24	31	17.20	34
9.8-17	50	13	75	17.22	61
9.9	22, 50	13.2	32	18.12	35
9.10	22	13.2-18	33	18.13-15	35
9.11	22	13.9-13	60	21.1	35
9.12	50	13.14-18	30	21.1-3	35
9.12-15	22	14.1-24	35	21.1-7	57, 60
9.16	22	15	61, 113	21.1-19	35
9.18-10.32	23	15.1	32, 38	21.6	35
9.19	23	15.1-21	32, 34, 35, 47,	21.7	35
10.1	23		50	21.8-21	35
10.1-32	23	15.2	32, 34	21.11	35
10.2-5	23	15.2-3	32	21.12	35
10.5	23, 25	15.2-4	34	21.17-21	36
10.6-20	23	15.2-6	30	21.18	36
10.20	23, 25	15.4	32, 33, 34, 45,	21.22-34	36
10.21-31	23		57, 60	22	75
10.31	23, 25	15.4-6	47	22.1	36, 45
10.32	10, 25	15.5	32, 33, 45	22.2	45
11.1	25	15.6	30, 32, 45	22.15-18	45
11.1-6	23	15.7	33, 50	22.18	75
11.1-9	23, 163	15.7-21	54	26–50	37
11.1-11	218	15.8	33	26.1-33	36
11.1	23	15.9-11	33	31.19	29, 30
11.2	23	15.13	33	31.32-35	29, 30
11.4	24	15.14	33	49	79
		15.18	30, 33, 50, 60	49.8-12	113

49.9	212	7.14-25	42	17.3	44, 52
49.10	65, 67	7.17	41	17.6	64
		8.1-15	42	17.8-14	57, 58
Exodus		8.16-19	42	17.11	57
1–15	40	8.20-32	42	17.13	57
1–18	48	8.30-35	49	18.1	64
1–40	45	9.1-7	42	19.1	64
1.1-7	37	9.8-12	42	19.1-2	46
1.7	37	9.13-35	43	19.5	50
1.9	37	10.1-20	43	19.5-6	40
1.10	37	10.21-29	43	19.16-18	52
1.11-14	37	12.1-51	145	20–24	60
1.11-22	40	12.1-28	43	20.1-2	47
1.15-22	37	12.29	43	20.2	48, 52
2.23-25	38	12.29-36	43	20.2-17	63
2.24	38	12.30	43	20.3-18	48
2.25-27	43	12.31	43	20.3-11	48
3.1	37	13.13	44	20.5	82
3.1-22	46, 58	13.17-22	52	20.6	82
3.2	37	14	18	20.8-11	144
3.3	37	14.1-9	44	20.12	48
3.4	37	14.1-31	52, 145	20.13	49
3.5	37	14.9	44	20.13-17	48
3.6	37	14.10-12	45	21.12	49
3.8	38	14.13	44	21.25	64
3.10	38	14.14	44	23.16	147
3.12	47	14.17	44	24.3	50
3.14-16	139, 147	14.26-28	44	24.7	52, 57
3.15	38	14.30	44	24.12-18	52
3.16	139	14.31	44, 45, 46, 54	25.19	49
4.6	49	15	45	28.17-20	227
4.7	49	15.1-18	44	32.1-10	81
4.22	41, 74, 113,	15.4	45	32.4	82
	128	15.10-12	37	32.33	82
4.23	41, 44	15.22	44, 45	33.20	228
5.1	41, 45	15.22-26	44, 46		
5.1–12.36	52	15.22–17.7	52	**Leviticus**	
5.2	41	15.23	44	11.44	210
5.2-18	45	15.24	44, 52	19.2	210
5.19-23	45	15.26	42	23.34	147
7.1-12.51	216	16	121		
7.3	42	16.1	46		
7.9	41	16.1-36	145	**Numbers**	
7.9-13	41	16.2	44, 52	11	52
7.10	42	17	119-20	11.1-3	53
7.12	42	17.1-17	46	11.1-14	52
7.13	42	17.2	44	11.4-6	53

Num. Cont'd

11.4-34	53
11.18	53
11.18-20	53
11.31-32	53
11.38	52
13.8	57
13.27	53
13.28	53
13.30	53
13.31-33	53
14	45
14.2	53
14.3	53, 54
14.8	57
14.9	54
14.22-23	54
14.26-35	58
14.45	45

Deuteronomy

1.19	47
4.40	49, 51, 57
5.12-15	144
6.4	82
6.10-11	94
8.1-16	36
8.1-20	13
8.7-9	93-94
8.16	36
17.14-20	65
18	64
18.15	58, 129, 135, 142, 148, 151
22.1	36
22.2	36
22.10-12	37
22.13	37
22.16-18	37
24	28
21.1	67
24.2	29
24.4	49
24.7	49
24.10	90
24.15	67
24.26	49

25.11	90
25.18	90
27–30	50
27.18-23	58
28.1-2	51
28.1-14	94
28.3	51
28.5	51
28.6	51
28.15	51
28.15-68	94
28.15-29.29	90
28.15-30.6	89
28.16	51
28.17	51
28.19	51
28.63	51, 101
29.6-7	91
29.10	91
29.11	91
29.12-14	91
30.1-2	89
30.3	89
30.4	89
30.5	90
30.6	90
30.15	101
32.39	147
34	52
34.9	58

Joshua

1.1	224-25
1.1-9	58
1–2	28
1–12	61
13–24	61
1–24	59, 60
1.4	59
1.13	59
2.1-24	58
2.9-11	58
3.1–4.24	58
4.26-31	58
5.1	58
5.13-15	58
6.2	58

8.1	58
8.30-35	61
10.8	58
10.10	59
10.11	59
10.14	59
11.8	59
11.23	59
12.7-24	59
13.7	59
13.13	59
13.14	59
13.15-16	60
13.24	59
23.5	59
24	61
24.1-28	61
24.2	29
24.15	61
24.21	61
24.24	61
24.26	49
24.27	61

Judges

2–16	62
2.6	62
2.10	62
2.11	62
2–16	64
3–16	63
3.7	62
3.7-11	62
3.8	62
3.9	62
3.10	62, 69
3.11	62
3.12	62, 63
3.12-31	63
3.14	63
3.15	63
3.30	63
4.1	63
4.1–5.31	63
4.2	63
4.3	63
4.4	63

Judges Cont'd

5.31	63
6.1	63
6.1–8.23	63
6.7	63
6.11	63
8.28	63
10.6	63
10.6–16.31	63
10.7	63
10.10-16	63
11.1	63
13–16	66
13.5	63
13.24	63
17–21	64
17.1-13	64
17.6	65
18.1-31	64
19.1-30	64
20.1-48	64
21.25	65
17.6	64
21.25	64

Ruth

4.17	65
4.18-22	70

1 Samuel

1.1	70
1.1-20	65
2.12	65, 66
2.35	65
4–6	66
7.15	65
8.1-20	65
8.3	67
8.4	67
8.5	67
8.7	67
8.8	67
8.11	68
8.11-17	68
8.16	68
8.18	68
8.19	68

8.20	68
9.1	69
9.1-2	69
9.1–31.13	69
9.2	73
9.15-17	65
9.16	70
10.1	69, 70
10.1-14	65
10.10	69
11.6	69
12	68
12.11-25	67
12.14	68
12.15	68
12.16	68
12.17	68
12.20	68
12.25	68, 86
13.11	73
13.12	70
13.8-13	70
13.13	73
13.13-17	65
13.14	70, 73
15.1-35	70
15.17	73
15.19-24	73
15.20	70
15.21	73
15.22	70
16.1	70
16.1-13	65
16.1-14	70
16.11	70
16.13	70
16.14	71
17	71
17.34	73
20.6-12	71
24.1-7	71
24.6-7	73

2 Samuel

1.11	71
1.12	71
2.1-4	73

2.8-11	73
3.1	73
5	71
5.1-4	73
5.5	73
5.6-10	73, 74, 122
6	71
6.1-19	74
7	113, 122
7.1	74
7.1-28	74
7.1-29	73
7.2	74
7.5	74
7.10	74
7.11	74
7.12	74
7.13	72
7.14	74, 128
7.16	65
8	71
8.1-18	73
9	71
11	71
11.4	73
11.14	73
11.17	73
12	72
12.1-24	73
12.3	71
12.13	73
12.14	73
12.24	72
23.2	70

1 Kings

1.1–11.43	72
1.34	72
1.38-40	113
2.11	70
2.25-33	78
3.1	80
3.3	73
3.14	83
3.28	72
6–8	72, 73
6.14	95

1 Kgs Cont'd
6.16   95
6.17   95
6.18   95
6.38   95
8.63   95
9.4-5   83
9.6-9   83
11.1-8   72
11.4   73, 83
11.9-13   73
11.9-40   72, 84
11.11   77
11.14-23   77
11.26   77
11.27-28   78
11.29   78
11.30-32   78
11.31   77
11.38   78
11.43   69
12.1   76
12.1-24   76
12.4   76
12.6   76
12.14   76
12.16   77
12.19   77
12.25-30   82
12.26-33   78
12.28   78
12.31   78
12.32-33   78
13.1-10   79
14.1-17   80
14.9   80
14.14   80
14.19   80
14.22   84
15.3   84
15.11   84
15.26   80
15.29   80
15.34   80
16.8   80
16.18   80
16.25   80

16.30   80
17   121
17.1-6   80
17.13   82
17.14-16   82
17.17-24   121
17.18   82
17.23   82
22.51   80

2 Kings
4   121
10.29   80
13.2   80
13.11   80
14.24   80
15.9   80
15.13   80
15.18   80
15.24   80
15.28   80
17.1   81
17.1-6   84, 101
17.1-18   77, 81
17.2   80, 81
17.5   81
17.6   81
17.7   82
17.7-25   121
17.8   82
17.9   82
17.12   82
17.17   82
17.23   77
18.1-2   84
18.3   84
18.4-8   84
21.1-26   84
21.2   84
21.3-7   84
21.9   84
21.10   84
21.10-15   85
21.12   85
21.13   85
21.14   85
21.22   84

22.2   84
23.25   85
23.26   86
23.27   86
23.32   86
24.10-25.30 83
25   92
25.21   51, 68, 86,
            101

1 Chronicles
36   28

2 Chronicles
33.10-13   85
33.12   85
33.13   85
36   61, 68

Ezra
1.1   98
1.1-4   96
1.2-3   92
1.6   93
1.7   98
1.7-11   93
2.1-70   98
2.2   93, 224
2.45   93
2.64   93
4.24   94
5.1   94
5.2   94
6.17   97
7.1-5   96
7.1-10   98
7.6   96, 97
7.7-9   97
7.9   97
7.10   96, 98
7.11-25   97, 98
7.16-20   97
7.21-23   97
7.25   97
8.1-20   97
8.1-36   98
8.21   97

Ezra Cont'd
8.22   97
8.24-30   97
8.35   97
8.36   97
9.1   97
9.2   97
9.3   97
9.4-15   97
9.15   98
10.2   98
10.3   98
10.4   98
10.5   98
10.9-17   98

Nehemiah
1.1   98
1.2   98
2.11   98, 99
2.12-20   98
2.17–4.23   99
5.19   100
6.15   99
7.7   93
8.3-4   99
8.7-8   99
8.9   98
8.14   99
8.17   99
8.18   99
9.1-38   99
9.33   99
9.38-10.27   99
10.29   99
10.32-39   99
11.1   99
13.1-3   99
13.4-9   99
13.10-14   99
13.14   100
13.15-22   99
13.22   100
13.23-29   99
13.30-31   99
13.31   100

Psalms
2.7   74, 128, 129,
              130
8   118
8.1-9   9
8.4   118
77.19   142, 145
77.21   142
78.13   145
78.21-33   142
78.24   145
90.10   14
95.7-11   54
110   125
110.1   75, 130
118.25   148
118.36   130

Ecclesiastes
3.1   10
3.2   11
3.4   11

Isaiah
6.2   210
7.14   113, 114
11.1   212
37.26-29   220
40.3   110
40.3-5   111
41.4   139, 147
42.1   128, 129
42.6   82, 186
44.27-28   220
44.28   92
44.28-45.7   92
45.2-3   92
45.18   139
46.4   147
49.6   82, 176, 186
51.10-12   145
59.7   196
61.1   160

Jeremiah
15.4   85
24.1   85

24.1-10   85
24.2-3   85
24.5   85
24.6-7   85
24.8   85
24.9   85
31.31   226
31.31-34   52
31.35   114

Ezekiel
1.10   210
2.1   118
18.13   182
37.3   88
47   228
47.1   228
47.4   228

Daniel
4.17   220
7   118
7.13   118, 119, 211,
              225
7.14   118, 212
7.25   212

Hosea
11.1   75, 113, 114,
              128

Joel
2.28-32   115

Micah
5.2   113, 114

Habakkuk
1.13   63

Haggai
1.1–2.23   96
1.12   93

Zechariah
6.9-15   96
6.11   96

Zech. Cont'd

6.12	96

Malachi

3.1	101, 106
3.2	101
3.4	101
4.2	101
4.4-6	101
4.5	106, 110, 111, 135

NEW TESTAMENT

Matthew

1	3, 225
1.1	112, 124, 224
1.2	124
1.2-17	112
1.6	124
1.10	120
1.11	120
1.16	113, 124
1.17	124
1.18	124
1.18-25	113
1.20	124
1.21	120, 132
1.22	113, 114, 120
1.23	113
1.23-34	120, 121
1.35	115
2.1-12	120
2.2	113, 124, 125
2.5	114
2.6	113
2.13-17	124
2.15	75, 114
2.17	114
2.19-23	124
3.2	126
3.3	114
3.13-19	120
4.1-31	120
4.17	126
4.41	121
5–7	144

5.1-34	121
5.1-43	121
5.1–7.37	121
5.2	126
5.20	126
5.45	13
6.9	126
7.11	159
7.13-14	84
8.10-12	127
9.27	124
11.11-13	126
12.1-8	125
12.3	125
12.4	125
12.18-21	125
12.22-28	126
12.23	124
12.35-37	75
13.3	164
13.11	126
13.16-17	126
13.39-42	127
13.49	127
13.50	127
15.22	124
16.16	126
16.28	126
17.1-8	126
19.28	156
20.30	125
21–22	125
21.3	113
21.9	125
21.15	125
22.14	125
22.15	125
25.31-41	127
27.11	125
27.27	125
28.18	157
28.19	157
28.20	157

Mark

1.1	117, 118, 199
1.11	119

1.18–2.12	119
1.21	119
1.21–4.41	120
1.22	119, 120
1.22-27	181
1.23-28	119, 120
1.27	120
1.29-34	119, 120
1.41	117
2.1-12	119
2.7	118, 120
2.10	117, 118, 119
2.11	118
2.12	120
2.18	120
2.23	120
2.24	118
2.28	118, 119
3.1-6	143
3.3	120
3.6	120, 143
3.21	120
4.35-41	119
4.41	118, 120
5.1–7.37	120
5.35-42	119
6.1-6	121
6.3	119
6.14	121
6.30-44	119
8.1–9.50	120, 121
8.27	121-22
8.28	121-22
8.29	122
8.31	118, 119
9.1-8	122
9.9	119
9.12	119
9.31	118, 119
10.1-11.11	122
10.1-16.20	120
10.1-16.25	122
10.17-27	197
10.26	197
10.27	197
10.33	118, 119
10.45	119, 123

Mark Cont'd

11.11	123
13.26	119
14.15	118
14.21	119
14.36	200
14.41	119
14.42	119
14.61	122
14.61-64	122
14.62	119, 122
14.63	122
14.64	122
15	18
15.9	122
15.12	123
15.13	123
15.16-39	123
15.17	123
15.18	123
15.26	123
15.32	123
15.39	119

Luke

1	225
1.1	134
1.5	174
1.5–2.41	115
1.5–2.42	119, 174
1.6	161
1.13	37, 111, 112
1.14	114
1.15	162
1.15-17	111, 112, 114
1.30	37, 132
1.31	128
1.32	110, 128, 129
1.32-35	75, 115, 157
1.33	129
1.34	128
1.35	110, 115, 128, 135
1.41	161, 162
1.46-55	162
1.47	131
1.67	114, 161, 162

1.69	131
1.71	132
1.76	110, 111, 115, 135
1.77	131
2	225
2.3	132
2.4	162
2.11	115, 132
2.15	113
2.25	161, 174
2.25-27	114, 131
2.29-32	177
2.30-32	132
3.1-2	111
3.3	111
3.4	111, 112
3.5	111
3.6	132
3.15	111
3.15-17	111
3.16	111, 112, 159
3.17	111, 159
3.18	111, 112
3.21	116, 128, 130, 157, 159
3.22	116, 128, 129, 130, 157, 159, 190
3.23	115
3.23-38	30
3.38	115, 128
4.1	130, 159
4.8	162
4.14	130, 157
4.18	116, 129, 130, 190, 197
4.16-21	130
4.18	157, 159
4.18-21	128
4.19	116
4.24	116, 130
4.24-30	177
4.25-27	116, 130
4.28-30	116
4.31	162
5.37	140

6	154
6.13	161
6.20	140
7.1-10	174
7.16	131
7.27	111
7.28	111
7.39	130
7.48-50	132
9.1-6	156
9.5	177
9.7-9	111
9.8	130
9.17	162
9.18-19	112
9.19	112, 130
9.32	129
9.28-36	128
9.29	128
9.31	129
9.35	129
9.51	128, 168
9.52	168
10.1-24	156
10.11	177
10.12	177
11.1-13	158
11.2	158
11.9-10	158
11.11	158
11.12	158
11.13	158
11.45-52	184
13.3	164
13.18-21	164
13.31-35	184
13.33	130
13.33-35	131
13.34	165
15.1	132
15.3-7	132
15.8-10	132
15.11-32	132
16.16	111
19.9	132
19.10	132
19.38	130

Luke Cont'd
21	216, 217
21.1-36	216
21.9	217
21.10	216
21.11	216
21.12	216
21.27	217
22.64	130
23.38	130, 131
24.1-24	129
24.19	130, 131, 140
24.20	130
24.48	157

John
1.1	143, 150
1.1-18	20
1.6	135
1.7	135
1.12	141, 150
1.15	135
1.18	75, 135, 142, 143
1.19	135
1.20	135
1.21	135
1.22	136
1.23	136
1.24	136
1.25-28	136
1.29	135
1.29-34	156
1.34	135
2–12	142
2.1-11	140, 143, 151
2.6	140
2.11	141, 149, 151
2.19	96
2.23	140, 145, 151
3.2	189, 190
3.16	134, 143, 150, 163
3.30	135
3.36	150
4.1-38	151
4.1-42	168

4.26	139
4.39-42	151, 168
4.46	141
4.46-54	143
4.47	143
4.48	141, 143
4.50	151
4.53	141, 151
5.1-9	143, 151
5.1-47	143, 144
5.16	11, 143
5.17	143, 149
5.18	143, 149
5.19-29	143
5.21	141
5.24	150
5.37	143
5.38	141, 151
5.39	141, 143
5.39-47	143
5.46	151
5.47	151
6	144
6.1-15	140, 141, 144, 149
6.1-71	143, 144
6.4	138, 145
6.9	141
6.13	141
6.14	145, 151
6.15	151
6.16-21	145
6.16-22	141
6.20	139, 142, 145
6.24	152
6.29	142, 151
6.35	138, 142, 145, 14
6.36	152
6.37	146
6.38	146
6.39	152
6.40	142, 150, 151
6.41	146
6.42	149
6.43	146
6.46	146

6.47	142
6.48	142, 146
6.51	146
6.52-58	146
6.60	146
6.64	151
6.66	146
6.68	141, 142, 146
6.69	141, 142, 146, 151, 152
7	144, 155
7.1–8.59	143
7.1–8.60	147
7.5	152
7.37	148
7.38	148
7.39	148
7.40	148
7.41	148
7.44	149
7.45	148
7.48	152
7.49	152
8	144
8.12	138, 148, 149, 151
8.18	147
8.24	139, 147, 148
8.28	147
8.38	139
8.56	30
8.58	38, 139, 147, 148
8.59	139, 148, 149
9.1-12	138
9.5	141, 151
9.5-7	149
9.18	152
9.35-41	149
9.38	141, 151, 152
10.7-9	138
10.10	189
10.11-14	138
10.22-39	143, 149
10.25	152
10.33	149
11.1-44	141

John Cont'd

11.25	138, 141, 151
11.27	152
11.38-44	138
11.45	141, 151
11.47-53	151
11.53	141
12.1	145
12.11	151
12.18	141
13–21	142
13.1	145
14.6	138
14.9	142
14.10	142
15.1-5	138
16.9	152
16.22	140
17.6	139
17.11	139
17.12	139
17.18	142, 156
17.21	142
17.22	139
17.25	142
18.4	139
18.5	139
18.6	139
18.6	38, 139
19.30	7
20.21	148, 156
20.22	141, 156
20.23	156
20.28	152
20.29	152
20.30	140, 156
20.31	134, 140, 141, 150, 151, 152, 156

Acts

1–7	167, 186
1.1-8	166
1.2	164
1.4	158, 174
1.4–7.60	164
1.5	158, 159, 161, 172, 174
1.8	157, 159, 164, 167, 172, 173, 174, 224
1.9-11	129, 158, 225
1.12–5.42	170
1.12–7.60	170
1.12–8.4	167
1.14	158
1.15	162, 164, 170
1.18	163
1.26	162, 164
2.1-4	141
2.1-9	165
2.1-21	159, 174, 185
2.1–7.60	170
2.1–8.4	170
2.2	159, 164
2.2–4.19	166
2.3	159, 164
2.4	158, 159, 161, 162, 164, 172, 183
2.5-11	162
2.9-11	167
2.16-18	162
2.17	109, 161
2.17-18	115, 172
2.22-25	157
2.29	183
2.33	129
2.36	132, 165, 167
2.39	167
2.43	165
2.47	165
3.1-9	166, 172
3.1–5.42	173
3.10-26	172
3.13	165
3.22	165
3.24	130
4.1–7.60	170
4.1–15.30	172
4.4	161, 165, 170
4.8	162
4.8-12	172
4.18	165
4.24	177
4.31	161, 176, 183
4.32	165
4.36	169
4.36-37	169
5.1-11	17, 165
5.11	170
5.12-16	172
5.14	165
5.40	165
6.1-7	168
6.8	165
6.8–7.60	166, 167
6.10	165
7.60	165
8–12	167
8–28	167
8.1-4	165, 168
8.1–28.31	164, 166
8.4-40	170, 186
8.5	165
8.5-13	166
8.5-25	168, 169
8.5-42	170
8.5–12.23	166
8.5–12.24	167
8.6-8	168
8.8	168
8.12	161, 168
8.14	174
8.14-17	169
8.14-25	170, 173
8.15	158
8.15-17	161
8.18-24	186
8.18-25	181
8.26	168
8.26-40	169
8.29	159, 166, 168
8.36	168
8.38	169
8.39	169
9.1-19	175
9.1-30	169
9.1–22.21	170, 185
9.15	161, 169, 204

Acts Cont'd
9.15-17   177, 178, 186
9.17   161, 169, 176, 183
9.20   190
9.26   190
9.27   183
9.32   173
9.32-35   172
9.32-43   171, 176, 180, 182
9.32–11.18 172, 173, 175, 179
9.33   173
9.35   166
9.36   173
9.36-43   172
9.37   173
9.40-42   173
9.42   166, 173
10.1-48   123, 171, 172
10.1–11.18 170
10.2   174
10.2-4   161
10.9-22   180
10.9-23   173
10.19   166
10.20   173
10.22   174
10.44-48   173, 174
10.46   161
11   190, 201
11.1   174
11.1-3   177, 178
11.1-18   171, 172
11.3   174
11.4-12   173
11.15-17   174
11.16   161
11.17   161, 173
11.18   174
11.22-24   169
11.24   176
11.32   193
12.24   166
12.25-28.31 167
13–28   167

13   190
13.1   169, 176, 185, 190
13.1-3   175, 182, 186
13.1-11   176
13.1-14.28 169
13.1-15.35 175, 179
13.1-22.21 171, 175
13.2   176, 180
13.2-4   166, 169
13.4   176
13.4-12   175
13.5   177
13.6-7   176
13.6-11   186
13.6-12   177, 181
13.9   177
13.12   181
13.13-52   171, 175
13.14-43   129
13.15-14.28 177
13.28-37   129
13.33   129
13.36-41   179
13.42   176
13.46   177
13.46-48   182
13.47   176, 177
13.51   177
13.52   177
14.1-7   175
14.3   176
14.4   176
14.8-18   175
14.17   13
14.19-28   175
14.27   177
15   190
15.1   178
15.1-5   182
15.1-35   175, 178
15.2   178
15.7   178
15.7-11   170
15.14-21   178
15.32   180, 185
15.36-41   179

15.36-16.10 179
15.36-18.23 179
15.39   123
16   201
16.1-5   179
16.1-40   179
16.6-8   183, 200
16.6-10   179, 180
16.7   180
16.8-10   180
16.11-40   171, 179
16.14   181
16.15   181
16.16   181
16.16-18   186
16.19-23   181
16.19-34   181
16.29-34   181
16.31   202
16.37   180
17.1-16   181
17.1-18.17 180
17.1-18.28 171
17.4   181
17.10-15   179
17.12   181
17.16-34   179
17.34   181
18–19   172
18.1-23   179
18.6   181, 182
18.8   181
18.9-17   181
18.18-21   183
18.22   182
18.24-28   179
18.25   190
19.1   161
19.1-7   182, 183
19.1-22.21 182
19.2   161
19.6   161
19.8-12   183
19.8-41   171, 182, 183
19.10   183
19.11-41   183
19.13-17   183

Acts Cont'd

19.18	183
19.21-41	183
19.23-41	186
20.1-3	184
20.1-6	182
20.1-22.21	171
20.7-12	182
20.7-17	184
21.8	169
20.13-38	182
20.22	184
20.22-24	185
20.23	184
20.26	184
21.1-6	182
21.1-14	185
21.7-14	184
21.15-22.21	182, 182
21.17	184
21.19	184
21.20	166, 184
21.21	184
21.22-25	185
22.26	185
24.49	157
27	201
28.11-31	170
28.31	164

Romans

1.1	189, 204
1.15	206
1.16	206
1.16–7.25	199
1.18-32	196
1.20	11
2.1–3.8	196
3.9	196
3.10-12	196
3.13-18	197
3.19	197
3.20	197
3.21–5.10	202
3.23	196, 208
3.24	198

3.25	198
5.12	15, 192, 196
5.12-21	192
5.14	192
5.15	192
6.1	192
7.14-21	205
7.14-25	199
7.24	197
8.1	199, 205
8.1-11	194, 200
8.1-27	199, 202
8.2	198, 199
8.3	198
8.4	194, 199
8.5	199
8.6	194, 199
8.9	199
8.11	199
8.12	200
8.12-17	200
8.13	200
8.14	200
8.15	200, 202
8.16	200
8.17	200, 202
8.18	200, 202
8.18-27	200
8.19	201
8.19-22	16
8.20	201
8.21	201
8.22	201
8.24	201
8.25	201
8.26	201, 202
8.27	202
8.28	18, 196, 202
8.28-39	199, 202
8.29	203, 204, 205
8.29-30	203
8.30	203, 205
8.31	205
8.31-34	204, 205
8.31-39	205
8.37	206

8.39	199, 206
11.29	52
11.33	199
11.33-36	206
13.13	195
13.14	195
16.7	190
16.27	206

1 Corinthians

1.1	189
3.6	189
9.1	190
12.10	202
12.13	159
12.14-28	193
13.1	202
14.1	202
15.45-49	192
15.44	192
15.58	193

2 Corinthians

3.1-27	205
3.18	205
5.20	189
11	201
11.21-33	200

Galatians

1.1	189
3.16	75
4.4	163, 198
4.4-6	107
4.5	163, 198
5.1	193
5.1-25	193
5.2	193
5.13	193
5.13-26	196
5.19	194
5.19-21	194
5.21	194
5.22	194
5.23	194
5.24	194

5.25	194	5.2	190	2.12	214
				2.14	215
Ephesians		**2 Peter**		2.18	215
1.5	204	3.18	189	2.19	212
2.26-28	193			3.1	212, 218
4.1–6.20	195	**1 John**		3.7	218
4.10	189	1.1	136	3.8	212
4.11	189, 190	1.1-4	136, 211	3.15	212
4.22-24	195	1.1-18	136	4–5	11
4.25	195	1.2	136	4.1-3	22
4.25-31	195	1.3	136, 137	4.1-11	209, 212
4.25-32	196	1.5	11, 228	4.1–5.14	7
4.27	196	1.7	136	4.2	210, 227
4.32	196	2.16	137	4.4	210
6.18	202	2.22	137	4.8	210
6.20	189	2.26	137	4.9	210
		2.27	137	4.11	210, 212, 218
Philippians		3.7	136	5.1	210, 212
2.5-11	225	4.1	137	5.1-11	213
		4.2	137	5.1-14	211, 212
Colossians		4.3	137	5.5	212
3.9-14	196	4.4	137	5.5-6	211
3.15	196	4.14	136	5.6	212
3.16	196	5.16	137	5.8	212, 213, 219
				5.9	212
1 Thessalonians		**Jude**		5.10	212
1.1	189	20		5.12	213
				5.13	213
Titus		**Revelation**		6–8	216
1.1	189	1.5	219	6–16	217
1.2	198	1.6	118	6.1	211, 212
1.3	198	1.7	225	6.1-8	210, 211
		1.8	38	6.1–16.21	214, 216, 218
Hebrews		1.9	212	6.2	216, 217
1.1	106	1.9-20	209	6.3-4	216, 217
1.1-2	115	1.10	118, 210	6.5-6	216, 217
1.2	106, 109	1.11	214	6.7-8	216, 217
3.7-19	54	1.12-16	213	6.8	211
8.6	226	1.12-18	211, 215	6.9-11	216, 217
8.6-13	52, 106	1.13-16	211	6.10	213, 217
8.13	226	1.17-19	211	6.12-17	216
11.37	85	2.1	214	7.6	219
12.11	208	2.1–3.22	210, 211, 214, 218	8.1	216, 217
				8.3-5	217
1 Peter		2.7	212	8.5	217
1.20	109	2.8	214	8.7	217
4.17	214	2.11	212	8.8	218

Rev. Cont'd

8.10-11	217
8.12	217
9.1	217
9.13	217
9.20	217
10.6	217
11.15	217
15.1	217
16.2	217
16.3	217
16.4	217
16.8-9	217
16.10-11	217
16.11	217
16.12-16	217
16.18	217
17.1	219
17.1-7	221
17.1-18	218, 219
17.1-18.24	214, 218, 220
17.2	218
17.3-5	219
17.5	218, 219
17.6	219
17.7	219
17.15	219
17.17	217, 219
18.1-24	219
18.2	220
18.7-19	219
18.8	220
18.20	220
19.1-7	221
19.1-10	213

19.1-20.15	214, 220
19.2	213
19.5	225
19.7	221
19.7-10	221
19.7-18	221
19.7-20.15	220
19.8	221
19.9	221
19.9-11	225
19.11	225
19.11-16	221
19.11-18	221
19.13	225
19.14	225
19.16	221
19.17	221
19.18	221
19.19-21	221
19.19-20.15	221
20	3
20.1-3	225
20.1-10	221
20.11-13	225
20.12-15	222
21	3, 18
21.1	7, 11, 16, 225, 226
21.2	226, 227
21.3	227
21.2-27	226
21.3-27	226
21.9	226
21.9-10	226
21.9-27	225

21.10	227
21.11	227
21.12	227
21.13	227
21.14	227
21.14-20	227
21.15	227
21.18-20	227
22	1, 3, 18
22.1	228
22.1-5	225, 227
22.3	228
22.4	228
22.5	228
22.20	225

OTHER ANCIENT SOURCES

The Martyrdom and Ascension of Isaiah

5.1-20	85

mShabbath

7.2	144
22.6	144

Nos

1–4	48
5–10	48

Tos Sota

8.5	114

INDEX OF AUTHORS

Brunson, A.C.   147
Calvin, J.   173
Dunn, J.   156
Hoehner, H.W.   184
Isbouts, J.-P.   42
Leivson, J.R.   181
McKnight, S.   178
Porter, S.E.   175
Tenney, M.   150
Veheyden, J.   131

CPSIA information can be obtained
at www.ICGtesting.com
Printed in the USA
LVOW10s1203260317

528501LV00008B/869/P